Teacher Edition

D1320533

GUM

Grammar, Usage, and Mechanics

Conventions of Standard English

ZB Zaner-Bloser

Grade Level Consultants

Margaret Bateman
Montgomery, Alabama

Cindy Daniel
Bothell, Washington

Suzanne Klein
Hilliard, Ohio

Nancy Morgan
Sharon, Pennsylvania

Joan Pawloski
Grand Rapids, Michigan

Illustration: Steve Botts, Tracy Greenwalt

ISBN: 978-1-4531-1216-8

Zaner-Bloser, Inc.
1-800-421-3018
www.zaner-bloser.com

ZB Code 16

Printed in the United States of America
2 3 4 5 6 27950 19 18 17 16 15

SUSTAINABLE FORESTRY INITIATIVE

Certified Sourcing
www.sfiprogram.org
SFI-01042

Teacher Edition Table of Contents

Grammar, Usage, and Mechanics

Conventions of Standard English

Grades 2–8

Are Your Students Ready to Write?

With *G.U.M. (Grammar, Usage, and Mechanics),* students master the **conventions of standard English** critical for success on **next-generation assessments** and **college- and career-ready** writing.

In as little as 15 minutes per day of **targeted, systematic, self-guided** instruction and practice, students will master these skills and meet the new academic standards.

The Right Choice for Grammar Instruction!

- Provides **targeted, systematic, self-guided** instruction and practice in **under 15 minutes a day**

- Meets 100% of the **conventions of standard English**

- Reinforces skills from grade to grade to ensure a **cumulative progression of skills and greater retention and skill development**

- Features **writing** and **spelling practice** in every unit

- Prepares students for high-stakes **next-generation assessments**

- Includes **English Language Learner support** in each lesson

- Fits easily into **any reading or language arts curriculum**

Five-Step Lessons for Self-Guided Instruction

The easy-to-follow, five-step lesson format provides explicit instruction in the conventions of standard English and includes opportunities for students to practice, apply, and reinforce skills.

Step 1
Provides an example of the skill in context for students to read and analyze

Step 2
Explains key skill information in clear, concise language

Step 3
Provides skill practice in the context of high-interest, nonfiction topics

Step 4
Provides an opportunity to apply skill knowledge

Step 5
Reinforces learning through writing, puzzles, and other fun activities

---

Read and Analyze

Titles

Unit 5: Lesson 53

Don't waste your money on the movie Temple of the Turtles. The short story "Froggy's Fandango" is quite funny. I used The Reptile Encyclopedia when I wrote my science report.

Circle the movie title. Draw a box around the story title. Tell how they are written differently. _____

Underline **book titles** and **movie titles** in handwritten work. Italicize book titles and movie titles when you write with a word processor. Use quotation marks around the titles of **songs, stories,** and **poems**. Capitalize the first word and last word in every title you write. Capitalize all other words except articles, prepositions, and conjunctions. Remember to capitalize forms of the verb *be*, such as *is* and *are*.

See Handbook Sections 1 and 3

Practice
Circle each lowercase letter that should be an uppercase letter. Draw a line through uppercase letters that should be lowercase letters. Underline or add quotation marks to the titles.

1. Sagit lent Jorge a book called cobra capers.

2. Sagit thought spitting mad was the best story in the book.

3. Lu loved the movie the ghosts of rattlesnake ranch.

4. The movie's t

5. Mark Twain

6. After reading

7. Nola wrote a

8. Brad set the p

9. Joelle read th

10. After dinner,

11. The poem wa

12. Then I read r

Lesson 53   Name _____

Apply
Read the titles below. Then write a title to answer each item. Be sure to write each title correctly.

13. Which book would tell you how to treat a snake bite? _____
_____

14. Make up a title for a short story that might appear in Reptile Tales. _____
_____

15. Which movie is likely to be a horror film? _____
_____

16. Which book might give you information about painted turtles? _____
_____

Reinforce
Draw a line to match each title in the first column with the item that best describes it in the second column.

17. "Ferdinand Frog's Life at the Plaza"   a movie about the life cycle of a turtle

18. Larry Lizard's Loud Act   a poem about a snake shedding its skin

19. "Marvin's Miraculous Molting"   a short story about a frog that lives in a fancy hotel

20. "Dot, the Silly Salamander"   a book about a singing lizard

21. The Life and Times of Tommy Turtle   a song about a spotted salamander

144

Assessment Options

The assessment options in *G.U.M. (Grammar, Usage, and Mechanics)* prepare students for next-generation, high-stakes tests and can be used for diagnostic, formative, and summative assessment.

Diagnostic Assessment

Unit Pretests can be used as a diagnostic tool to help you determine students' existing knowledge and skill proficiency prior to instruction.

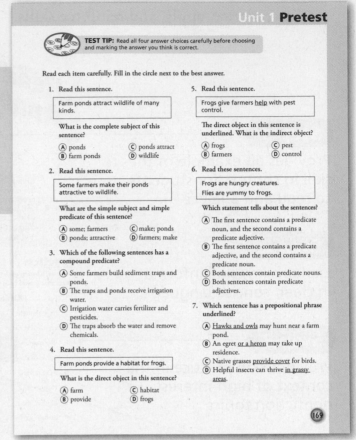

Unit 1 **Pretest**

TEST TIP: Read all four answer choices carefully before choosing and marking the answer you think is correct.

Read each item carefully. Fill in the circle next to the best answer.

1. Read this sentence.

   Farm ponds attract wildlife of many kinds.

   What is the complete subject of this sentence?

   Ⓐ ponds
   Ⓑ farm ponds
   Ⓒ ponds attract
   Ⓓ wildlife

2. Read this sentence.

   Some farmers make their ponds attractive to wildlife.

   What are the simple subject and simple predicate of this sentence?

   Ⓐ some; farmers
   Ⓑ ponds; attractive
   Ⓒ make; ponds
   Ⓓ farmers; make

3. Which of the following sentences has a compound predicate?

   Ⓐ Some farmers build sediment traps and ponds.
   Ⓑ The traps and ponds receive irrigation water.
   Ⓒ Irrigation water carries fertilizer and pesticides.
   Ⓓ The traps absorb the water and remove chemicals.

4. Read this sentence.

   Farm ponds provide a habitat for frogs.

   What is the direct object in this sentence?

   Ⓐ farm
   Ⓑ provide
   Ⓒ habitat
   Ⓓ frogs

5. Read this sentence.

   Frogs give farmers <u>help</u> with pest control.

   The direct object in this sentence is underlined. What is the indirect object?

   Ⓐ frogs
   Ⓑ farmers
   Ⓒ pest
   Ⓓ control

6. Read these sentences.

   Frogs are hungry creatures.
   Flies are yummy to frogs.

   Which statement tells about the sentences?

   Ⓐ The first sentence contains a predicate noun, and the second contains a predicate adjective.
   Ⓑ The first sentence contains a predicate adjective, and the second contains a predicate noun.
   Ⓒ Both sentences contain predicate nouns.
   Ⓓ Both sentences contain predicate adjectives.

7. Which sentence has a prepositional phrase underlined?

   Ⓐ <u>Hawks and owls</u> may hunt near a farm pond.
   Ⓑ An egret <u>or a heron</u> may take up residence.
   Ⓒ Native grasses <u>provide cover</u> for birds.
   Ⓓ Helpful insects can thrive <u>in grassy areas</u>.

169

Unit 1

Review

Subjects and Predicates

Underline the complete subject in each sentence. Draw a circle around the simple subject.

1. Rain is one kind of precipitation.

2. Regions with very little rain have few large animals.

Underline the complete predicate in each sentence. Draw a circle around the simple predicate.

3. Polar regions get most of their precipitation in the form of snow.

4. Winter snowpacks hold a great amount of water.

Draw one line under each compound subject in these sentences. Draw two lines under each compound predicate.

5. Texas and several neighboring states suffered terrible floods during the summer of 2007.

6. Thunderstorms flashed and boomed in June and July.

7. Creeks and rivers surged over their banks.

8. The Brazos River flooded homes and carried away cars.

Prepositions

Underline the prepositional phrase in each sentence. Draw a circle around the preposition.

9. Water surged into homes.

10. Some people climbed onto their roofs.

11. Volunteers in small boats rescued many people.

Relative Pronouns and Adverbs

Decide whether the boldfaced word in each sentence is a relative pronoun (RP) or a relative adverb (RA). Write *RP* or *RA* after each sentence to identify the boldfaced word.

12. Warning signs are posted at spots **where** visitors must be especially careful. _____

13. Hikers **who** are careful seldom have problems. _____

31

Formative Assessment

Unit Reviews allow you to check students' progress and help you determine when targeted instruction and support for individual learners are needed.

Summative Assessment

Unit Posttests, modeled after next-generation assessments, can be used as a summative assessment to evaluate students' achievement.

1 Students read a short text that contains errors in grammar, usage, and mechanics.

2 Questions require students to analyze the errors in the text they read.

3 Students read sentences and short paragraphs, analyze them for errors, and answer questions.

Unit 1 Posttest

Read this text and answer the questions on the next page.

A Twister Is Formed

1 An unusually hot and humid afternoon in mid-May.
2 The sun has been shining but now there are storm clouds in the
3 west. Suddenly, your weather radio
4 There is a tornado warning. You kn
5 do you know what is happening in
6 Most likely, a large thunderstorm
7 is very unstable. Warm air near the
8 higher, cooler air. The water molecu
9 form of a gas. When those molecu
10 change into a liquid and fall as rain
11 the water molecules change. This ca
12 upward currents of air.
13 Something called wind shear is
14 is created when winds at different h
15 directions or at different speeds. Th
16 directions cause a tube of spinning
17 Conditions are now perfect. For
18 The updraft can pull on the spinnin
19 vertical to the ground. The tube tig
20 turns into a twister capable of dama

Unit 1 Posttest

Name _____

Read each item carefully. Fill in the circle next to the best answer.

1. What change, if any, should be made to the underlined words in line 1?
   - Ⓐ NO CHANGE
   - Ⓑ Is an unusually
   - Ⓒ Is an unusual
   - Ⓓ It is an unusually

2. What change, if any, should be made to the underlined words in lines 2–3?
   - Ⓐ NO CHANGE
   - Ⓑ shining, but now
   - Ⓒ shining, now
   - Ⓓ shining but, now

3. What change, if any, should be made to the underlined words in lines 4–5?
   - Ⓐ NO CHANGE
   - Ⓑ at the atmosphere
   - Ⓒ from the atmosphere
   - Ⓓ of the atmosphere

4. What change, if any, should be made to the underlined words in lines 6–7?
   - Ⓐ NO CHANGE
   - Ⓑ approaching the air
   - Ⓒ approaching. The air
   - Ⓓ approaching; The air

5. What change, if any, should be made to the underlined words in lines 9–10?
   - Ⓐ NO CHANGE
   - Ⓑ cool off. They
   - Ⓒ cool off? They
   - Ⓓ cool off, they

6. What change, if any, should be made to the underlined words in lines 13–15?
   - Ⓐ NO CHANGE
   - Ⓑ is created. When winds
   - Ⓒ is created which winds
   - Ⓓ is created, when winds

7. What change, if any, should be made to the underlined words in line 17?
   - Ⓐ NO CHANGE
   - Ⓑ perfect for the
   - Ⓒ perfect; for the
   - Ⓓ perfect, for the

8. What change, if any, should be made to the underlined words in lines 19–20?
   - Ⓐ NO CHANGE
   - Ⓑ faster, it turns
   - Ⓒ faster, but it turns
   - Ⓓ faster. It turns

220

Unit 1 Posttest

Read each item carefully. Fill in the circle next to the best answer.

9. Read the following sentences.

   > The shark swam gracefully around the tank. Only the glass separated it from us.

   What part of the sentence is underlined?
   - Ⓐ complete subject
   - Ⓑ complete predicate
   - Ⓒ simple subject
   - Ⓓ simple predicate

10. Read the following sentences.

    > The full moon shone very brightly. It was more like day than night!

    What part of the sentence is underlined?
    - Ⓐ complete subject
    - Ⓑ complete predicate
    - Ⓒ simple subject
    - Ⓓ simple predicate

11. Read the following sentences.

    > I'm surprised Kyle did not win the writing contest. His story was hilarious!

    What part of the sentence is underlined?
    - Ⓐ direct object
    - Ⓑ indirect object
    - Ⓒ predicate noun
    - Ⓓ predicate adjective

12. Read the following sentences.

    > Fossils are the remains of animals preserved in rock. They give people an idea of what ancient species looked like.

    What part of the sentence is underlined?
    - Ⓐ direct object
    - Ⓑ indirect object
    - Ⓒ predicate noun
    - Ⓓ predicate adjective

13. Read the following paragraph.

    > [1] The skin is the body's largest organ. [2] It protects you. [3] It keeps you warm. [4] Your skin is important, so keep it healthy.

    What is the best way to combine sentences 2 and 3?
    - Ⓐ It protects you, and keeps you warm.
    - Ⓑ It protects you and keeps you warm.
    - Ⓒ It protects you, it keeps you warm.
    - Ⓓ It protects you but keeps you warm.

14. Read the following sentences.

    > The ants crawled ____. There must have been hundreds of them!

    Which is a prepositional phrase that completes the first sentence?
    - Ⓐ and gathered together
    - Ⓑ across the floor
    - Ⓒ when the light hit them
    - Ⓓ frantically

221

ext to the best answer.

18. Read the following paragraph.

    > [1] Although she loves dogs, Missy prefers cats. [2] The thing Missy likes most about felines is that they are proud and quiet. [3] They are also easy to care for.

    Where is the best place to add the following sentence?

    > They do not run wildly and bark like dogs.

    - Ⓐ Before sentence 1
    - Ⓑ After sentence 1
    - Ⓒ After sentence 2
    - Ⓓ After sentence 3

19. Read the following sentences.

    > Pedro sings in the local children's ____ once a week.

    Which words and punctuation best complete the sentences?
    - Ⓐ choir, they practice
    - Ⓑ choir. They practice
    - Ⓒ choir. Practice
    - Ⓓ choir. They practice

20. Read the following sentences.

    > The engine sputtered and died, the car wouldn't start again. Mom went inside to call the mechanic.

    Why is the first sentence incorrect?
    - Ⓐ It is a fragment.
    - Ⓑ It is a run-on sentence.
    - Ⓒ It should be a question.
    - Ⓓ It is a comma splice.

Ⓑ Sentence 2
Ⓒ Sentence 3
Ⓓ Sentence 4

222

Practice and Application Options

G.U.M. (Grammar, Usage, and Mechanics) includes a variety of options for more practice with targeted skills and application of skill knowledge to reinforce learning and extend it to students' own writing.

Extra Practice

Additional practice exercises for each lesson in the back of the Student Edition can be used to reteach targeted skills.

Proofreading Practice

At the end of each unit, students proofread a text for errors.

Proofreading Checklist

A proofreading checklist helps students apply targeted skills to their own writing.

Lesson 1 Underline the complete subject in each sentence once. Underline the complete predicate twice.

1. Hot sand covered Zoe's feet.
2. She rested beside a pile of driftwood.
3. This hidden beach was her favorite place.
4. Zoe fell asleep.
5. A noisy sea gull landed at her feet.
6. Someone's radio blasted loud music.
7. Some teenagers set up a volleyball net.
8. A crowd gathered.
9. Everyone cheered the players.
10. A quiet place is hard to find.

Lesson 2 In each sentence, draw one line under the simple subject and two lines under the simple predicate.

1. My alarm rang at 6:30 this morning.
2. I looked out the window.
3. Heavy black clouds threatened rain.
4. I dressed in warm clothes.
5. My father prepared a hot breakfast for everyone.
6. My mother packed an umbrella in my backpack.
7. A crowd waited impatiently for the bus.
8. The first raindrops were huge.
9. My umbrella snapped in the wind.
10. Randy shared his umbrella with me.

Extra Practice

189

Proofreading Practice

Read this report about wetlands and find the mistakes. Use the proofreading marks below to show how each mistake should be fixed. Use a dictionary to check and correct spellings.

Proofreading Marks

Mark	Means	Example
✄	take away	Bogs and swamps are are two types of wetlands.
∧	add	Bogs and swamps are two types of wetlands.
≡	make into an uppercase letter	bogs and swamps are two types of wetlands.
/	make into a lowercase letter	Bogs and Swamps are two types of wetlands.
⊙	add a period	Bogs and swamps are two types of wetlands⊙
ⓢⓟ	fix spelling	Boggs and swamps are two types of wetlands.

Wetlands

Wetlands are low-lying areas that are saturated with water for long periods. wetlands are classified according to the tipes of vegetation that grow in them. Swamps are wetlands that have many trees, marshes are wetlands where mostly grasses grow. Bogs are filled with different types of mosses. All three types, havens for many kinds of wildlife.

Birds throughout the world they depend on wetlands as a place to live and raise young. Many migrating birds rely on wetlands as a resting place on they're long migrations. The prairie fringed orchid and other rare plants thrive in wet, mossy bogs. Wetlands provide a natural clasroom where scientist can study a wide variety of Plant and animal life

Wetlands also teaches us about the past the chemical composition of most bogs is ideal for preserving remains. Scientists have discovered well-preserved animals and other preserved life forms in bogs all over the world. One group of scientists in florida found artifacts of a Native American people who lived 7,000 to 8,000 years ago. The items revealed that this group had advanced weaving and tool-making skills.

Although milliones of acers of wetlands in the United States been destroyed by pollution or drained for farming or industry. Many groups are working to preserve the Wetlands that remain.

35

Name _____

Proofreading Checklist

You can use the list below to help you find and fix mistakes in your own writing. Write the titles of your own stories or reports in the blanks on top of the chart. Then use the questions to check your work. Make a check mark (✓) in each box after you have checked that item.

Proofreading Checklist for Unit 1

	Titles			
Have I joined compound sentences correctly?				
Does each sentence have both a subject and a predicate?				
Have I avoided run-on sentences, comma splices, and fragments?				
Does each sentence end with the appropriate end punctuation?				

Also Remember…

Does each sentence begin with an uppercase letter?				
Did I use a dictionary to check and correct spellings?				
Have I used commas correctly?				

Your Own List

Use this space to write your own list of things to check in your writing.

Spelling Practice

Each unit includes a spelling practice lesson that focuses on grade-level spelling skills and strategies as required by the new standards.

Spelling Practice

Read and Analyze

Liz took a **photograph** of a lizard that was ten **centimeters** long.

Circle the word in bold type that has a Greek root that means "to measure."

Greek and Latin Roots

Many words in English have major parts, or **roots**, that come from the ancient Greek and Roman languages. For example, *telephone, photocopy, graphics,* and *millimeter* contain the Greek roots *tele* ("distant"), *photo* ("light"), *graph* ("written"), and *meter* ("measure"). *Inspect, describe, disrupt, export, eject,* and *dictate* contain the Latin roots *spec* ("see"), *scrib* ("write"), *rupt* ("break apart"), *port* ("carry"), *ject* ("throw"), and *dict* ("speak").

Word Sort

Use the words below to complete the word sort.

| predict | prescribe | telecast | photocopy | thermometer |
| prospect | reject | erupt | import | photograph |

Greek roots (*tele, photo, graph, meter*)	Latin roots (*spec, scrib, rupt, port, ject, dict*)

161

Name _____

Pattern Practice

| dictionary | telescope | biography | portable |
| inspector | photocopy | erupt | |

Write the word that answers each question.

1. Which word has a Greek root that means "light"? _____
2. Which word has a Latin root that means "break apart"? _____
3. Which word has a Latin root that means "speak"? _____
4. Which word has a Greek root that means "written"? _____
5. Which word has a Latin root that means "see"? _____
6. Which word has a Greek root that means "distant"? _____
7. Which word has a Latin root that means "carry"? _____

Write the word from above that best completes each sentence.

8. You should read this _____ about Ben Franklin's life.
9. It is hard to tell when the volcano will _____ again.
10. Because the speakers are _____, I can take them anywhere.
11. Lily tracks the movement of the stars with her _____.
12. Use a _____ to check the word's meaning.

Use the Dictionary

Write three words that begin with each Greek or Latin root. Use a dictionary to find words and check spellings.

13. photo _____
14. spec _____
15. tele _____

162

> Students practice **word sorting** or using **spelling words in context**.

> Activities focus on **pattern practice** and **dictionary skills**.

School Home Connection

School Home Connection

In Unit 1 of *Grammar, Usage, and Mechanics,* we are learning about different types of sentences and about the important parts of a sentence. The activities on this page give extra practice with some of the concepts we're learning. You can help your child use the information he or she is learning in school by choosing one or more activities to complete with your child at home.

Sentence Scramble (Complete Subjects and Complete Predicates)

With your child, read the weather forecasts in your local newspaper. Ask your child to copy four sentences from the forecasts onto strips of paper. Have your child underline the complete subject and circle the complete predicate. (The subject is the part of the sentence that tells whom or what the sentence is about. The predicate is the part of the sentence that tells what happens.)

Example   Wednesday will be sunny.

Rain is expected by Friday.

Then snip the strips in half between the subject and predicate, and scramble the parts to make silly new sentences.

Example   Rain will be sunny.

Wednesday is expected by Friday.

Back Then (Simple Subjects and Simple Predicates)

These activities can be sent home anytime during the unit to reinforce unit skills and to involve families in student learning.

Differentiating Instruction

The Teacher Edition features lesson plans that make it easy to differentiate and target instruction to meet the needs of individual learners.

Lesson 3 (student pages 11–12)
Compound Subjects and Compound Predicates

Objectives
- To learn that a compound subject is two or more subjects joined by a conjunction (*and* or *or*) and that a compound predicate is two or more verbs joined by a conjunction
- To identify the simple subjects that make up each compound subject and the verbs that make up each compound predicate in sentences
- To combine phrases to form sentences with compound subjects or compound predicates
- To write a sentence with a compound subject or a compound predicate

English Language Learners
Ask students to study the picture on page 11 and to suggest living things that are affected by the change of tides, such as seashore creatures and beachgoers.

Read the sentences in **Practice** aloud. In item 1, model how to identify the two simple subjects (ports and harbors). Ask volunteers to reread the other sentences aloud and to identify the compound subject or compound predicate in each one.

Invite volunteers to read the sentences in **Apply** aloud. Model combining the first sentence pair to form a new sentence with a compound predicate. (Example: Visitors to the beach can swim at high tide or dig clams at low tide.) Then have students work with partners to complete the section.

Have students work independently or in pairs to unscramble the words in **Reinforce.**

Speaking and Listening
Ask students to choose two classroom objects and create sentences with compound subjects. (Example: Pictures and **posters** decorate the walls.) Have students follow a similar procedure for compound predicates. (Example: We *eat* lunch and then *go* outside.)

Extra Practice
For more practice, see page 190.

 Language Standard(s): L.5.1

Lesson 4 (student pages 13–14)
Direct Objects

Objectives
- To discover that a direct object receives the action of the verb
- To learn that in a compound direct object, more than one word receives the action of the verb
- To identify direct objects and compound direct ...

English Language Learners
Read aloud the caption and discuss the picture on page 13. Invite students who have been to the ocean to describe their experiences.

Read each sentence in **Practice** aloud and explain any unfamiliar terms, such as *reefs, container ships,* and *luxury liners.* Then ask volunteers to reread each sentence orally and to identify the direct object(s) in it. Help students identify the direct object by saying the verb in each sentence and asking "What?" or "Whom?" (Example: item 2: *explore* what? *reefs*).

For **Apply,** read aloud the words in the word bank, and read each sentence. Work as a group to choose a direct object that makes sense for each sentence. Invite students to draw pictures or to pantomime the action described in the sentence to illustrate the relationship between the verb and the direct object.

Display pictures of underwater scenes before students complete **Reinforce.** Explain any unfamiliar terms in the word bank. After students draw, have them work independently to write their descriptive sentences.

Speaking and Listening
Read aloud several sentences from a book or other source that contains action verbs and direct objects. Omit reading the direct objects. Ask students to add new direct objects that make sense.

English Language Learners
Teaching suggestions provide scaffolding for English language learners.

Each lesson plan includes basic information on topics that may be unfamiliar to students.

Speaking and Listening
These activities develop oral communication skills.

Students practice building on others' ideas and expressing their own ideas clearly—skills that are important for meeting the new language standards.

Speaking Alert
The megaphone signals specific skills that relate to both oral and written communication.

When the megaphone appears, encourage students to discuss how the lesson topic applies to their spoken language.

Read and Analyze

Subject and Object Pronouns
Unit 4: Lesson 37

Auto racing fans admire the sleek cars before the race. **They** watch **them** closely during the warm-up period.

Which boldfaced word replaces the phrase *auto racing fans*? _____

Which boldfaced word replaces the phrase *the sleek cars*? _____

Which boldfaced word is the subject of the sentence? _____

A pronoun can be the subject or the object in a sentence. **Subject pronouns** include *I, he, she, we,* and *they.* **Object pronouns** can be used after an action verb or a preposition. Object pronouns include *me, him, her, us,* and *them.* The pronouns *it* and *you* can be either subjects or objects. **Remember to use this information when you speak, too.**

See Handbook Section 16

Practice
Circle each boldfaced word that is a subject pronoun. Underline each boldfaced word that is an object pronoun.

1. My friends and **I** watch the Indy 500 every year on TV.
2. The speed, the noise, and the excitement thrill **us.**
3. **You** might know that only three drivers have four Indy victories to their credit.
4. Can you name **them?**
5. **They** are A.J. Foyt, Jr., Al Unser, Sr., and Rick Mears.

Z12

Grammar, Usage, and Mechanics
Scope and Sequence

Grade	2	3	4	5	6	7	8
Sentence Structure							
subjects							
subject	•	•	•	•	•	•	•
simple and complete subjects	•	•	•	•	•	•	•
understood *you*					•	•	•
compound subject				•	•	•	•
predicates							
predicate	•	•	•	•	•	•	•
simple and complete predicates	•	•	•	•	•	•	•
compound predicate			•	•	•	•	•
predicate nouns and predicate adjectives			•	•	•	•	•
sentences							
simple sentences	•	•	•	•	•	•	•
compound sentences	•	•	•	•	•	•	•
complex sentences		•	•	•	•	•	•
compound-complex sentences						•	•
complete sentences	•	•	•	•	•	•	•
declarative and interrogative sentences	•	•	•	•	•	•	•
imperative and exclamatory sentences	•	•	•	•	•	•	•
choosing sentence structures						•	•
word order in sentences							•
parallel structure							•
combining sentences	•	•	•	•	•	•	•
producing, expanding, and rearranging sentences	•	•	•	•	•	•	•
phrases and clauses							
prepositional phrases	•	•	•	•	•	•	•
adjectival and adverbial prepositional phrases						•	•
participial phrases						•	•
infinitive phrases						•	•
gerund phrases						•	•
dependent and independent clauses				•	•	•	•
adjective and adverb clauses						•	•
noun clauses							•
restrictive and nonrestrictive clauses					•	•	•
analyzing phrases and clauses						•	•
appositives							
appositives					•	•	•
restrictive vs. nonrestrictive						•	•
correcting sentences							
sentence fragments	•	•	•	•	•	•	•
run-on sentences		•	•	•	•	•	•
comma splice			•	•	•	•	•
ramble-on sentences					•	•	•
misplaced and dangling modifiers						•	•
misplaced subordinate clauses						•	•
objects							
direct object			•	•	•	•	•

Grade	2	3	4	5	6	7	8
Sentence Structure (continued)							
indirect object				•	•	•	•
object of the preposition				•	•	•	•
object complement							•
Parts of Speech							
nouns							
concrete vs. abstract nouns	•	•	•	•	•	•	•
common nouns, proper nouns	•	•	•	•	•	•	•
singular and plural nouns	•	•	•	•	•	•	•
irregular plural nouns	•	•	•	•	•	•	•
possessive nouns	•	•	•	•	•	•	•
collective nouns	•	•	•	•	•	•	•
verbs							
action verbs and linking verbs	•	•	•	•	•	•	•
simple tense (present, past, future)	•	•	•	•	•	•	•
irregular verbs	•	•	•	•	•	•	•
perfect tenses (present, past, future)				•	•	•	•
progressive forms (present, past, future)			•	•	•	•	•
main verbs and helping (auxiliary) verbs			•	•	•	•	•
modal auxililaries			•	•	•	•	•
transitive and intransitive verbs						•	•
active and passive voice					•	•	•
shifts in verb tense				•	•	•	•
shifts in verb voice							•
verb moods							•
shifts in verb moods							•
verbals							
gerunds						•	•
participles						•	•
infinitives						•	•
pronouns							
personal pronouns	•	•	•	•	•	•	•
reflexive pronouns	•	•	•	•	•	•	•
intensive pronouns					•	•	•
demonstrative pronouns		•			•	•	•
interrogative pronouns					•	•	•
subject pronouns/subjective case pronouns	•	•	•	•	•	•	•
object pronouns/objective case pronouns	•	•	•	•	•	•	•
possessive pronouns/possessive case pronouns	•	•	•	•	•	•	•
indefinite pronouns	•	•	•	•	•	•	•
relative pronouns			•	•	•	•	•
adjectives							
adjectives	•	•	•	•	•	•	•
order of adjectives			•	•	•	•	•
demonstrative adjectives	•	•	•	•	•	•	•
proper adjectives				•	•	•	•
comparative and superlative adjectives		•	•	•	•	•	•
coordinate adjectives						•	•
absolute adjectives						•	•
adverbs							
adverbs	•	•	•	•	•	•	•

Scope and Sequence (continued)

Grade	2	3	4	5	6	7	8
Parts of Speech (continued)							
comparative and superlative adverbs		•	•	•	•	•	•
relative adverbs					•	•	•
conjunctions							
coordinating conjunctions	•	•	•	•	•	•	•
subordinating conjunctions		•	•	•	•	•	•
correlative conjunctions						•	•
prepositions	•	•	•	•	•	•	•
interjections				•	•	•	•
Usage							
homophones							
your and *you're*		•	•	•	•	•	•
their, they're, there; its and *it's*	•	•	•	•	•	•	•
whose and *who's*					•	•	•
to, two, too			•	•	•	•	•
than and *then*						•	•
problem words							
myself and *yourself*	•						
very and *real*					•		
good and *well*			•		•		
who and *whom*					•	•	•
doesn't and *don't*			•	•	•	•	
learn and *teach*					•		
set and *sit*					•	•	•
like, you know, go, and *all*					•	•	•
who, which, and *that*					•	•	•
leave, let, rise, and *raise*					•	•	•
lie and *lay*						•	•
less and *fewer; over* and *more than*							•
determiners							
articles: *a* and *an*	•	•	•	•	•	•	•
demonstratives: *this, that, these, those*	•	•	•	•	•	•	•
recognizing variations from standard English					•	•	•
Grammar							
pronouns							
subject and object pronouns	•	•	•	•	•	•	•
pronouns in pairs	•	•	•	•	•	•	•
I and *me*	•	•	•	•	•	•	•
pronoun-antecedent agreement			•	•	•	•	•
correcting vague pronouns					•	•	•
shifts in number and person					•	•	•
avoiding extra pronouns					•	•	•
verbs							
subject-verb agreement	•	•	•	•	•	•	•
subject-verb agreement (special cases)						•	•
using helping (auxiliary) verbs	•	•	•	•	•	•	•
using modal auxiliaries			•	•	•	•	•
agreement with compound subjects					•	•	•
negatives							
avoiding double negatives		•	•	•	•	•	•

Nonfiction Topics by Unit

Each unit of *G.U.M.* features the following nonfiction topics.

Unit 1
The World Outside: Water

Unit 2
Looking Back: United States History

Unit 3
Unforgettable Folks: Athletes

Unit 3 *(continued)*

Unit 4

Grab Bag: Cars

Unit 5

Beasts & Critters: Amphibians and Reptiles

Correlation to the Conventions of Standard English

Each grade level of *G.U.M.* meets grade-specific language standards as well as the standards for all previous grades, ensuring that students retain and further develop the conventions of standard English taught in previous grades. This cumulative progression of skills prepares students to meet college and career readiness expectations.

Grade 5 Conventions of Standard English	Grade 5 *G.U.M.* Page Numbers
Anchor Standard 1: Demonstrate command of the conventions of standard English grammar and usage when writing or speaking.	
L.5.1a Explain the function of conjunctions, prepositions, and interjections in general and their function in particular sentences.	**Student Book:** 19–22, 25, 26, 31, 38, 59–62, 64, 70, 147, 148, 192, 193, 200, 216 **Teacher Edition:** T6, T7, T16, T17, T38
L.5.1b Form and use the perfect (e.g., *I had walked; I have walked; I will have walked*) verb tenses.	**Student Book:** 115–118, 127, 210 **Teacher Edition:** T30, T33
L.5.1c Use verb tense to convey various times, sequences, states, and conditions.	**Student Book:** 49–52, 64, 70, 109–120, 127, 133, 197, 198, 208–211 **Teacher Edition:** T13, T14, T17, T28–T31, T33
L.5.1d Recognize and correct inappropriate shifts in verb tense.	**Student Book:** 119, 120, 127, 211 **Teacher Edition:** T31, T33
L.5.1e Use correlative conjunctions (e.g., *either/or, neither/nor*).	**Student Book:** 61, 62, 64, 200 **Teacher Edition:** T16, T17
Anchor Standard 2: Demonstrate command of the conventions of standard English capitalization, punctuation, and spelling when writing.	
L.5.2a Use punctuation to separate items in a series.	**Student Book:** 147, 148, 159, 166, 216 **Teacher Edition:** T38
L.5.2b Use a comma to separate an introductory element from the rest of the sentence.	**Student Book:** 149, 150, 159, 166, 216 **Teacher Edition:** T38
L.5.2c Use a comma to set off the words *yes* and *no* (e.g., *Yes, thank you*), to set off a tag question from the rest of the sentence (e.g., *It's true, isn't it?*), and to indicate direct address (e.g., *Is that you, Steve?*).	**Student Book:** 149, 150, 159, 166, 216 **Teacher Edition:** T38
L.5.2d Use underlining, quotation marks, or italics to indicate titles of works.	**Student Book:** 143, 144, 159, 163, 215 **Teacher Edition:** T37
L.5.2e Spell grade-appropriate words correctly, consulting references as needed.	**Student Book:** 33–34, 65–66, 97–98, 129–130, 161–162 **Teacher Edition:** T9, T17, T25, T33, T41
Grade 4 Conventions of Standard English	**Grade 5 *G.U.M.* Page Numbers**
Anchor Standard 1: Demonstrate command of the conventions of standard English grammar and usage when writing or speaking.	
L.4.1a Use relative pronouns (*who, whose, whom, which, that*) and relative adverbs (*where, when, why*).	**Student Book:** 27, 28, 31, 99, 194 **Teacher Edition:** T8
L.4.1b Form and use the progressive (e.g., *I was walking; I am walking; I will be walking*) verb tenses.	**Student Book:** 113, 114, 127, 209 **Teacher Edition:** T29
L.4.1c Use modal auxiliaries (e.g., *can, may, must*) to convey various conditions.	**Student Book:** 51, 52, 64, 198 **Teacher Edition:** T14
L.4.1d Order adjectives within sentences according to conventional patterns (e.g., *a small red bag* rather than *a red small bag*).	**Student Book:** 57, 58, 64, 199 **Teacher Edition:** T15
L.4.1e Form and use prepositional phrases.	**Student Book:** 19, 20, 31, 38, 192 **Teacher Edition:** T6
L.4.1f Produce complete sentences, recognizing and correcting inappropriate fragments and run-ons.	**Student Book:** 7–10, 29, 30, 32, 189, 194 **Teacher Edition:** T3, T8
L.4.1g Correctly use frequently confused words (e.g., *to, too, two; there, their*).	**Student Book:** 35, 67, 71–76, 83–88, 95, 96, 99, 101, 102, 201, 202, 204, 205 **Teacher Edition:** T19, T20, T22, T23

Grade 4 Conventions of Standard English *(continued)*	Grade 5 *G.U.M.* Page Numbers
Anchor Standard 2: Demonstrate command of the conventions of standard English capitalization, punctuation, and spelling when writing.	
L.4.2a Use correct capitalization.	**Student Book:** 35, 67, 135–144, 153–158, 160, 163, 165, 166, 213–215, 217, 218 **Teacher Edition:** T35–T37, T39, T40
L.4.2b Use commas and quotation marks to mark direct speech and quotations from a text.	**Student Book:** 153–156, 159, 163, 217, 218 **Teacher Edition:** T39, T40
L.4.2c Use a comma before a coordinating conjunction in a compound sentence.	**Student Book:** 21, 22, 32, 35, 38, 59, 60, 64, 67, 70, 149, 150, 159, 166, 192, 200, 216 **Teacher Edition:** T6, T16, T38
L.4.2d Spell grade-appropriate words correctly, consulting references as needed.	**Student Book:** 33, 34, 35, 36, 65, 66, 67, 68, 97, 98, 99, 100, 129, 130, 131, 132, 161, 162, 163, 164 **Teacher Edition:** T9, T17, T25, T33, T41

Grade 3 Conventions of Standard English	Grade 5 *G.U.M.* Page Numbers
Anchor Standard 1: Demonstrate command of the conventions of standard English grammar and usage when writing or speaking.	
L.3.1a Explain the function of nouns, pronouns, verbs, adjectives, and adverbs in general and their functions in particular sentences.	**Student Book:** 7–18, 27, 28, 31, 35, 37, 39–58, 63, 64, 67, 69, 70, 89–94, 95, 96, 99, 101, 102, 103–120, 123–126, 127, 128, 131, 133, 134, 137, 138, 141, 142, 160, 165, 189–191, 194, 195–199, 205, 206, 207–211, 212, 213, 214 **Teacher Edition:** T3–T5, T8, T11–T15, T23, T24, T27–T31, T32, T35, T36
L.3.1b Form and use regular and irregular plural nouns.	**Student Book:** 41, 42, 63, 70, 195 **Teacher Edition:** T11
L.3.1c Use abstract nouns (e.g., *childhood*).	**Student Book:** 43, 44, 63, 196 **Teacher Edition:** T12
L.3.1d Form and use regular and irregular verbs.	**Student Book:** 47–50, 64, 70, 83, 84, 89, 90, 96, 101, 109–112, 127, 133, 197, 204, 205, 208, 209 **Teacher Edition:** T13, T22, T23, T28, T29
L.3.1e Form and use the simple (e.g., *I walked; I walk; I will walk*) verb tenses.	**Student Book:** 111, 112, 127, 209 **Teacher Edition:** T529
L.3.1f Ensure subject-verb and pronoun-antecedent agreement.	**Student Book:** 93, 94, 95, 107, 108, 128, 134, 206, 208 **Teacher Edition:** T24, T28
L.3.1g Form and use comparative and superlative adjectives and adverbs, and choose between them depending on what is to be modified.	**Student Book:** 123–126, 128, 131, 134, 212 **Teacher Edition:** T32
L.3.1h Use coordinating and subordinating conjunctions.	**Student Book:** 21, 22, 25, 26, 32, 35, 38, 59, 60, 64, 67, 70, 192, 193, 200 **Teacher Edition:** T6, T7, T16
L.3.1i Produce simple, compound, and complex sentences.	**Student Book:** 21, 22, 25, 26, 32, 35, 38, 67, 192, 193 **Teacher Edition:** T6, T7
Anchor Standard 2: Demonstrate command of the conventions of standard English capitalization, punctuation, and spelling when writing.	
L.3.2a Capitalize appropriate words in titles.	**Student Book:** 143, 144, 160, 163, 165, 215 **Teacher Edition:** T37
L.3.2b Use commas in addresses.	**Student Book:** 157, 158, 159, 218 **Teacher Edition:** T40
L.3.2c Use commas and quotation marks in dialogue.	**Student Book:** 153, 154, 217 **Teacher Edition:** T39
L.3.2d Form and use possessives.	**Student Book:** 41, 42, 63, 70, 145, 146, 159, 163, 195, 215 **Teacher Edition:** T11, T37
L.3.2e Use conventional spelling for high-frequency and other studied words and for adding suffixes to base words (e.g., *sitting, smiled, cries, happiness*).	**Student Book:** 97, 98 **Teacher Edition:** T25
L.3.2f Use spelling patterns and generalizations (e.g., *word families, position-based spellings, syllable patterns, ending rules, meaningful word parts*) in writing words.	**Student Book:** 33, 34, 65, 66, 97, 98, 129, 130, 161, 162 **Teacher Edition:** T9, T17, T25, T33, T41
L.3.2g Consult reference materials, including beginning dictionaries, as needed to check and correct spellings.	**Student Book:** 33, 34, 35, 36, 65, 66, 67, 68, 97, 98, 99, 100, 129, 130, 131, 132, 161, 162, 163, 164 **Teacher Edition:** T9, T17, T25, T33, T41

Grade 2 Conventions of Standard English	Grade 5 *G.U.M.* Page Numbers
Anchor Standard 1: Demonstrate command of the conventions of standard English grammar and usage when writing or speaking.	
L.2.1a Use collective nouns (e.g., *group*).	**Student Book:** 43, 44, 63, 196 **Teacher Edition:** T12
L.2.1b Form and use frequently occurring irregular plural nouns (e.g., *feet, children, teeth, mice, fish*).	**Student Book:** 41, 42, 70, 195 **Teacher Edition:** T11
L.2.1c Use reflexive pronouns (e.g., *myself, ourselves*).	**Student Book:** 91, 92, 96, 206 **Teacher Edition:** T24
L.2.1d Form and use the past tense of frequently occurring irregular verbs (e.g., *sat, hid, told*).	**Student Book:** 83, 84, 89, 90, 101, 95, 96, 199, 200 **Teacher Edition:** T22, T23
L.2.1e Use adjectives and adverbs, and choose between them depending on what is to be modified.	**Student Book:** 53–58, 64, 69, 77, 78, 95, 102, 123–126, 128, 134, 198, 199, 202, 212 **Teacher Edition:** T14, T15, T20, T32
L.2.1f Produce, expand, and rearrange complete simple and compound sentences (e.g., *The boy watched the movie; The little boy watched the movie; The action movie was watched by the little boy*).	**Student Book:** 8, 10, 12, 14, 16, 18, 20, 22, 24, 26, 28, 30, 189–194 **Teacher Edition:** T3–T8
Anchor Standard 2: Demonstrate command of the conventions of standard English capitalization, punctuation, and spelling when writing.	
L.2.2a Capitalize holidays, product names, and geographic names.	**Student Book:** 141, 142, 160, 163, 165, 214 **Teacher Edition:** T36
L.2.2b Use commas in greetings and closings of letters.	**Student Book:** 157, 158, 160, 163, 166, 218 **Teacher Edition:** T40
L.2.2c Use an apostrophe to form contractions and frequently occurring possessives.	**Student Book:** 145, 146, 159, 163, 165, 166, 215 **Teacher Edition:** T37
L.2.2d Generalize learned spelling patterns when writing words (e.g., *cage → badge; boy → boil*).	**Student Book:** 33, 34, 65, 66, 97, 98 **Teacher Edition:** T9, T17, T25
L.2.2e Consult reference materials, including beginning dictionaries, as needed to check and correct spellings.	**Student Book:** 34, 35, 36, 66, 67, 68, 98, 99, 100, 130, 131, 132, 162, 163, 164 **Teacher Edition:** T9, T17, T25, T33, T41

Notes

The World Outside: Water

Unit 1 Sentence Structure

Building Grammar Awareness

Write this phrase on the chalkboard and ask a volunteer to read it aloud: Is in.

Ask students whether this phrase makes sense by itself. (no) Invite students to suggest some words that might be added to this phrase to create a group of words that makes sense. (Examples: The bird is in its cage; A frog is in the pond.) Then tell students that in Unit 1 they will learn about the different parts that make up a sentence. They will also learn how to combine short sentences into longer ones and how to correct sentences that are too long or are incomplete thoughts. Point out that knowing what a sentence is and how it is put together can help them when they speak and write.

Introduce the Unit Theme

Explain to students that the title of Unit 1 is "The World Outside" and that each lesson gives information about water—an important life-giving substance on Earth. Invite students to suggest ways people use water and to name some forms or forces of water. List their ideas in a chart such as this:

Water	
Uses	**Forms or Forces**
drinking	rain snow
washing	flood hail

Assessment Options

Unit Pretest

The **Unit Pretest** (pp. 169–172) is intended to be used as a diagnostic assessment to help you determine, prior to instruction, your students' existing knowledge and skill proficiency. Follow this procedure for administering the Unit Pretest:

1. Read aloud the test instructions. (**Note:** For additional scaffolding, you may wish to read the test questions and answer choices aloud.)

2. Tell students that they will have 20 minutes to read and answer the questions independently.

3. When time is up, collect and correct the tests. Use the results to determine which lessons to teach for targeted instruction or which lessons to spend extra time on during whole-class instruction if you are teaching all lessons in the unit.

Unit Posttest

The **Unit Posttest** (pp. 219–222) helps you judge students' achievement while providing students with practice for high-stakes tests. When you are ready to administer the test, ask students to carefully tear it out of their books. (**Note:** If the test has already been removed, distribute copies to students.) Read aloud the directions for each section and make sure students understand how to answer the questions. Ask students to work independently to complete the test.

Students who miss two questions focusing on the same grammar element may need additional help understanding the concept. Reteach the concept, following this procedure:

1. Review **Read and Analyze.**

2. Review the rule statement for the concept.

3. Guide students through the items a second time. Ask the students to explain why each right answer is correct.

4. Refer students to the **G.U.M. Handbook** for further reinforcement.

Lesson 1 (student pages 7–8)
Complete Subjects and Complete Predicates

Objectives
- To learn that every sentence has a subject and a predicate
- To learn what words make up the complete subject and what words make up the complete predicate
- To identify the complete subject and the complete predicate in sentences
- To complete sentences by adding subjects or predicates to phrases
- To compose original sentences

English Language Learners
Explain to students that every living thing is made up of water and that without it there would be no life on Earth. Introduce the words *beverages, industries, agriculture, cultivation,* and *treatment plants.* Use drawings or actual containers to acquaint English Language Learners with the units of measurement mentioned.

Read aloud the sentences in **Practice,** and then have volunteers reread the sentences orally and identify the complete subject and the complete predicate in each.

Invite volunteers to read each phrase in **Apply** aloud and to suggest a subject or a predicate to make a complete sentence. (Example: item 13: **A thirsty person** needs water.) Then have students work with English-proficient partners to complete the section.

Students can work with the same partners to complete the writing activity in **Reinforce.** Suggest that partners first talk about their favorite water activity and then work together to write their sentences.

Speaking and Listening
Ask students to read aloud the sentences they composed in **Reinforce.** Ask listeners to identify the complete subject and the complete predicate in each. List the water activities students mentioned. Have them orally compose safety tips for each.

Extra Practice
For more practice, see page 189.

Lesson 2 (student pages 9–10)
Simple Subjects and Simple Predicates

Objectives
- To learn that the simple subject is the most important word or words in the complete subject and the simple predicate is the word or words that tell what the subject did, does, or will do
- To identify simple subjects and simple predicates in sentences
- To write sentences using simple subjects and simple predicates
- To write a descriptive paragraph, and to identify each simple subject and simple predicate in it

English Language Learners
Ask students to study the picture on page 9 as you read the caption aloud. Encourage them to identify the form of each item shown in the picture: ice cube (solid), glass of water (liquid), steam (gas). Note that the steam represents water vapor, which is the invisible gas form of water.

Help students name the forms of the verb *be* and list them on the board. Make sure they understand the difference between **complete subject/predicate** and **simple subject/predicate.** Read all the sentences in **Practice** aloud. Ask volunteers to reread each sentence orally and to identify the simple subject and the simple predicate.

In **Apply,** model using a simple subject and a simple predicate from the word bank to compose an oral sentence. (Example: *Hailstones clatter* on the rooftop.) Then have partners work together to complete **Apply.**

For **Reinforce,** list a word bank of "winter weather words" students might use to write their descriptions.

Speaking and Listening
Have students find weather forecasts in newspapers or online and read the forecasts, pretending to be weather announcers. Ask listeners to identify the simple subjects and the simple predicates.

Extra Practice
For more practice, see page 189.

Lesson 3 (student pages 11–12)
Compound Subjects and Compound Predicates

Objectives
- To learn that a compound subject is two or more subjects joined by a conjunction (*and* or *or*) and that a compound predicate is two or more verbs joined by a conjunction
- To identify the simple subjects that make up each compound subject and the verbs that make up each compound predicate in sentences
- To combine phrases to form sentences with compound subjects or compound predicates
- To write a sentence with a compound subject or a compound predicate

English Language Learners
Ask students to study the picture on page 11 and to suggest living things that are affected by the change of tides, such as seashore creatures and beachgoers.

Read the sentences in **Practice** aloud. In item 1, model how to identify the two simple subjects (ports and harbors). Ask volunteers to reread the other sentences aloud and to identify the compound subject or compound predicate in each one.

Invite volunteers to read the sentences in **Apply** aloud. Model combining the first sentence pair to form a new sentence with a compound predicate. (Example: Visitors to the beach can swim at high tide or dig clams at low tide.) Then have students work with partners to complete the section.

Have students work independently or in pairs to unscramble the words in **Reinforce.**

Speaking and Listening
Ask students to choose two classroom objects and create sentences with compound subjects. (Example: **Pictures** and **posters** decorate the walls.) Have students follow a similar procedure for compound predicates. (Example: We *eat* lunch and then *go* outside.)

Extra Practice
For more practice, see page 190.

Lesson 4 (student pages 13–14)
Direct Objects

Objectives
- To discover that a direct object receives the action of the verb
- To learn that in a compound direct object, more than one word receives the action of the verb
- To identify direct objects and compound direct objects in sentences
- To choose direct objects to complete sentences
- To compose descriptive sentences with direct objects about a picture

English Language Learners
Read aloud the caption and discuss the picture on page 13. Invite students who have been to the ocean to describe their experiences.

Read each sentence in **Practice** aloud and explain any unfamiliar terms, such as *reefs, container ships,* and *luxury liners.* Then ask volunteers to reread each sentence orally and to identify the direct object(s) in it. Help students identify the direct object by saying the verb in each sentence and asking "What?" or "Whom?" (Example: item 2: *explore* what? *reefs*).

For **Apply,** read aloud the words in the word bank, and read each sentence. Work as a group to choose a direct object that makes sense for each sentence. Invite students to draw pictures or to pantomime the action described in the sentence to illustrate the relationship between the verb and the direct object.

Display pictures of underwater scenes before students complete **Reinforce.** Explain any unfamiliar terms in the word bank. After students draw, have them work independently to write their descriptive sentences.

Speaking and Listening
Read aloud several sentences from a book or other source that contains action verbs and direct objects. Omit reading the direct objects. Ask students to add new direct objects that make sense.

Extra Practice
For more practice, see page 190.

Lesson 5 (student pages 15–16)
Indirect Objects

Objectives
- To learn that an indirect object is a noun or pronoun that comes before a direct object and that it appears only in sentences that have direct objects
- To identify indirect objects in sentences
- To rewrite words in sentences as indirect objects
- To compose sentences that include indirect objects

English Language Learners
Read the caption on page 15 aloud and, if possible, show students a picture of a bayou. Also display pictures of other bodies of water, such as ponds, lakes, creeks, rivers, and estuaries.

Read aloud the sentences in **Practice**. Explain that a pothole is a natural depression in the ground that often fills with water. Reread the sentences and have volunteers identify the indirect object in each. Model "testing" whether a word is the indirect object by moving it after the direct object and putting the word *to* in front of it. (Example: item 1: Potholes offer resting places **to migrating ducks**.)

Discuss the directions and example in **Apply**. Have a volunteer read the first sentence aloud and model rewriting it. (Example: item 15: Eddie sold Rachel his kayak.) Ask student pairs to complete the section.

In **Reinforce**, make sure students know what a canoe trip is and what the items in the word bank mean. Pair students with English-proficient partners to compose and write their sentences.

Speaking and Listening
Write this sentence frame on the board:
___ gave ___ (a/some/the) ___.
Have students take turns creating oral sentences by filling in the blanks. (Examples: Roger gave his dog a bone; I gave my mom some flowers.) Write the sentences on the board as students say them. Then call on volunteers to identify the direct and indirect objects.

Extra Practice
For more practice, see page 191.

Lesson 6 (student pages 17–18)
Predicate Nouns and Predicate Adjectives

Objectives
- To discover that predicate nouns follow linking verbs and rename the subject, and predicate adjectives follow linking verbs and describe the subject
- To identify predicate nouns and predicate adjectives in sentences
- To add predicate nouns or predicate adjectives to complete sentences
- To write a question and an answer using a predicate noun or a predicate adjective

English Language Learners
Write *glacier* on the board. Direct students to the picture on page 17 and read the caption aloud.

Review what a linking verb is and list examples on the board (Examples: is, are, was, were, become, seem, feel). Read each sentence in **Practice** aloud and have students identify the predicate noun or predicate adjective and the linking verb before they write their answers.

Before beginning **Apply**, tell students the *Titanic* was a British ship that sank in 1912 when it struck an iceberg. Read the first sentence aloud, and model how to complete it. (Example: A floating chunk of ice from a glacier becomes **an iceberg**.) Have students work in pairs to complete the section.

Read aloud the directions for **Reinforce**. Have student pairs role-play survivors and reporters before they write their questions and answers.

Speaking and Listening
Write these sentence starters on the board:
My dog is ___.   My friend is ___.
Ask students to suggest at least two endings for each one: one with a predicate noun and one with a predicate adjective. (Examples: My dog is a Great Dane; My dog is big.)

Extra Practice
For more practice, see page 191.

Lesson 7 (student pages 19–20)
Prepositional Phrases

Objectives
- To discover that a prepositional phrase can tell how, what kind, when, how much, or where
- To learn that a prepositional phrase begins with a preposition and ends with a noun or pronoun that is the object of the preposition
- To identify prepositions and prepositional phrases in sentences
- To add prepositional phrases to sentences
- To use prepositions to complete a puzzle

English Language Learners
Invite students to describe lakes they know of or have visited. Then read aloud the caption on page 19. Discuss how the Great Lakes and their connecting waterways might be vital to the American and Canadian economies (Examples: transporting goods to many ports; providing shipping routes to the sea).

Next, read aloud all the sentences in **Practice**. Then ask a volunteer to reread each sentence, identifying the prepositional phrase in it and the preposition that begins the phrase.

Read the phrases in **Apply** aloud. Have students complete this section in small groups. Ask group members to decide which prepositional phrase to use in each sentence. Invite each group to share its rewritten sentences.

Finally, have student pairs complete **Reinforce**. To help English Language Learners, write the answers in a word bank on the board and ask students to identify which preposition belongs in each sentence.

Speaking and Listening
Display a picture that shows many objects and events, such as a picture of a fair or a circus. Ask students to orally describe the scene. Remind them to use prepositional phrases in their sentences. Ask listeners to identify the prepositional phrases.

Extra Practice
For more practice, see page 192.

Lesson 8 (student pages 21–22)
Simple and Compound Sentences

Objectives
- To learn that a compound sentence is two simple sentences, or independent clauses, joined either by a comma and a conjunction or by a semicolon
- To identify compound sentences and to rewrite pairs of simple sentences as compound sentences
- To combine independent clauses to form compound sentences

English Language Learners
Explain that many canals have locks that enable ships to move from one water level to another. Read aloud the caption and discuss the diagram on page 21.

Read aloud each sentence in **Practice**. To help students determine which items are compound sentences, have a volunteer try to restate the two items separated by commas or semicolons as two separate sentences. Ask students to tell how the independent clauses in the compound sentences are joined.

For **Apply**, read the first pair of sentences aloud and discuss which conjunction to use (and) to combine sentences and why. Have student pairs orally compose possible compound sentences for each item before they write.

Have students work in small groups to complete **Reinforce**. Remind them to refer to the page 21 diagram as they reorder the sentences.

Speaking and Listening
Write these sentence frames on the board:
    Last summer we went ___.
    This summer we may go ___.
Ask students to complete the frames orally by describing a real or imaginary trip to a river or other body of water. Have them expand each to form a compound sentence. (Example: Last summer we went to Lake Erie, and I had a great time fishing.) Have volunteers tell where to place the comma or semicolon in each.

Extra Practice
For more practice, see page 192.

Objectives

- To review that an independent clause is a sentence that makes sense by itself
- To learn that a dependent clause has a subject and a verb but cannot stand alone and that it begins with words such as *although, because, if, as,* or *when*
- To identify dependent clauses and independent clauses and the conjunctions that join them
- To match dependent clauses with independent clauses to create new sentences
- To add independent clauses to dependent clauses to make sentences

English Language Learners

Read the caption on page 23 aloud; discuss how waves can carve cliffs or other formations in rock. Ask students how they think ocean waves are created.

Read the sentences in **Practice** aloud. Clarify the terms *tracking equipment* and *overboard.* Ask volunteers to reread each sentence aloud, to identify the dependent clause and the independent clause, and to explain how they determined the two. Have them also identify the word that begins each dependent clause.

In **Apply,** read aloud each pair of sentences. Explain that students will be combining each pair of sentences to form a sentence that has a dependent and an independent clause. Have a volunteer complete item 11. Then have students work in pairs to complete items 12–14. Afterward, have volunteers identify the clauses in each sentence.

Have students work in pairs or small groups to complete **Reinforce.** Suggest students brainstorm possible independent clauses before they write their sentences.

Speaking and Listening

Write these words on separate index cards: after, although, because, if, as, when, unless, before, since, while. Distribute a card to each student. Ask students to compose a sentence containing a dependent and an independent clause using the word on their card.

Extra Practice

For more practice, see page 193.

Objectives

- To discover that a complex sentence is made up of an independent clause and a dependent clause
- To identify complex sentences and to join clauses to form complex sentences
- To compose a paragraph with at least one complex sentence

English Language Learners

Discuss with students the sport of surfing. Guide them to describe the movements of surfers as they paddle out, catch a wave, and ride it in to shore. Read aloud the caption on page 25; explain that some expert surfers specialize in riding very large waves.

Read aloud the underlined part of the sentence in **Read and Analyze.** Ask students if it expresses a complete thought. (no) Point out that this group of words has a subject (waves) and a verb (form), but it does not make sense by itself. Next, read aloud the boldfaced part. Ask students if it expresses a complete thought. (yes) Point out that this group of words has a subject (you) and a verb (will find), and could stand alone as a sentence. Read aloud the rule statement, and have students reread it with you.

In **Practice,** read aloud the instructions and sentences. Guide students to look for an independent clause and a dependent clause in each sentence. Have students work in pairs to complete the activity.

In **Apply,** read aloud each clause and have students reread it with you. Have a volunteer complete item 11. Then have students work in pairs to complete items 12–14. Afterward, have partners rearrange the order of the clauses in each sentence and decide which version is clearer.

In **Reinforce,** have students work in pairs to brainstorm sports to write about. Next, have students work independently to write their paragraphs. Afterward have students work with partners to read aloud, expand, and rearrange the sentences in their paragraphs to make them more interesting.

Speaking and Listening

Have students read aloud the paragraphs they wrote in **Reinforce.** Encourage listeners to ask questions about each sport's thrills and challenges.

Extra Practice

For more practice, see page 193.

Lesson 11 (student pages 27–28)
Relative Pronouns and Relative Adverbs

Objectives
- To discover that *who, whom, whose, that,* and *which* can be used as relative pronouns
- To discover that *when, where,* and *why* can be used as relative adverbs
- To identify relative pronouns and relative adverbs
- To use dependent clauses with relative pronouns and dependent clauses with relative adverbs in sentences

English Language Learners
Show students the location of Idaho, the Salmon River, and the Snake River on a map of the United States. Next, read aloud the example sentences in **Read and Analyze.** Guide students to recognize that the adverb *where* begins a dependent clause that provides information about the noun *state,* and the pronoun *who* begins a dependent clause that provides information about the noun *pilot.* Read aloud the rule statement to students, and then have them read it with you.

Read aloud each sentence in **Practice.** Ask students to identify the first word in each boldfaced clause and tell whether it is a relative pronoun or a relative adverb. Next, read aloud the instructions, clauses, and incomplete sentences in **Apply.** Have students work in pairs to complete this activity. The same student pairs can work together on the scrambled word activity in **Reinforce.**

Speaking and Listening
Lead a class discussion of rivers in your region and what activities are associated with each of them. Have students compose oral sentences about these rivers using relative pronouns or relative adverbs.

Extra Practice
For more practice, see page 194.

Lesson 12 (student pages 29–30)
Avoiding Fragments, Run-ons, Comma Splices

Objectives
- To learn that a sentence fragment does not express a complete thought, that a run-on sentence is a compound sentence missing a comma and a conjunction, and that a comma splice is a run-on sentence that has a comma but no conjunction
- To identify and correct sentence fragments, run-ons, and comma splices

English Language Learners
Review with students what they learned about waves in Lesson 9. Explain that a *tsunami* is a series of huge, destructive waves.

Read the paragraph in **Practice** aloud, one sentence at a time. Ask students to examine each sentence to determine whether it expresses one or more complete thoughts. Have them circle any fragments. Ask students to determine whether the clauses are joined and punctuated properly.

Pair students with English-proficient partners to complete **Apply.** Remind them how the fragment at the beginning of the paragraph in **Practice** should be corrected. (Example: A tsunami is not a single wave but a series of waves sometimes called a wave train.) Then model correcting the comma splice that follows the fragment. Suggest that partners compose their sentences orally before they write them.

Students can work with the same partners to complete **Reinforce,** using a dictionary if needed.

Speaking and Listening
Have students form groups of three. Assign each student one of the following topics: comma splice, run-on, fragment. Ask students to prepare a short presentation describing their assigned error, giving an example of it, and explaining how to correct it.

Extra Practice
For more practice, see page 194.

Unit Review (student pages 31–32)

The **Unit Review** allows you to check students' progress and determine when reteaching is necessary. The review pages may be completed in class or as homework. If a student responds incorrectly to two or more items involving the same skill, you may want to work directly with the student to review the relevant lesson. The lesson number to which each review item relates appears in parentheses on the review pages in the Teacher Edition.

Assign the **Extra Practice** activities (pp. 189–194) to reteach targeted skills in a more focused way.

Spelling Practice (student pages 33–34)

Spelling Patterns: Final Schwa with *l*

Read aloud the example sentences and the directions in **Read and Analyze**. Have students reread the example sentences with you. Ask which spelling for the /əl/ sound can be found in the words in bold type. (le) Read the rule statement aloud.

Have students work in small groups to complete the **Word Sort** and share their results with the class. For the first **Pattern Practice** activity, read aloud the directions and the words in the word bank. Have student pairs complete items 1–6. Ask them to present their answers to the class. For the second **Pattern Practice** activity, read aloud the directions and have students work independently to write the word that completes each sentence. Ask students to identify the /əl/ spelling in each word from the word bank. (rural—al, fossil—il, humble—le, parcel—el, syllable—le, loyal—al)

Read aloud the directions in **Use the Dictionary**. Have students work independently to complete the words.

English Language Learners

Have students work with a partner who is fluent in English for the spelling activities. Make flash cards for ten of the words from these activities. Write the following headings on the board: **le, al, el,** and **il**. Work with students to categorize the ten words by their /əl/ spelling. Hold up a flash card. Have students read the word aloud, and then have a volunteer write the word in the proper column based on its /əl/ spelling.

Proofreading (student pages 35–36)

Proofreading Practice

Review the **Proofreading Marks** chart and the examples. Read the first two sentences aloud. Discuss the first error (The w in **wetlands** should be an uppercase letter.) and how it should be marked. Ask students to correct the remaining errors using proofreading marks. You may wish to have students correct the spelling errors, too. After they have completed the activity, ask volunteers to read each sentence aloud and to identify the errors. **Note:** Some errors can be corrected in more than one way.

Proofreading Checklist

Ask students to select a recent piece of their own writing and to write the title of that piece at the top of the chart. Ask students to put a check mark next to each item in the checklist after they have checked it in their work. Students might first work independently and then trade papers with a partner to double-check each other's work. You might model, or ask a student to model, using the **G.U.M. Handbook** (beginning on page 239) to clarify a concept or rule.

Suggest that students look at the errors they did not find in the proofreading activity and add them to the checklist. Also ask students to think about other kinds of errors they make and to add these to the checklist.

English Language Learners

Have students work with partners who are fluent in English for the proofreading activities.

School Home Connection (student pages 37–38)

These pages provide quick, fun activities that review and reinforce the skills and concepts taught in Unit 1. You might utilize the **School Home Connection** pages in one of the following ways:

- Ask students to take the pages home, choose one or two activities to do, and then ask their parents to sign and return the pages.
- Send the pages home without asking that they be returned.
- Ask students to do one activity at school and then send the pages home.

Looking Back:
United States History

Unit 2 Parts of Speech

Building Grammar Awareness

Write these words on the board and ask a volunteer to read them aloud:

     played Joey well the in game

Have students work in pairs to put the words in an order that makes sense. (Joey played well in the game.) Write this sentence on the board. Explain to students that different words have different jobs in sentences. Ask volunteers to look at the sentence and find a word that names a particular person (Joey), a word that tells of an action (played), and a word that names a thing (game). Inform students that in Unit 2 they will learn about the parts of speech that make up a sentence. Point out that learning about different kinds of words and using them correctly in sentences can help them to be better understood when speaking and writing.

Introduce the Unit Theme

Inform students that the title of Unit 2 is "Looking Back." Explain that each lesson tells about the history, land, or culture of the United States. Invite students to name some American symbols (apple pie, stars and stripes, bald eagle, the Liberty Bell), celebrations (Thanksgiving, Fourth of July), and tourist attractions (Grand Canyon, Mount Rushmore, Statue of Liberty). You might use a web to record their responses. Encourage students to share what they know about each item they suggest.

Assessment Options
Unit Pretest

The Unit Pretest (pp. 173–176) is intended to be used as a diagnostic assessment to help you determine, prior to instruction, your students' existing knowledge and skill proficiency. Follow this procedure for administering the Unit Pretest:

1. Read aloud the test instructions. (**Note:** For additional scaffolding, you may wish to read the test questions and answer choices aloud.)

2. Tell students that they will have 20 minutes to read and answer the questions independently.

3. When time is up, collect and correct the tests. Use the results to determine which lessons to teach for targeted instruction or which lessons to spend extra time on during whole-class instruction if you are teaching all lessons in the unit.

Unit Posttest

The **Unit Posttest** (pp. 223–226) helps you judge students' achievement while providing them with practice for high-stakes tests. When you are ready to administer the test, ask students to carefully tear it out of their books. (**Note:** If the test has already been removed, distribute copies to students.) Read aloud the directions for each section and make sure students understand how to answer the questions. Ask students to work independently to complete the test.

Students who miss two questions focusing on the same grammar element may need additional help understanding the concept. Reteach the concept, following this procedure:

1. Review **Read and Analyze**.

2. Review the rule statement for the concept.

3. Guide students through items a second time. Ask the students to explain why each correct answer belongs in each sentence.

4. Refer students to the **G.U.M. Handbook** for further reinforcement.

Objectives

- To learn that a common noun names any person, place, thing, or idea
- To discover that a proper noun names a particular person, place, thing, or idea
- To identify common and proper nouns in sentences, and to write sentences using them
- To find hidden nouns in a word search and then identify them as common nouns or proper nouns

English Language Learners

Point out the figure on page 39, and explain that Uncle Sam symbolizes the United States government. Inform students that a meatpacker named Sam Wilson was the inspiration for this national symbol.

Read the sentences in **Practice** aloud and clarify any unfamiliar concepts or words, such as *packing, friendliness, inspector,* and *curious.* Ask volunteers to read each sentence aloud, to identify which words are common and proper nouns, and to tell how they know.

In **Apply,** be sure students understand what each symbol refers to. If possible, show pictures of the Great Seal (on which the bald eagle appears), the Liberty Bell, and the White House. Explain that a sea captain gave the name "Old Glory" to the national flag in 1824. Pair students with English-proficient partners to orally compose and then write their sentences.

Partners can work together to complete the word search in **Reinforce.** (across: fireworks, flag, Lincoln, America; down: independence, Jefferson, parade, Washington)

Speaking and Listening

Have small groups of students work together to brainstorm and list common and proper nouns that refer to people, to places, to things, and to ideas. Have students copy the listed words onto the board under the headings Common Nouns and Proper Nouns.

Extra Practice

For more practice, see page 195.

Objectives

- To discover that a plural noun names more than one person, place, thing, or idea and that some nouns change spelling in the plural form
- To learn that a possessive noun shows ownership, and to form possessives from plural nouns
- To identify plural and possessive nouns in sentences, and to write the plural and the plural possessive forms of given nouns
- To write a paragraph using plural and possessive nouns

English Language Learners

Read the caption on page 41 aloud. Then, if necessary, introduce and explain the terms *colonists/colony, Pilgrims,* and *harvest.*

In **Practice,** ask volunteers to read each sentence; to find a word that names more than one person, place, thing, or idea; and to explain how they know the words are plural nouns. Repeat the procedure with possessive nouns. Have students complete **Practice.**

Read the sentences in **Apply** aloud. Discuss the meaning of the word *matches* in item 16. (games, contests) Model completing item 13 and have students work with partners to complete the remaining items.

For **Reinforce,** invite students to share what they know about the first Thanksgiving. Pair students with English-proficient partners to compose their paragraphs.

Speaking and Listening

Ask each student to write five nouns that name a person or a thing on separate index cards. Place all the cards in a bag. Have student pairs take turns selecting two cards from the pile. Partners then have one minute to come up with sentences that include both nouns, using their plural or possessive forms. (Examples: *Peter's basketball* is flat. *Peter* has two *basketballs.*)

Extra Practice

For more practice, see page 195.

Lesson 15 (student pages 43–44)
Concrete, Abstract, and Collective Nouns

Objectives
- To discover that a collective noun can name a group of people or things
- To discover that a concrete noun can name something you can see, hear, smell, or touch
- To discover that an abstract noun can name a thing that can be sensed, or an idea
- To identify concrete, abstract, and collective nouns and use them appropriately in sentence context
- To discover special collective nouns for groups of animals

English Language Learners
Guide students to share what they know about pioneers who traveled to the West in wagon trains in the 1840s and 1850s.

Read aloud the example sentence and the directions in **Read and Analyze.** Have students reread the example sentence with you. Ask which boldfaced word names a collection of people. (group) Then ask which of the other boldfaced words names an idea. (danger) Read the rule statement aloud, and then have students read it with you.

Next, read the **Practice** instructions and each numbered sentence. Have students read each sentence to themselves, decide which boldfaced noun is the type of noun specified, and circle it.

For **Apply,** ask volunteers to read the questions aloud. Ask pairs of students to work together to complete the activity. In **Reinforce,** have the same pairs work together to complete the matching activity. You may want to have students do research on the Internet to determine the correct answers.

Speaking and Listening
Point out to students that pioneer families who traveled west in wagon trains could carry only a very limited amount of goods with them on the journey. Guide students to generate a list of goods they think their family would have taken with them if they had traveled west in a wagon train. Invite students to present their lists to the class, explaining why each item would have been appropriate to take.

Extra Practice
For more practice, see page 196.

Lesson 16 (student pages 45–46)
Personal and Possessive Pronouns

Objectives
- To learn that personal pronouns such as *I* and *me* can be used to refer to oneself, and that personal pronouns such as *she* and *they* can be used to refer to others
- To learn that pronouns such as *his, its,* and *our* show possession
- To identify personal and possessive pronouns in sentences
- To rewrite sentences by replacing nouns with pronouns
- To use personal and possessive pronouns in expository sentences

English Language Learners
Play recordings of "America the Beautiful" and "The Star-Spangled Banner," and introduce the words *melody, anthem, verses,* and *patriotic.*

Read the sentences in **Practice** aloud. Ask volunteers to identify the pronoun in each and tell whether it is personal or possessive. Call on other volunteers to identify the noun to which each pronoun refers.

In **Apply,** ask students to rephrase each sentence orally before they write pronouns to replace the underlined words. Point out that the apostrophes in items 11, 12, 14, and 15 show that possessive pronouns are needed. Note: Students may choose either the inclusive terms *us* and *We,* or *them* and *They* in their answers for items 12 and 13.

For **Reinforce,** students might dictate their sentences to you, an aide, or a peer tutor.

Speaking and Listening
Invite students to briefly tell about their favorite songs or singers. Ask listeners to identify the personal and possessive pronouns each speaker uses.

Extra Practice
For more practice, see page 196.

Lesson 17 (student pages 47–48)
Action Verbs and Linking Verbs

Objectives
- To discover that an action verb tells what the subject of a sentence does and that a linking verb tells what the subject is or is like
- To identify action verbs and linking verbs in context and to use them in original sentences
- To write a descriptive paragraph that includes action and linking verbs

English Language Learners
Point out the map on page 47. Explain to students that the Mississippi River is the longest river in the United States, and that most rivers between the Rocky Mountains and the Appalachians flow directly or indirectly into the Mississippi.

Read aloud the example sentences and the directions in **Read and Analyze.** Have students reread the example sentences with you. Have volunteers identify the words that indicate actions and the words that link subjects to words that tell about them. Read aloud the rule statement, and then have students read it with you.

Next, read the paragraphs in **Practice** aloud. Describe and, if possible, show pictures of barges and tugboats. Have volunteers read aloud each sentence and tell whether the boldfaced word is an action verb or a linking verb.

For **Apply,** pair students with English-proficient partners to complete the sentences and identify the type of verb used. Finally, read aloud the instructions for **Reinforce.** Have students work independently to write their paragraphs. Afterward, have students join with their English-proficient partners, and read aloud, expand, and rearrange sentences in their paragraphs to make them more expressive.

Speaking and Listening
Display a photograph or a painting showing activity on or near a river. Have students compose oral sentences describing things and actions in the picture. Ask listeners to identify verbs in the sentences and tell whether they are action verbs or linking verbs.

Extra Practice
For more practice, see page 197.

Lesson 18 (student pages 49–50)
Main Verbs and Helping Verbs

Objectives
- To learn that a main verb is the most important verb in a sentence and that a helping verb comes before the main verb
- To differentiate between main verbs and helping verbs in sentences
- To write sentences using helping verbs
- To find helping verbs in a word search puzzle

English Language Learners
Discuss with students that there are many serious illnesses. Explain that leukemia is a type of cancer that involves blood cells. Tell students that scientists called *biochemists* work to discover better treatments for these and other illnesses.

Read aloud the example sentences and the directions in **Read and Analyze.** Ask a student to identify the boldfaced main verbs and helping verbs. Point out that in the first sentence, the adverb *not* appears between the helping verb and the main verb. Read the rule statement aloud, and then have students reread it with you.

Next, read aloud each sentence in **Practice,** and ask students to orally identify the main verb and the helping verb before they mark their answers. After students complete the activity, discuss the prejudice Gertrude Elion faced, and the ways in which she was able to overcome this prejudice.

Read aloud the instructions and questions in **Apply.** Have students work with partners; have them discuss answers to the questions before writing responses. Have students continue to work with partners to identify and write the 23 helping verbs in the word search puzzle in **Reinforce.**

Speaking and Listening
Ask students to scan a paragraph and look for main verbs in a book they are currently reading. Elicit several examples and write each one on an index card. Write each of these helping verbs on index cards: is, are, was, were, will, may, can, has, have. Place both sets of cards facedown on a table. Ask students to take turns picking a card from each pile and composing oral sentences with these main verbs and helping verbs.

Extra Practice
For more practice, see page 197.

Lesson 19 (student pages 51–52)
Modal Auxiliaries

Objectives

- To discover that certain helping verbs called *modal auxiliaries* have special functions
- To identify modal auxiliaries and their functions in sentences
- To use modal auxiliaries in sentence context
- To write sentences with modal auxiliaries

English Language Learners

Read aloud the caption as students look at the picture on page 51. Invite students to tell what they know about General Robert E. Lee and the American Civil War. Then read aloud the example sentences in **Read and Analyze.** Help students identify the function of each helping verb. Read aloud the rule statement; then have students read it with you.

Read aloud each sentence in **Practice** and identify the main verb and helping verb in it. Have students work in mixed-proficiency pairs to circle each modal auxiliary and identify its function.

In **Apply,** ask volunteers to read the words in the word bank and the sentences aloud. Have students continue to work in pairs to complete this activity and the writing activity in **Reinforce.**

Speaking and Listening

Display a timeline showing events in a certain period of American history. Ask volunteers to tell what events the timeline includes and what information it gives about these events. Then have students suggest ways that they could create a more informative timeline about this period by adding facts and visuals.

Extra Practice

For more practice, see page 198.

Lesson 20 (student pages 53–54)
Adjectives

Objectives

- To learn that adjectives describe nouns and pronouns, and that there are different kinds of adjectives
- To identify descriptive adjectives, demonstrative adjectives that tell how many, and articles as adjectives in sentences
- To use adjectives to complete sentences
- To use adjectives to complete a puzzle

English Language Learners

Read the caption on page 53 aloud. Ask a volunteer to find North Carolina on a United States map. Point out the Outer Banks, a chain of islands that buffers the mainland from the Atlantic Ocean.

Read the sentences in **Practice** aloud. Then have volunteers read the sentences aloud, one at a time. Ask students to study each boldfaced word in item 1 and identify what type of adjective it is. Be sure students understand the four-part process in the directions as they complete the section.

Read aloud the word bank in **Apply.** Then have students work in pairs to complete the sentences. Suggest that they complete the sentences orally before they write their answers.

Students can work with the same partners to complete the puzzle in **Reinforce.** Suggest that they refer to the rule statement (in the gray box) on page 53 for information about adjectives.

Speaking and Listening

Have students work in pairs to brainstorm three or more sentences that describe themselves, using adjectives that tell how many. (Examples: I have *three* sisters. I like *many* sports. I have a collection of *twenty* comic books.) Give students five minutes. Then ask volunteers to share their sentences and to identify the adjectives in them.

Extra Practice

For more practice, see page 198.

Lesson 21 (student pages 55–56)
Adverbs

Objectives
- To learn that adverbs tell more about verbs or adjectives by explaining *how, when, where,* or *to what extent* (*how much*)
- To learn that many adverbs end in *-ly*
- To identify adverbs in sentences, and to tell how they are used
- To find adverbs in a word search and then write sentences using them

English Language Learners
Explain that whaling—the hunting of whales for profit—was a major industry in America in the early 1800s. Then read the caption on page 55 aloud.

Invite volunteers to help you read the sentences in **Practice** aloud. Make sure students understand the words *abandoned, declined, species,* and *extinct.* Ask students to identify the verb and the adverb in the first sentence. (hunted; first) Have them tell what the adverb explains. (when) Then have students work in pairs to find the remaining adverbs.

Before student pairs begin **Apply**, make sure they understand the terms *prey, entangled, starves, frantically,* and *shreds.* Read aloud all the sentences. Model identifying the adverb in item 14 and telling what it explains. (yearly; **when** whales migrate)

For **Reinforce**, students might complete the word search independently and then work with English-proficient partners to compose their sentences. List on the board the words students should look for. (across: recently, there; down: sometimes, very, slowly)

Speaking and Listening
Provide pictures showing various activities. Ask students to compose oral sentences for each picture, using adverbs that help describe the action. List on the board some adverbs students might use. (Examples: quickly, happily, hungrily, extremely, only)

Extra Practice
For more practice, see page 199.

Lesson 22 (student pages 57–58)
Ordering Adjectives

Objectives
- To discover that pairs of adjectives should be used in a natural-sounding order
- To identify pairs of adjectives used in an order that sounds natural
- To use pairs of adjectives in a natural-sounding order
- To write a paragraph about a national symbol

English Language Learners
Direct students' attention to the illustration on page 57. Next, read aloud the two example sentences in **Read and Analyze.** Have a volunteer identify the sentence that sounds more natural. Tell students that an adjective that tells how many should always be used before an adjective that tells what quality. Read aloud the rule statement. Tell students that adjectives describing origin, such as *American,* should be placed immediately before the nouns they describe.

Read aloud each sentence in **Practice** twice, inserting a different answer each time. Ask students to identify which choice produces a more natural-sounding sentence.

Pair students with English-proficient partners for the activity in **Apply.** Encourage students to read their completed sentences aloud quietly, to make sure they sound natural. Have partners continue to work together on the **Reinforce** activity. Encourage them to do Internet research on the symbol they choose before they write their paragraphs.

Speaking and Listening
Use objects in the classroom to give students practice in generating and ordering adjectives. You might pick up a softball and ask students what words they might use to describe it. Write students' responses on the board; for example, *white, round.* Have a volunteer then use these adjectives to describe the softball in a sentence: *That is a round white ball.* Note that students may offer some nouns that can function as adjectives, such as *rubber.* Guide students to place these closest to the noun; for example, *That is a round white rubber ball.*

Extra Practice
For more practice, see page 199.

Objectives

- To discover that coordinating conjunctions connect words or groups of words that are similar
- To learn that subordinating conjunctions, such as *although* and *because*, show how one clause is related to another clause in a sentence
- To identify coordinating and subordinating conjunctions in sentences, and to use them to complete sentences

English Language Learners

Read the caption on page 59 aloud and help students identify the four presidents in the illustration. (George Washington, Thomas Jefferson, Theodore Roosevelt, Abraham Lincoln) To help students fully appreciate the size of the monument, explain that the head of Washington is as high as a five-story building.

Read aloud and discuss the sentences in **Practice**. If necessary, explain the meanings of *statues, peak,* and *blast away*. Then help students identify the coordinating or subordinating conjunction in each sentence before they mark their answers.

Before students complete **Apply**, read the conjunctions in the word bank aloud. Then have student pairs work together to complete the section.

In **Reinforce**, have pairs work together to read the descriptions, to write the names of the presidents on the lines, and to circle the conjunctions.

Speaking and Listening

Write and, or, and but as well as several subordinating conjunctions on separate index cards. Have students pick a card and compose a sentence. Each sentence should contain the conjunction that was selected. (Examples: We go to the computer room on Tuesdays *and* Thursdays. We can't play outside *because* it is raining.)

Extra Practice

For more practice, see page 200.

Objectives

- To learn that correlative conjunctions always appear in pairs and that they connect words or groups of words
- To identify correlative conjunctions in sentences
- To rewrite groups of sentences as a single sentence with correlative conjunctions
- To write a paragraph using correlative conjunctions

English Language Learners

Ask students whether any of them have heard of the Tuskegee Airmen. Discuss with students why it would be both challenging and exciting to be a military pilot.

Next, read aloud the example sentence in **Read and Analyze** and have a volunteer identify the correlative conjunctions. Read aloud the rule statement and then have students reread it with you.

Read aloud the instructions and the sentences in **Practice**. If necessary, explain that discrimination means not treating people of a certain group fairly. Then call on students to identify conjunctions and tell whether they are coordinating conjunctions or correlative conjunctions.

Have students work with English-proficient partners to complete **Apply**. Point out that they may have to delete some words and add others when they rewrite each sentence pair as one sentence. For the **Reinforce** activity, have students continue to work with partners. Point out that students can write about someone who has served bravely in a branch of the U.S. military, someone who has helped many people while working in a branch of government, or someone who has helped Americans while working in another type of employment.

Speaking and Listening

Write a pair of correlative conjunctions on index cards. Have student pairs pick a card and use the correlative conjunctions in sentences about events in American history.

Extra Practice

For more practice, see page 200.

Unit Review (student pages 63–64)

The **Unit Review** allows you to check students' progress and determine when reteaching is necessary. The review pages may be completed in class or as homework. If a student responds incorrectly to two or more items involving the same skill, you may want to work directly with the student to review the relevant lesson. The lesson number to which each review item relates appears in parentheses on the review pages in the Teacher Edition.

Assign the **Extra Practice** activities (pp. 195–200) to reteach targeted skills in a more focused way.

Spelling Practice (student pages 65–66)

Spelling Patterns: Final Schwa + *n*, Final Schwa + *r*

Read aloud the example sentence and the directions in **Read and Analyze**. Have students reread the example sentence with you. Ask which words in the sentence end with the /ər/ sound. (remember, governor) Read the rule statement aloud.

Have students work in small groups to complete the **Word Sort** and share their results with the class. For the first **Pattern Practice** activity, read aloud the directions and have student pairs complete items 1–8. Ask them to present their answers to the class. For the second **Pattern Practice** activity, read aloud the directions and have students work independently to write the word that completes each sentence. Ask students to identify the /ər/ or /ən/ spelling in each word from the word bank. (common—on, remember—er, profession—ion, bother—er, citizen—en, major—or, solution—ion, differ—er)

Read aloud the directions in **Use the Dictionary**. Have students work independently to complete the words.

English Language Learners

Have students work with a partner who is fluent in English for the spelling activities. Students whose first language is Spanish are accustomed to stressing every syllable in a word and will not be familiar with the unstressed syllable in English. The vowel in this syllable is often pronounced as the schwa sound, regardless of how it is spelled. There is, therefore, no sound clue to the spelling. Have students whose first language is Spanish practice saying each syllable of a word as if it were a word itself. This will help clarify the schwa spelling.

Proofreading (student pages 67–68)

Proofreading Practice

Review the **Proofreading Marks** chart and the examples. Read the first sentence aloud. Discuss the first error (*is* should be *has*) and how it should be marked. Ask students to correct the remaining errors using proofreading marks. You may wish to have students correct the spelling errors, too. After students have completed the activity, ask volunteers to read each sentence aloud and identify the errors. **Note:** Some errors can be corrected in more than one way.

Proofreading Checklist

Ask students to select a recent piece of their own writing and to write the title of that piece at the top of the chart. Ask students to put a check mark next to each item in the checklist after they have checked it in their work. Students might first work independently and then trade papers with a partner to double-check each other's work. You might model, or ask a student to model, using the **G.U.M. Handbook** (beginning on page 239) to clarify a concept or rule.

Suggest that students look at the errors they did not find in the proofreading activity and add them to the checklist. Ask students to think about other kinds of errors they make and to add these to the checklist.

English Language Learners

Have students work with partners who are fluent in English for the proofreading activities.

School Home Connection (student pages 69–70)

These pages provide quick, fun activities that review and reinforce the skills and concepts taught in Unit 2. You might utilize the **School Home Connection** pages in one of the following ways:

- Ask students to take the pages home, choose one or two activities to do, and then ask their parents to sign and return the pages.
- Send the pages home without asking that they be returned.
- Ask students to do one activity at school and then send the pages home.

Unforgettable Folks:
Athletes

Unit 3 Usage

Building Usage Awareness

Write these sentences on the board:

Sports flash! Get you're tickets now if your going to the championship finals. There selling fast!

Invite a volunteer to read the sentences aloud. Ask students if the words in the sentences **sound** correct. Then ask if all the words in the sentences **look** correct. Invite volunteers to identify those they think are used incorrectly. (you're, your, there) Help students write the correct words above the incorrect words. Explain to students that in Unit 3, they will learn how to correctly use words that sound alike but have different meanings and spellings. They will also learn about other words that are often used incorrectly in writing. Inform students that using the correct words and word forms can help other people understand what they say and write.

Introduce the Unit Theme

Tell students that the title of Unit 3 is "Unforgettable Folks" and that each lesson highlights the achievements of one or more athletes in the United States and around the world. Invite students to name some athletes they admire. You might create a web around the title "Unforgettable Sports Figures." Use questions such as these to guide discussion:

- Do you think sports are an important part of a school, a town, or a country? Why or why not?

- Do you think athletes can be considered heroes or role models? Why or why not?

- What are some traits that most great athletes have?

Assessment Options
Unit Pretest

The **Unit Assessment** (pp. 177–180) is intended to be used as a diagnostic assessment to help you determine, prior to instruction, your students' existing knowledge and skill proficiency. Follow this procedure for administering the Unit Pretest:

1. Read aloud the test instructions. (**Note:** For additional scaffolding, you may wish to read the test questions and answer choices aloud.)

2. Tell students that they will have 20 minutes to read and answer the questions independently.

3. When time is up, collect and correct the tests. Use the results to determine which lessons to teach for targeted instruction or which lessons to spend extra time on during whole-class instruction if you are teaching all lessons in the unit.

Unit Posttest

The **Unit Posttest** (pp. 227–230) helps you judge students' achievement while providing them with practice for high-stakes tests. When you are ready to administer the test, ask students to carefully tear it out of their books. (**Note:** If the test has already been removed, distribute copies to students.) Read aloud the directions for each section and make sure students understand how to answer the questions. Ask students to work independently to complete the test.

Students who miss two questions focusing on the same grammar element may need additional help understanding the concept. Reteach the concept, following this procedure:

1. Review **Read and Analyze.**

2. Review the rule statement for the concept.

3. Guide students through items a second time. Ask the students to explain why each right answer is correct.

4. Refer students to the **G.U.M. Handbook** for further reinforcement.

Lesson 25 (student pages 71–72)
Their, There, They're

Objectives
- To discover that *their, there,* and *they're* sound the same but have different spellings and meanings
- To learn that *their* is a possessive pronoun, *there* is an adverb, and *they're* is a contraction of the words *they* and *are*
- To choose *their, there,* or *they're* to complete sentences, and to write sentences using these words
- To complete clues to a riddle using *their, there,* and *they're* correctly

English Language Learners
Read the caption on page 71 aloud. Explain that Billy Mills (a member of the Lakota, or Sioux, nation in South Dakota) won a gold Olympic medal in the track-and-field competition at the 1964 Olympics.

Read aloud the information in **Practice** about Mills's race. Then ask volunteers to reread each sentence aloud, to identify the word in parentheses that correctly completes that sentence, and to explain the reason for their choice. Point out that if *they are* makes sense in a sentence, then the contraction *they're* is correct.

For **Apply**, ask students to work in small groups to discuss races before they write their sentences. Have volunteers read their completed sentences aloud and spell out *their, there,* and *they're* to indicate which word was used in each sentence.

Have groups continue to work together to complete **Reinforce**. Remind them to capitalize a word that begins a sentence.

Speaking and Listening
Invite students to work in small groups to compose riddles using *their, there,* and *they're,* as in Reinforce. Group members can then take turns saying the sentences in their riddle aloud while classmates identify the use of *their, there,* and *they're* in the sentences.

Extra Practice
For more practice, see page 201.

Lesson 26 (student pages 73–74)
Its and *It's*

Objectives
- To discover that *its* and *it's* sound the same but have different spellings and meanings
- To learn that *its* is a possessive pronoun and *it's* is a contraction of *it* and *is*
- To distinguish between *its* and *it's,* and to use each correctly in sentences
- To complete clues to a riddle using *its* and *it's*

English Language Learners
Ask how many students have played table tennis. Encourage them to talk about the skills a person would need to become a champion table tennis player. Then explain to students that in this lesson they will read about one of the world's greatest table tennis players, Jan-Ove Waldner (YAHN-OH•vuh VAHLD•nehr).

Write *its* and *it's* on the board. Then read aloud the sentences in **Practice,** one at a time. Have students read each sentence after you. Ask group members to identify which word from the board belongs in each sentence.

Have students work in pairs to read aloud each sentence in **Apply,** explaining whether *its* or *it's* belongs in the blank before they write their responses.

Have student teams of two or more compete to solve the riddle in **Reinforce.** Remind them to capitalize a word that begins a sentence.

Speaking and Listening
Divide the class into two teams. Have one member from each team come to the front of the class, listen as you read aloud a sentence containing *its* or *it's,* and identify which word is used. The first student to raise his or her hand and spell the right answer scores a point. Continue until all students have had a chance to compete.

Extra Practice
For more practice, see page 201.

Lesson 27 (student pages 75–76)
Your and *You're*

Objectives
- To discover that *your* and *you're* sound the same but have different spellings and meanings
- To learn that *your* is a possessive pronoun and *you're* is a contraction of the words *you* and *are*
- To distinguish between *your* and *you're* in sentences, and to answer questions using *your* and *you're* correctly
- To compose a pep talk using *your* and *you're*

English Language Learners
Ask students to identify the skater on page 75. (Michelle Kwan) If possible, obtain a video about figure skating to show to the class.

Read the sentences in **Practice** aloud. Then have volunteers reread the sentences aloud. After each sentence, ask students to identify the correct word in parentheses and to explain their answer. Point out that if *you are* makes sense in the sentence, then the contraction *you're* is correct.

For **Apply**, have students work in pairs to compose oral responses to the questions before they write sentences. Model the process with the help of a student volunteer. (Example: Is my coach here yet? No, **your** coach isn't here.)

Have students discuss the meaning of *pep talk* before they work independently to complete **Reinforce**. If necessary, students might dictate their sentences to you, an aide, or a peer tutor.

Speaking and Listening
Challenge students to use *your* and *you're* in oral sentences about safety tips for a sport or other activity. Model the process using examples such as these:

> Wear **your** helmet when **you're** riding a bike.
> When **you're** learning to ski, keep **your** knees bent.

Ask students to identify which word is used at each occurrence.

Extra Practice
For more practice, see page 202.

Lesson 28 (student pages 77–78)
Comparing With *Good* or *Bad*

Objectives
- To learn how to make comparisons using forms of *good* and *bad*
- To understand that *better* and *worse* are used to compare two people, things, or actions and *best* and *worst* are used to compare three or more people, things, or actions
- To choose the correct form of *good* or *bad* in sentences
- To complete sentences, and to write a comparison using forms of *good* and *bad* correctly

English Language Learners
Read the caption on page 77 aloud. Explain to students that in Lesson 28 they will find out about two baseball players, Ichiro Suzuki and Jackie Robinson.

Work with students to complete **Practice**. Discuss how many things are being compared in each sentence. Ask students to choose a word to complete each sentence, and have a volunteer read the sentence aloud.

For **Apply**, review the words in the word bank and ask volunteers to use them in oral sentences. Have students discuss with a partner how many things are being compared in each sentence before they write.

For **Reinforce**, draw a Venn diagram on the board and show students how to use it to make comparisons. Have students work in pairs to make diagrams comparing two sports before they write their paragraphs.

Speaking and Listening
Ask volunteers to name their favorite and least favorite foods. Record their responses on the board. Then have students use these responses to make oral comparisons between two or more things, using the correct forms of *good* and *bad*. (Examples: Pizzas are *better* than hot dogs. Celery is the *worst* food of all.)

Extra Practice
For more practice, see page 202.

Objectives

- To learn that *that* is used to refer to either people or things, *which* is used to refer to things, and *who* is used to refer to people
- To choose *that, which,* or *who* in sentences
- To complete sentences and clues using *that, which,* or *who* correctly

English Language Learners

Read the caption on page 79 aloud. Explain that Jim Plunkett was one of the first Mexican American players to become a star in the National Football League. Tell students that Plunkett was very good at several sports but had to choose just one to focus on.

In **Practice**, ask students to pick the word they think belongs in each sentence and to explain their choice. Remind them that they can test whether to use *that* or *which* by reading the sentence without the clause to see if the sentence still makes sense.

For **Apply**, ask students to read each sentence and discuss their choices with a partner before they fill in the blanks.

Then divide the class into teams of two or more, and have them work cooperatively to solve the riddle poem in **Reinforce.**

Speaking and Listening

Help students brainstorm lists of different sports, pieces of sports equipment, and athletes. Ask students to compose oral sentences that contain an item from one or more of the lists and the pronoun *that, which,* or *who.* (Examples: Football, *which* is a popular sport, is very exciting to watch. The position *that* requires the greatest strength is nose tackle. Jim Plunkett, *who* was an exceptional player, helped make the Raiders successful.)

Extra Practice

For more practice, see page 203.

Objectives

- To learn that *real* is an adjective that means "actual" and that *very* is an adverb that means "extremely"
- To identify correct and incorrect usage of *real* and *very*
- To write sentences, and to complete a poem using *real* and *very* correctly

English Language Learners

Invite students to share what they know about hockey. Discuss the picture of Canadian Mario Lemieux on page 81 and help students pronounce his name (MAH•ree•oh luh•MYOO). Tell students that Lemieux enjoyed a long and highly successful career despite disabling injuries and a serious illness.

Read each sentence in **Practice**. After each one, ask students to tell whether *real* or *very* is used correctly. Ask volunteers to correct the sentences that have the wrong words and then to reread them aloud.

For **Apply**, invite students to complete each item orally. (Example: item 11: Basketball is *very* exciting to watch.) Have student pairs compose oral sentences using *real* and *very* before they write.

Have students work with the same partners to solve the riddle poem in **Reinforce.** Invite students to read the poem chorally after it has been completed.

Speaking and Listening

Guide students in telling a round-robin story using *real* or *very* in each sentence. You might write the sentences below on the board as story starters and have small groups of storytellers choose which one they would like to use.

One day Joshua found a real gold coin.

Anna was very happy to see the brown envelope on the desk.

Extra Practice

For more practice, see page 203.

Lesson 31 (student pages 83–84)
Set and *Sit*

Objectives
- To learn how to use the verbs *set* and *sit* correctly
- To choose a correct form of *set* or *sit* in sentences
- To rewrite sentences with correct forms of *set* or *sit*
- To write lists that reflect correct use of *set* and *sit*

English Language Learners

Read the illustration caption on page 83 aloud. Inform students that Carly Patterson, of Baton Rouge, Louisiana, won two silver medals in the 2004 Olympics. Then invite students who may be involved in gymnastics or who may have seen gymnastic competitions to describe the equipment and events related to the sport.

Read each sentence in **Practice** aloud twice, using a different answer choice each time. Have students underline the answer choice that correctly completes the sentence. If students have difficulty, remind them to ask themselves, "Set what?" If they cannot answer that question, then the correct word is *sit*.

For **Apply,** suggest that students ask themselves the same question ("Set what?") before they write their answers. Then ask a volunteer to model rewriting item 12. (Example: The members of the audience...*sat down.*) Have students complete the remaining items with partners.

Have students work independently to complete **Reinforce.** Invite volunteers to compose oral sentences using the items they listed and the word *set* or *sit.*

Speaking and Listening

Invite students to take turns pantomiming actions that involve *sitting* or *setting* things down. Ask other students to compose oral sentences describing each action that uses forms of *set* or *sit* correctly.

Extra Practice

For more practice, see page 204.

Lesson 32 (student pages 85–86)
Learn and *Teach*

Objectives
- To understand that the verbs *learn* and *teach* are both related to knowledge and to learn how to use the two words correctly
- To choose a form of *learn* and *teach* in sentences, and to write answers to questions using the correct forms of these words
- To write a paragraph using correct forms of *learn* or *teach*

English Language Learners

Ask students what they have *learned* about how to play soccer, and who *taught* them. Then read the caption on page 85 aloud and discuss the picture.

Read each sentence in **Practice** aloud twice, inserting a different answer choice each time. Allow students to answer orally before they underline their answers. Write *goalie, goalkeeper,* and *goaltender* on the board. Explain that these are synonyms.

For **Apply,** invite students to respond orally before they write their answers.

Then have students work independently or in pairs to write their paragraphs in **Reinforce.** Invite volunteers to read their paragraphs aloud.

Speaking and Listening

Ask students to compose oral sentences about subjects they are studying or activities they are involved in, using present and past tense forms of *learn* and *teach.* (Examples: I *learn* about athletic champions in class. I *taught* my mother how to use the computer.)

Extra Practice

For more practice, see page 204.

Objectives

- To learn that *two, to,* and *too* sound the same but have different spellings and meanings
- To distinguish between *two, to,* and *too* in context and to use them correctly in sentences
- To write a sentence using *two, to,* and *too* correctly

English Language Learners

Direct students' attention to the sketch on page 87. Read the caption aloud. Ask students to identify similarities and differences between softball and baseball. List students' responses in a Venn diagram. Then have volunteers summarize the similarities and differences.

Read aloud the example sentence in **Read and Analyze.** Have volunteers identify the words called for in the directions below the sentence. Then read aloud the rule statement. Have students reread it with you.

Next, read the paragraphs in **Practice** aloud. Then ask volunteers to read each sentence aloud and identify the correct word in parentheses. After a student identifies a choice, ask another student why the choice is or is not correct.

Read each sentence in **Apply** aloud. Have students work in pairs to complete the activity. Have students write their sentences for **Reinforce** independently. Then have partners check each other's work. You may want to give an award to the student who writes the sentence in which *two, to,* and *too* are used the most times correctly.

Speaking and Listening

Ask students to tell about a sporting event they have attended. Each time a student says the word *two, to,* or *too,* signal the speaker to stop and have the class spell out the word the student used.

Extra Practice

For more practice, see page 205.

Objectives

- To learn that the irregular verbs *know* and *grow* change spelling in the past tense
- To choose a form of *know* or *grow* in sentences, and to write answers to questions using correct forms of these words
- To complete a crossword puzzle using correct forms of *know* and *grow*

English Language Learners

Ask students to state some rules for staying safe in and around water. Then ask students to brainstorm ways that swimming regularly could help a person.

In **Practice,** review the verb forms on page 89. Read each sentence from **Practice** aloud twice, saying a different answer choice each time. Have students pick the correct word and reread the complete sentence aloud.

Read aloud the questions in **Apply** and invite volunteers to respond orally to each one. Model this process with the help of a student volunteer. Students might then work independently or in pairs to discuss and write their answers.

Have students work cooperatively to complete the puzzle in **Reinforce.** Suggest that they refer to the rule statement (in the gray box) on page 89 if they need help remembering the forms of *know* and *grow.*

Speaking and Listening

Invite students to tell about themselves. Ask them to use as many different forms of *know* and *grow* as possible. Write the verb forms on the board and review them before students begin. You might prompt their responses with questions such as *What is something you know a lot about?* and *In what year did you grow the most in height?* After each speaker is finished, have listeners identify the forms of *know* and *grow* that were used.

Extra Practice

For more practice, see page 205.

Lesson 35 (student pages 91–92)
Reflexive and Indefinite Pronouns

Objectives

- To recognize that reflexive pronouns are used to refer back to the subject of a sentence
- To recognize that indefinite pronouns refer to persons or things that are not identified as individuals
- To recognize reflexive and indefinite pronouns and use them correctly in sentences

English Language Learners

Direct students' attention to the illustration on page 91. Read the caption aloud. Have volunteers explain when basketball players get to shoot free throws, and what a player must do to be able to shoot free throws accurately. Read aloud the example sentences in **Read and Analyze.** Have students then reread the example sentences with you. Ask students which sentences are written correctly. (the first pair) Read the rule statement aloud, and then have students reread it with you.

Next, read the **Practice** instructions and each sentence aloud. Tell students to read each sentence to themselves, decide which word in parentheses is correct, and circle that word. Then read aloud the instructions and incomplete sentences in **Apply.** Work as a class to complete item 11. Then have student pairs complete the remaining items. Finally, read aloud the instructions for **Reinforce.** Have students work with partners to unscramble and classify the pronouns.

Speaking and Listening

Invite students to name their favorite sports and describe particular skills having to do with the sport that they practice in order to improve their game. Encourage listeners to ask specific questions about technique and practice routines.

Extra Practice

For more practice, see page 206.

Lesson 36 (student pages 93–94)
Pronoun-Antecedent Agreement

Objectives

- To discover that an antecedent is the word or words that a pronoun refers to, and that pronouns and antecedents must agree in number and gender
- To select pronoun forms that agree with antecedents in sentences
- To write sentences using personal pronouns that agree with their antecedents

English Language Learners

Have students look at the picture on page 93 and read the caption. Discuss with students what would be challenging about climbing a mountain in a wheelchair. Ask them to speculate on why a person might try to do this despite the difficulty involved. Next, read aloud the example sentences and the directions in **Read and Analyze.** Have students reread the example sentences with you. Ask which words in the first sentence could replace the word *he* in the second sentence. (Bob Coomber) Guide students to circle these words and draw an arrow from the boldfaced pronoun to them. Follow the same procedure for the boldfaced pronoun *it* in the third sentence. Read the rule statement aloud and have students read it with you.

Read aloud the sentences in **Practice.** Work with students to complete the first item. Explain that *Bob Coomber's wheelchair* is the phrase that the pronoun *it* takes the place of in the second sentence. Then have students work in pairs to complete the remaining items.

Have students complete **Apply** in pairs. Then have students work independently to write sentences in **Reinforce.**

Speaking and Listening

Encourage students to identify and discuss trails and paths in your region that they could hike. If possible, invite a ranger, park employee, or other outdoor recreation expert to give students tips on hiking safety.

Extra Practice

For more practice, see page 206.

Unit Review   (student pages 95–96)

The **Unit Review** allows you to check students' progress and determine when reteaching is necessary. The review pages may be completed in class or as homework. If a student responds incorrectly to two or more items involving the same skill, you may want to work directly with the student to review the relevant lesson. The lesson number to which each review item relates appears in parentheses on the review pages in the Teacher Edition.

Assign the **Extra Practice** activities (pp. 201–206) to reteach targeted skills in a more focused way.

Spelling Practice   (student pages 97–98)

Adding Suffixes: *-er, -est, -ed, -ing*

Read aloud the example sentences and the directions in **Read and Analyze**. Have students reread the example sentences with you. Ask which word in bold type has a suffix that means "the most." (calmest) Discuss the meanings of other suffixes in the sentences. Read the rule statement aloud.

Have students work in small groups to complete the **Word Sort** and share their results with the class. For the first **Pattern Practice** activity, read aloud the directions and have student pairs complete items 1–7. Ask them to present their answers to the class. For the second **Pattern Practice** activity, read aloud the directions. Have students work independently to add the suffixes and write the new words in the sentences. Ask which words students formed. (sunniest, trimming, removed, kinder, admitted, traveled, carrying)

Read aloud the directions and the words in **Use the Dictionary**. Have students work independently to write the base words.

English Language Learners

Have students work with a partner who is fluent in English for the spelling activities. In the Spanish language, there is no final **-ing** spelling, though there is the word ending **-ante**, which serves the same function. Additionally, the pronunciation of **-ing** should not be too problematic as Spanish has an **/ng/** sound. In Spanish the final **d** has a slightly different pronunciation than it has in English.

Proofreading   (student pages 99–100)

Proofreading Practice

Review the **Proofreading Marks** chart and the examples. Read the second sentence in the second paragraph aloud. Discuss the error (*which* should be *who*) and how it should be marked. Ask students to correct the remaining errors using proofreading marks. You may wish to have students correct the spelling errors, too. After students have completed the activity, ask volunteers to read each sentence aloud and to identify the errors. **Note:** Some errors can be corrected in more than one way.

Proofreading Checklist

Ask students to select a recent piece of their own writing and to write the title of that piece at the top of the chart. Ask students to put a check mark next to each item in the checklist after they have checked it in their work. Students might first work independently and then trade papers with a partner to double-check each other's work. You might model, or ask a student to model, using the **G.U.M. Handbook** (beginning on page 239) to clarify a concept or rule.

Suggest that students look at the errors they did not find in the proofreading activity and add them to the checklist. Ask students to think about other kinds of errors they make and to add these to the checklist.

English Language Learners

Have students work with partners who are fluent in English for the proofreading activities.

School Home Connection   (student pages 101–102)

These pages provide quick, fun activities that review and reinforce the skills and concepts taught in Unit 3. You might utilize the **School Home Connection** pages in one of the following ways:

- Ask students to take the pages home, choose one or two activities to do, and then ask their parents to sign and return the pages.
- Send the pages home without asking that they be returned.
- Ask students to do one activity at school and then send the pages home.

Grab Bag:
Cars

Unit 4 Grammar

Building Grammar Awareness

Write this sentence on the board and ask a volunteer to read it aloud:

My mom, dad, aunt, and uncle took my brother, sister, and me to the car races.

Ask students whether there is a shorter, easier way to say this sentence. (*They* took *us* to the car races.) Tell students that in Unit 4 they will learn how to use words such as *they* and *us* in sentences. Explain that they will also learn how to use different types of verbs, comparing words, and words that mean "no." Tell students that using words correctly in sentences can help other people understand what is meant when writing and speaking.

Introduce the Unit Theme

Explain that each lesson in Unit 4 gives information about auto racing and cars. Invite students to name some racecars or car races they know of. List their responses in a web labeled "Cars." Use questions such as those below to guide discussion.

- How is driving a racecar different from driving a normal car on a city street?
- What safety precautions do racecar drivers need to take?

Assessment Options
Unit Pretest

The **Unit Pretest** (pp. 181–184) is intended to used as a diagnostic assessment to help you determine, prior to instruction, your students' existing knowledge and skill proficiency. Follow this procedure for administering the Unit Pretest:

1. Read aloud the test instructions. (**Note:** For additional scaffolding, you may wish to read the test questions and answer choices aloud.)

2. Tell students that they will have 20 minutes to read and answer the questions independently.

3. When time is up, collect and correct the tests. Use the results to determine which lessons to teach for targeted instruction or which lessons to spend extra time on during whole-class instruction if you are teaching all lessons in the unit.

Unit Posttest

The **Unit Posttest** (pp. 231–234) helps you judge students' achievement while providing them with valuable practice for high-stakes tests. When you are ready to administer the test, ask students to carefully tear it out of their books. (**Note:** If the test has already been removed, distribute copies to students.) Read aloud the directions for each section and make sure students understand how to answer the questions. Ask students to work independently to complete the test.

Students who miss two questions focusing on the same grammar element may need additional help understanding the concept. Reteach the concept, following this procedure:

1. Review **Read and Analyze.**
2. Review the rule statement for the concept.
3. Guide students through items a second time. Ask the students to explain why each right answer is correct.
4. Refer students to the **G.U.M. Handbook** for further reinforcement.

Lesson 37 (student pages 103–104)
Subject and Object Pronouns

Objectives
- To discover that a subject pronoun takes the place of a noun in a sentence
- To learn that object pronouns can be used after action verbs or prepositions
- To identify subject and object pronouns in sentences, and to rewrite sentences using subject and object pronouns
- To write descriptive sentences using subject and object pronouns

English Language Learners
Write Indy 500 on the board. Explain that it is the short name for the Indianapolis 500-mile car race that is held every Memorial Day weekend in Indiana.

In **Practice**, ask students to read each sentence and to tell whether the boldfaced word is a subject or an object pronoun. **Note:** For item 4, because *you* can be either a subject or an object pronoun, model changing the question into a statement to find the subject.

For Apply, have student pairs read each sentence aloud, decide which pronoun should replace each boldfaced phrase, and then rewrite the sentence.

Before students begin **Reinforce**, list on the board the subject and object pronouns from the rule statement on page 103. Have students work in groups of three or four to compose sentences using subject and object pronouns. Suggest that they begin by brainstorming things they might see, hear, and feel at the Indy 500.

Speaking and Listening
Encourage students to find pictures of racecars and car races in magazines. Have them use subject and object pronouns to describe the pictures.

Extra Practice
For more practice, see page 207.

Lesson 38 (student pages 105–106)
Pronouns in Pairs

Objectives
- To learn how to use subject and object pronouns correctly in sentences
- To choose appropriate subject or object pronouns to complete sentences
- To rewrite sentences, substituting nouns with appropriate subject or object pronouns
- To complete a crossword puzzle, using pronouns as clues

English Language Learners
Explain that *drag* can be a slang term for a street or road (for example, the main *drag*). Then ask students what a *drag race* is (a high-speed car race on pavement). Explain that usually two cars race at a time to determine which can accelerate faster.

Before students mark their answers in **Practice**, ask them to identify whether the answer choices are part of the subject or part of an object. To help students determine the correct pronoun, suggest that they say each sentence without *and* and the name of the other person. (Example: item 1: Take away **Betty and** and read the sentence as (*He/Him*) takes turns driving their dragster.) Have students identify the pronoun that fits.

For **Apply,** help students determine which subject or object pronoun each boldfaced noun should be replaced with. Explain that a "funny car" (in item 13) is one of three types of professional drag-racing cars.

For **Reinforce,** tell students that the answers to the crossword puzzle are the names of the people in **Apply.**

Speaking and Listening
Ask students to describe races they have watched. Encourage speakers to use as many personal pronouns as they can, and have listeners identify each as a subject or an object pronoun.

Extra Practice
For more practice, see page 207.

Lesson 39 (student pages 107–108)
Subject-Verb Agreement

Objectives
- To learn that the subject and the verb of a sentence must agree
- To learn how to make present tense regular verbs agree with singular and plural subjects
- To choose verb forms that agree with the subjects to complete sentences and puzzle clues

English Language Learners
Point out the picture and caption on page 107. Explain that Formula One races feature cars with one seat, a rear engine, and front and back wings.

In **Practice,** ask students to identify each simple subject and to identify the correct verb.

Have students complete **Apply** with partners. You may need to introduce *series* and *Grand Prix*. Explain that the Grand Prix series is made up of about 15 races held in Canada, France, the United States, and other countries.

Have pairs of students work cooperatively to complete the puzzle in **Reinforce.**

Speaking and Listening
Write subject/verb pairs on separate index cards. Each subject should be singular and each verb should have the *s* or *es* ending (Examples: The Formula One car/zooms, The fan/cheers). Give one card to each pair of students. Ask each pair to compose a sentence using the subject/verb pair on the card. (Example: *The Formula One car zooms* around the curve.) Write it on the board, and read it aloud. Ask a volunteer to restate the sentence with a plural subject and write it under the original. Discuss how the subject and verb must agree as you review each pair of sentences.

Extra Practice
For more practice, see page 208.

Lesson 40 (student pages 109–110)
Forms of *Be*

Objectives
- To learn which forms of *be* to use with singular subjects and plural subjects
- To choose the correct form of *be* to complete sentences
- To write sentences using forms of *be*

English Language Learners
Have students look at the picture on page 109 as you read the caption aloud. Tell students that "banked corners" refers to the angle of incline of the track. The incline helps a stock car get around a curve.

Read the sentences in **Practice** aloud, saying both answer choices. Help students identify whether the subject of each sentence is singular or plural before having them underline their answers. Ask volunteers to reread the sentences aloud with the correct answer choices in place.

Before students complete **Apply,** have them identify the singular and plural subjects in the sentences in the paragraph. **Note:** To help students decide which verb fits the first sentence, you might have them rephrase the question as a statement: You _____ at the NASCAR races last Saturday.

Have pairs of students compose the sentences in **Reinforce.** Suggest that partners describe what auto racers are like before they write their sentences. (Example: Auto racers are brave. I am a brave auto racer.)

Speaking and Listening
Write each form of *be* on a separate index card and place the cards facedown in a pile. Have students take turns picking a card and using the verb form in an oral sentence about themselves or their classmates.

Extra Practice
For more practice, see page 208.

Language Standard(s): L.5.1, L.5.1c

Objectives

- To discover that the present tense is used to tell about something that is taking place now or is true now and to write the present tense form of verbs
- To learn that past tense verbs tell about actions that have already happened and to write the past tense form of regular and irregular verbs
- To learn that future tense verbs tell about actions that are going to happen and to use the helping verb *will* to form the future tense
- To identify verbs in past, present, and future tense in sentences, and to rewrite sentences using correct tense forms of verbs
- To write sentences with past, present, and future tense forms of verbs

English Language Learners

Write *Ferrari* and *Porsche* on the board and ask volunteers to pronounce the names and describe these sports cars. Point out that these two sports cars are among the fastest race cars in the world.

Read aloud the example paragraph in **Read and Analyze.** Have volunteers respond to the directions. Then read aloud the rule statement, and have students read it aloud with you.

Read each sentence in **Practice.** Ask students to identify the verb and tell whether it is in the past, present, or future tense.

Read the caption on page 112 aloud. Remind students that the 24 Hours of Daytona held in Daytona Beach, Florida, is a famous endurance race. Then read the sentences in **Apply** aloud. Have student pairs reread each sentence aloud, first with the present tense verb in place and then with the past tense verb, before they write their answers. Have partners complete the activity in **Reinforce.**

Speaking and Listening

Challenge students to compose oral sentences about ten things they did last week. Then challenge them to predict ten things they will do next week.

Extra Practice

For more practice, see page 209.

Objectives

- To discover that progressive verb forms show continuing action
- To learn how to form progressive verbs
- To distinguish among present, past, and future progressive verb forms in sentences
- To complete sentences by writing the correct progressive forms of verbs
- To write sentences with progressive forms of verbs

English Language Learners

Ask students whether they have ever watched a demolition derby. Ask those who have seen such an event to describe its sights and sounds.

Read aloud the example paragraph in **Read and Analyze.** Have volunteers tell how the verbs should be marked. Next, read aloud the rule statement; then have students read it with you.

Read aloud the sentences in **Practice.** Point out that progressive forms of verbs end in *-ing* and use forms of *be* as helping verbs. Have students reread the first sentence and tell which progressive form is used. (past progressive) Have student pairs complete the remaining items.

For **Apply,** call on volunteers to tell which helping verb from the word bank is appropriate for each item. Have student pairs complete the sentences. Then have students work independently to write answers to the questions in **Reinforce.**

Speaking and Listening

Point out that events such as auto races and demolition derbies are dangerous. Invite students to discuss the risks involved in different motor sports, and the safety measures that drivers, event organizers, and motor sports organizations have instituted to reduce the risk of injury. Encourage interested students to do Internet research on protective devices and safety equipment used in motor sports and report their findings to the class.

Extra Practice

For more practice, see page 209.

Objectives

- To learn that verbs in the present perfect tense show action that began in the past and may still be continuing in the present
- To learn how to form the present perfect tense by adding *has* or *have* to the past participle of a verb
- To identify verbs in the present perfect tense in sentences
- To complete sentences using verbs in the present perfect tense

English Language Learners

Have students look at the drawing of the globe on page 115. Read the caption aloud. Ask students which continents the contestants crossed. (North America, Asia, Europe)

Read aloud the example sentences in **Read and Analyze.** Have volunteers tell which verb should be circled. Next, read aloud the rule statement; then have students read it with you.

Read aloud the sentences in **Practice.** Point out that the verb in sentence 1 is *has attracted*, which is a present perfect tense verb. Have students work with partners to identify and mark the present perfect tense verbs in the remaining sentences.

For **Apply,** have students continue to work in pairs. Tell students to compose answers orally before they write their responses. For **Reinforce,** have students work with partners to complete the activity.

Speaking and Listening

Play a game about movies, songs, and books. Have teams of students write questions. Call on teams, one by one, to read the questions aloud. Students should begin with the question *Have you seen . . .?, Have you heard . . .?,* or *Have you read . . .?* Then, if the answer is *yes,* they should ask a question about that movie, song, or book. (If the answer is *no,* they must start over.) The opposing team has to answer the second question correctly to score a point.

Extra Practice

For more practice, see page 210.

Objectives

- To learn that the past perfect tense indicates action that was completed by a certain time in the past
- To learn that the future perfect tense indicates action that will be completed by a certain time in the future
- To identify and use past perfect tense and future perfect tense verbs in sentences
- To write sentences with past perfect tense and future perfect tense verbs

English Language Learners

Explain that a jet dragster is a racing car that has an engine of the kind used to power modern airliners. Invite a volunteer to explain how a jet engine works.

Read aloud the example paragraph in **Read and Analyze.** Have volunteers respond to the directions. Then ask students to identify the tense of the remaining boldfaced verb, *has excited.* (present perfect tense) Read aloud the rule statement, and have students read it aloud with you.

Read each sentence in **Practice.** Have a volunteer identify the tense of the verb in sentence 1 (past perfect tense) and explain how she or he determined this. (This verb includes the helping verb *had* and the past participle form of the verb *prove*.) Have students work independently to complete the activity.

Read aloud the instructions and sentences in **Apply.** Have students work with English-proficient partners to complete this activity. Have students continue to work with their partners to write the sentences called for in **Reinforce.**

Speaking and Listening

Challenge students to compose oral sentences about goals they had accomplished by the time they celebrated their tenth birthday. Then ask them to compose oral sentences about goals they probably will have accomplished by the time they celebrate their twentieth birthday.

Extra Practice

For more practice, see page 210.

Objectives

- To learn that events happening in the same time frame should be described using verbs in the same tense
- To learn that events happening at different times should be described using verbs in different tenses that make clear the order of these events
- To identify and correct inappropriate tense shifts in sentences and paragraphs
- To write a paragraph using verb tenses correctly to indicate different time frames

English Language Learners

Read aloud the caption on page 119. Guide students in a dicussion on go-karts and explain what go-kart drivers must do to stay safe while driving these vehicles.

Read aloud the example sentences in **Read and Analyze.** Have a volunteer respond to the questions and read the corrected sentence aloud. Then read aloud the rule statement.

Read aloud each sentence in **Practice.** Ask students to identify the first verb in the first sentence (*writes*) and tell what tense it is in. (present tense) Then ask them whether a verb that follows this first verb shifts the time frame inappropriately, and if so, how it does this. (Yes. *Chose* shifts the time frame incorrectly from present to past.) Have a volunteer correct the error and read the corrected sentence aloud. Then have students work with English-proficient partners to complete the activity.

Next read aloud the instructions and the paragraph in **Apply.** Have students continue working with English-proficient partners to complete this activity. Then read aloud the instructions for **Reinforce.** Have students work with their partners to plan and write drafts. Afterward, have students work with partners to read aloud and revise their paragraphs, noting the correct use of verb tenses.

Speaking and Listening

Have students role-play race announcers using present-tense verbs to describe events in an auto race as they are happening. Then have students role-play announcers recapping the events in an auto race that has just concluded, using past tense verbs to describe what happened.

Extra Practice

For more practice, see page 211.

Objectives

- To learn that a negative is a word that means "no" or "not" and that the words *no, not, nothing, none, never, nowhere,* and *nobody* are negatives
- To learn that using two negatives in a sentence should be avoided
- To identify double negatives in context, and to rewrite sentences to eliminate double negatives
- To find negatives in a word search and write them

English Language Learners

Explain that the Mille Miglia was a grueling 1,000-mile cross-country auto race that started and ended in Brescia, Italy. Have students look at the map of the race route on page 121. Explain that Taruffi, nicknamed the "Silver Fox" for his gray hair, was the victor (after many previous failures) in the final race held in 1957.

Read aloud the sentences in **Practice** and ask students to identify the negative(s) in each. Then have them mark the incorrect sentences. Ask volunteers to correct the sentences containing double negatives.

Have students identify the negatives in each sentence in **Apply.** Ask volunteers to model correcting item 13 in two different ways. (Examples: After 1957, the Mille Miglia wasn't held anymore. The Mille Miglia was not held after 1957.)

Student pairs can complete the word search in **Reinforce.** Ask students to identify contractions with the word *not* (Examples: don't, doesn't, weren't, and isn't).

Speaking and Listening

Invite students to play a "Negatives" game by using negative expressions to make silly observations about people or things. (Examples: *Nobody* can hang upside down from the classroom ceiling. The chairs have legs, but *none* of them can walk.)

Extra Practice

For more practice, see page 211.

Lesson 47 (student pages 123–124)

Comparative and Superlative Adjectives

Objectives

- To learn that comparative forms of adjectives compare two or more people, places, or things and are often followed by the word *than*
- To learn that superlative forms of adjectives compare three or more people, places, or things and often follow the word *the*
- To learn how to create the comparative and superlative forms of adjectives
- To choose the correct forms of adjectives in sentences, and to complete sentences using these forms
- To find adjectives in a word search, and to identify the comparative or superlative form of each

English Language Learners

Explain that a soap box race is for 9- to 16-year-olds who build their own motorless racecars that they coast downhill.

In **Practice,** have volunteers correct the first two items. Then have student pairs complete the activity.

Help students identify what is being compared in each sentence in **Apply** before pairs complete the activity. Help students determine whether to use *more* or *most* or the endings *-er* or *-est.*

Students can work independently to complete the word search in **Reinforce.** (across: wildest, earliest, faster; down: lowest, softer, highest)

Speaking and Listening

Ask students to orally compose comparisons about racecars and races. Each sentence should use a comparative or a superlative adjective. (Example: The *most difficult* race was the New York-to-Paris race in 1908. That Porsche may be the *fastest* of all the cars at this race.)

Extra Practice

For more practice, see page 212.

Lesson 48 (student pages 125–126)

Comparative and Superlative Adverbs

Objectives

- To learn that adverbs that end in *-ly* are preceded by *more* in the comparative form and are followed by the word *than*
- To learn that adverbs that end in *-ly* are preceded by *most* in the superlative form
- To choose the correct forms of adverbs in sentences, and to complete sentences using these forms
- To write a comparison using a comparative or a superlative adverb

English Language Learners

Read the caption on page 125. If any students have driven a midget car, have them describe the experience.

Review the meaning of *comparative* and *superlative.* Then read the sentences in **Practice** aloud, and help students clarify how many people or things are being compared in each (Example: item 2: two: the last lap and the first lap). Have student pairs reread each sentence aloud, decide which adverb form correctly completes the sentence, and underline their answer.

In **Apply,** suggest that partners read each sentence aloud and determine what is being compared before they complete the activity.

Read the directions in **Reinforce** aloud. Ask students to name different competitions. Then list them on the board (Examples: car races, track-and-field events, swimming, gymnastics, figure skating). Have partners compose their sentences orally before they write them.

Speaking and Listening

Write several comparative and superlative forms of adverbs on the board (Examples: **comparative:** faster, more carefully; **superlative:** fastest, most carefully). Invite students to suggest words and phrases of their own. Then ask students to use these forms in oral sentences.

Extra Practice

For more practice, see page 212.

Unit Review (student pages 127–128)

The **Unit Review** allows you to check students' progress and determine when reteaching is necessary. The review pages may be completed in class or as homework. If a student responds incorrectly to two or more items involving the same skill, you may want to work directly with the student to review the relevant lesson. The lesson number to which each review item relates appears in parentheses on the review pages in the Teacher Edition.

Assign the **Extra Practice** activities (pp. 207–212) to reteach targeted skills in a more focused way.

Spelling Practice (student pages 129–130)

Homophones

Read aloud the example sentences and the directions in **Read and Analyze**. Have students reread the example sentences with you. Ask which word in bold type means "stops working properly." (breaks) Then ask which one means "parts that cause a machine to stop." (brakes) Ask students what these words have in common. Read the rule statement aloud.

Have students work in small groups to complete **Words in Context** and share their answers with the class. For the first **Pattern Practice** activity, read aloud the directions and have student pairs complete items 9–12. Ask them to present their answers to the class. For the second **Pattern Practice** activity, read aloud the directions and the words in the word bank. Have students work independently to write the word that matches each meaning. Ask students to use each homophone in a sentence.

Read aloud the directions in **Use the Dictionary**. Have students work independently to complete each homophone.

English Language Learners

Have students work with a partner who is fluent in English for the spelling activities. Make flash cards for the words in these activities. Introduce the words using real objects, gestures, and pictures to provide context and support meaning. Have students choose five sets of homophones from the list and write sentences using each word. Allow time for volunteers to read their sentences to the rest of the class.

Proofreading (student pages 131–132)

Proofreading Practice

Review the **Proofreading Marks** chart and the examples. Read the first few sentences aloud. Discuss the errors and how they should be marked. Ask students to correct the remaining errors using proofreading marks. You may wish to have students correct the spelling errors, too. After students have completed the activity, ask volunteers to read each sentence aloud and to identify the errors. **Note:** Some errors can be corrected in more than one way.

Proofreading Checklist

Ask students to select a recent piece of their own writing and to write the title of that piece at the top of the chart. Ask students to put a check mark next to each item in the checklist after they have checked it in their work. Students might first work independently and then trade papers with a partner to double-check each other's work. You might model, or ask a student to model, using the **G.U.M. Handbook** (beginning on page 239) to clarify a concept or rule.

Suggest that students look at the errors they did not find in the proofreading activity and add them to the checklist. Also ask students to think about other kinds of errors they make and to add these to the checklist.

English Language Learners

Have students work with partners who are fluent in English for the proofreading activities.

School Home Connection (student pages 133–134)

These pages provide quick, fun activities that review and reinforce the skills and concepts taught in Unit 4. You might utilize the **School Home Connection** pages in one of the following ways:

- Ask students to take the pages home, choose one or two activities to do, and then ask their parents to sign and return the pages.
- Send the pages home without asking that they be returned.
- Ask students to do one activity at school and then send the pages home.

Language Standard(s): L.5.1, L.5.1b, L.5.1c, L.5.1d, L.5.2, L.5.2e

Beasts & Critters:
Amphibians and Reptiles

Unit 5 Mechanics

Building Mechanics Awareness

Write this sentence on the board and ask a volunteer to read it aloud:

> James asked, "Do you have the book called <u>Snake</u> by Caroline Arnold?"

Ask students to point out the different punctuation marks they see in the sentence. Inform students that in Unit 5 they will learn how to use these and other punctuation marks that make writing easier to read. Explain that they will also learn some rules for capitalizing words, and for writing initials, abbreviations, titles, quotations, friendly letters, and e-mails. Point out to students that using correct punctuation and capitalization can make their sentences and paragraphs easier to understand.

Introduce the Unit Theme

Explain to students that the title of Unit 5 is "Beasts & Critters: Amphibians and Reptiles," and that each lesson gives information about a different amphibian or reptile. Invite students to name some amphibians and reptiles they have seen or read about, and to describe features of each. Write their responses in a chart with the headings Amphibians and Reptiles. Use questions such as these to guide discussion:

- How are reptiles different from amphibians?
- What kind of climate is good for an alligator? a snake? a frog?
- What special features have some amphibians and reptiles developed that help them survive?

Assessment Options
Unit Pretest

The **Unit Pretest** (pp. 185–188) is intended to be used as a diagnostic assessment to help you determine, prior to instruction, your students' existing knowledge and skill proficiency. Follow this procedure for administering the Unit Pretest:

1. Read aloud the test instructions. (**Note:** For additional scaffolding, you may wish to read the test questions and answer choices aloud.)

2. Tell students that they will have 20 minutes to read and answer the questions independently.

3. When time is up, collect and correct the tests. Use the results to determine which lessons to teach for targeted instruction or which lessons to spend extra time on during whole-class instruction if you are teaching all lessons in the unit.

Unit Posttest

The **Unit Posttest** (pp. 235–238) helps you judge students' achievement while providing students with valuable practice for high-stakes tests. When you are ready to administer the test, ask students to carefully tear it out of their books. (**Note:** If the test has already been removed, distribute copies to students.) Read aloud the directions for each section and make sure students understand how to answer the questions. Ask students to work independently to complete the test.

Students who miss two questions focusing on the same grammar element may need additional help understanding the concept. Reteach the concept, following this procedure:

1. Review **Read and Analyze.**

2. Review the rule statement for the concept.

3. Guide students through items a second time. Ask the students to explain why each right answer is correct.

4. Refer students to the **G.U.M. Handbook** for further reinforcement.

Lesson 49 (student pages 135–136)
Writing Sentences Correctly

Objectives
- To learn the names of the different sentence types, and to correctly punctuate and capitalize each
- To identify types of sentences, and to correct capitalization and punctuation errors in sentences
- To compose imperative, interrogative, declarative, and exclamatory sentences
- To add correct end punctuation

English Language Learners
Point out the picture of the turtle on page 136. Explain that the leatherback, the largest living turtle, is one of seven species of sea turtles.

Read aloud the sentences in **Practice**, one at a time. Use voice inflection to emphasize the end mark in each sentence. Ask students to listen to your voice to help them decide whether the end punctuation in the sentence is correct. Have students discuss the correct end mark and any changes in capitalization that should be made. Point out that commands usually begin with a verb, and have students identify the verbs that begin items 1 and 10.

Have students review the four sentence types before they begin **Apply**. Read aloud the caption on page 136 and encourage students to comment on the features of the leatherback turtle. Then brainstorm sentence ideas with students before they begin writing.

Ask student pairs to read aloud the sentences and to complete the activity in **Reinforce**.

Speaking and Listening
Encourage students to think about the most unusual animal that they have ever seen. Ask them to describe the animal. Speakers should try to use all four kinds of sentences, and listeners should identify each type the speakers use.

Extra Practice
For more practice, see page 213.

Lesson 50 (student pages 137–138)
Proper Nouns and Proper Adjectives

Objectives
- To learn that a proper noun names a specific person, place, or thing and a proper adjective is an adjective formed from a proper noun
- To learn that a title of respect is used before a person's name and that titles of respect, proper nouns, and proper adjectives are capitalized
- To correct capitalization errors in sentences
- To rewrite sentences to correct capitalization errors
- To find proper nouns, proper adjectives, and titles of respect in a word search, and to write a sentence using them

English Language Learners
In **Practice**, ask volunteers to read the sentences aloud, one at a time; identify the words that contain capitalization errors; and explain each of their choices. Encourage students to identify the proper nouns, proper adjectives, and titles of respect in the sentences.

For **Apply**, invite students to identify the capitalization errors aloud before they rewrite the sentences. Ask them to identify each corrected word as a proper noun, a proper adjective, or a title of respect.

Students can work independently to complete the word search in **Reinforce** and then work with partners to write sentences.

Speaking and Listening
Distribute pages from a newspaper or a nature magazine to pairs of students. Ask them to look for proper nouns and proper adjectives as well as titles of respect and to share them with the group. Have them tell whether each proper noun names a person, a place, or a thing and what each proper adjective describes.

Extra Practice
For more practice, see page 213.

Objectives

- To learn that an abbreviation is a shortened form of a word and usually begins with an uppercase letter and ends with a period
- To learn that an initial takes the place of a name and is written as an uppercase letter followed by a period
- To correct capitalization and punctuation errors in abbreviations and initials in sentences
- To rewrite words using abbreviations and initials
- To address an envelope

English Language Learners

Invite students to describe snakes they have seen or kept as pets. Have students name different kinds of snakes and share what is known about snakes' habits.

For **Practice**, write the first sentence on the board. Invite a volunteer to model marking errors according to the directions. Have student pairs complete the remaining items. You may need to explain what *inc* (item 4) and *corp* (item 6) stand for.

Read the items in **Apply** aloud. Before student pairs rewrite the items, discuss which items can be abbreviated and where initials can be used. Suggest that pairs refer to the corrections in **Practice** to help them recall how certain words are abbreviated.

Have students work independently to write the names and addresses on the envelope in **Reinforce**. Display an addressed envelope, and discuss what goes on each line before students begin.

Speaking and Listening

Distribute an advertisement to student pairs. Ask partners to look for abbreviations and titles of respect and then to share with the group what each abbreviation or title of respect stands for. Then have pairs speculate about what names are represented by the initials they found.

Extra Practice

For more practice, see page 214.

Objectives

- To recognize that all the important words in names of people, places, holidays, important events, companies, and products should be capitalized
- To identify and properly write words that should be capitalized in sentences
- To write a paragraph in response to a prompt, using correct capitalization
- To expand and rearrange sentences in a paragraph for clarity and interest

English Language Learners

Ask students why auto manufacturers might choose certain animal names for car models. Read aloud the example sentences in **Read and Analyze** and have a volunteer respond to directions. Read aloud the rule statement with students.

Next, read the **Practice** instructions and each sentence aloud. Have students work in pairs to identify the words that should be capitalized. Then read aloud the instructions for **Apply** and **Reinforce.** Have students complete these activities independently. When students complete their paragraphs, have them work with partners to read aloud, expand, and rearrange the sentences in their paragraphs to produce a clearer, more informative description.

Speaking and Listening

Have students form small groups. Challenge each group to imagine and describe a new model for an automobile manufacturer. Tell them to name their model after an animal, a fish, a bird, an insect, or a reptile. Have them work cooperatively to create and present a video ad for this car, telling what it's called, what it does, and why people will like it.

Extra Practice

For more practice, see page 214.

Lesson 53 (student pages 143–144)
Titles

Objectives
- To discover that book and movie titles are underlined and that quotation marks are used around titles of songs, stories, and poems
- To learn which words in a title should be capitalized
- To identify and correct the capitalization and punctuation in titles
- To complete a matching activity containing titles

English Language Learners
Invite students to describe books, movies, poems, or short stories they have seen or read about snakes, lizards, frogs, or other amphibians and reptiles. Then display pictures of a cobra, a rattlesnake, and a newt and help students identify each.

In **Practice**, ask volunteers to read each sentence aloud, to identify the title, and to tell whether it is the title of a book, movie, story, poem, or song. Have a volunteer model completing the first item before student pairs complete the remaining items.

In **Apply**, invite a volunteer to read aloud the titles on the bookshelf. Then have students work with partners to respond to each item. Make sure students understand the meaning of *treat, horror film,* and *painted turtles.*

Student pairs can continue working together to complete **Reinforce**.

Speaking and Listening
Invite students to take a poll of favorite books, poems, movies, and songs among students in other classes. Have students record the information in a chart. Remind them to use proper capitalization and punctuation when writing titles. Encourage students to share their results.

Extra Practice
For more practice, see page 215.

Lesson 54 (student pages 145–146)
Apostrophes

Objectives
- To learn how to form possessive nouns and contractions using apostrophes
- To identify possessive nouns and contractions, and to choose the correct possessive noun or contraction to complete sentences
- To rewrite sentences using apostrophes correctly in possessive nouns and contractions
- To find words in a word search and then use them to form possessive nouns and contractions

English Language Learners
Point out the picture and the caption on page 145. Explain that frogs are among some 3,000 species that make up the animal group called *amphibians.*

In **Practice**, ask volunteers to read each sentence aloud and to tell whether the words in parentheses are possessives or contractions. Then have them identify each correct choice and explain why it is correct.

For **Apply**, have students identify the sentences that should be rewritten using a possessive noun and those that require a contraction. Introduce the word *caecilians* (suh•SIHL•yunz) in item 17 and help students pronounce it. Explain that few biologists have seen a live caecilian.

Students can work independently to complete the activity in **Reinforce** and then work with partners to check each other's word search and list.

Speaking and Listening
Write these nouns and phrases on the board: girls, boys, chair, is not, will not, they are. Ask students to pick a word or phrase and compose oral sentences including a contraction or possessive form of the word(s) they chose. (Examples: The *girls'* team is practicing now. We *won't* have time to finish our project today.) After students write their sentences on the board, have volunteers verify the correct use of the apostrophes.

Extra Practice
For more practice, see page 215.

Language Standard(s): L.5.2, L.5.2d

Lesson 55 (student pages 147–148)
Uses of Commas

Objectives

- To discover that a series is a list of three or more words or phrases and that commas separate items in a series
- To learn that interjections are words that express emotions
- To discover that a mild interjection at the beginning of a sentence should be set off by a comma
- To add missing commas in a series and to delete unnecessary commas
- To compose and complete sentences using commas and interjections correctly

English Language Learners

Discuss the picture and caption on page 147. Explain to students that the spotted salamander is one of about 360 species of salamander. Invite students who have seen salamanders to describe them.

Read aloud the sentences and questions in **Read and Analyze.** Have volunteers answer the questions. Then read aloud the rule statement.

Read aloud the sentences in **Practice,** pausing where commas are needed. Have students tell whether any commas are missing or misplaced and how the errors should be corrected. You may want to clarify the words *grubs, mold, acid rain,* and *larvae.*

For **Apply,** have students work with partners to read the sentences aloud and to brainstorm answers before they write their responses. Read the adjectives in the word bank in **Reinforce** aloud, and then have students work independently to complete the activity. Have them draw on another sheet of paper.

Speaking and Listening

Ask students to find three or more similar objects in the classroom (Examples: three round things; four things on a table; three blue things). Ask students to compose sentences that begin with *I spy* followed by the list of objects. Have them say the sentence aloud and then write it on the board. Listeners should check it for proper use of commas and guess what characteristic the objects have in common.

Extra Practice

For more practice, see page 216.

Lesson 56 (student pages 149–150)
More Uses of Commas

Objectives

- To learn that commas are used to indicate a pause and to separate introductory words and elements, nouns of direct address, tag questions, and independent clauses
- To correct and explain comma usage in sentences
- To rewrite sentences and to write a paragraph using commas correctly

English Language Learners

Read the caption on page 149 aloud. Explain that some frogs live mostly in or near water, others live mostly on land, and some live in underground burrows.

Read aloud the example paragraph in **Read and Analyze.** Have volunteers respond to the questions. Read aloud the rule statement and have students read it with you.

Read the sentences in **Practice** aloud, pausing briefly where commas belong. After each sentence is read, ask students where and why the pause occurred before having them add the comma. Then have them write *I, D, T,* or *C* to indicate why a comma is needed in the sentence.

For **Apply,** ask student pairs to read each sentence aloud, including the words in parentheses. Have them discuss how the sentence should be rewritten, including the placement of the comma, before they write their answers. Read the directions in **Reinforce** aloud. Review with students what they have learned about amphibians in Unit 5 (Lessons 54, 55, and 56). Then have students work with English-proficient partners to write their paragraphs. Suggest that students discuss the information they want to include in their paragraphs before they write. If possible, have students do Internet research to learn more about amphibians.

Speaking and Listening

Ask student pairs to look in fiction and nonfiction books to find an example of each of the rules for commas they learned about in Lesson 56. Have them read each example aloud to the group, write it on the board, and explain what rule it follows.

Extra Practice

For more practice, see page 216.

Language Standard(s): L.5.1, L.5.1a, L.5.2, L.5.2a, L.5.2b, L.5.2c

Lesson 57 (student pages 151–152)
Using Semicolons

Objectives
- To learn that a semicolon can be used instead of a comma and a conjunction to separate independent clauses in compound sentences
- To add semicolons to separate clauses in sentences, and to combine sentences using semicolons
- To write sentences using a semicolon to separate independent clauses

English Language Learners
Write chameleon on the board and help students pronounce it. Ask students what they know about this reptile. (a lizard that can change its color) Then have students look at the chameleon pictured on page 151 and describe its features.

Be sure students understand what an independent clause is. Then read each sentence in **Practice** aloud, pausing where a semicolon is needed. Ask volunteers to identify the two independent clauses in each sentence and to tell where the semicolon belongs.

For **Apply,** read the sentences aloud. Ask students to work with partners to match the sentences and to discuss how they will combine them. Invite a volunteer to model the process with one sentence pair. Remind students to check capitalization in their sentences.

Discuss possible answers to the questions in **Reinforce,** and then have students work in pairs to complete the activity.

Speaking and Listening
Hold up a book and say something about it, such as This is a nature book. Ask a volunteer to say something more about the book. (Example: It tells about plants and animals.) Write both sentences on the board. Invite a volunteer to form a compound sentence using a semicolon to separate the clauses. Follow a similar procedure with other objects that you or the students choose.

Extra Practice
For more practice, see page 217.

Lesson 58 (student pages 153–154)
Direct and Indirect Quotations

Objectives
- To discover that a direct quotation, or direct speech, is a speaker's exact words and an indirect quotation is a retelling of a speaker's words
- To identify indirect quotations, to add missing punctuation to direct quotations, and to correct capitalization in sentences
- To rewrite indirect quotations as direct quotations and vice versa
- To write dialogue to go with pictures

English Language Learners
Point out the picture on page 153 and read the caption aloud. Inform students that there are about 30 species of rattlesnake; some are large, and some are small. If necessary, explain the meaning of *hibernate*.

Read the sentences in **Practice** aloud, one at a time. Ask volunteers to identify each sentence as a direct or an indirect quotation. If the sentence is a direct quotation, ask the volunteer to read aloud only the part that is spoken by the character. Then have students decide where to add the missing punctuation.

Have volunteers read aloud and model completing items 13 and 14 in **Apply.** (Example: item 13: Nico asked Joe how a rattlesnake makes its rattling sound. item 14: Joe said, "A rattlesnake sheds its skin a few times every year.") Ask partners to complete the section.

Before they draw their pictures and write their dialogue to complete **Reinforce,** have partners brainstorm what might happen next to Joe, Nico, and Tony.

Speaking and Listening
Have students take turns restating the indirect quotations in **Practice** as direct quotations and vice versa. They should tell where the quotation marks belong in each direct quotation. (Items 1, 3, 6, and 10 should become direct quotations; the other items should become indirect quotations.)

Extra Practice
For more practice, see page 217.

Lesson 59 (student pages 155–156)
Quotations From a Text

Objectives

- To discover that a quotation from a text is a writer's exact words
- To learn to punctuate quotations from texts correctly
- To write quotations from texts and punctuate them correctly

English Language Learners

Read aloud the example paragraph in **Read and Analyze.** Ask students to identify which words were said by Wendell Berry. Have volunteers point out the punctuation marks that indicate that these words are a quotation. Then read aloud the rule statement.

Read aloud the instructions for **Practice.** Next, read aloud the items, one at a time. Have students add necessary punctuation marks to each quotation. Then invite students to discuss its message; explain references and terms as necessary. Ask students whether they agree with each.

For **Apply,** have students work with English-proficient partners to add and correctly punctuate the appropriate quotations. Have students work with English-proficient partners to brainstorm sentences for their paragraph before writing it in **Reinforce.**

Speaking and Listening

Write on the board "Every day is Earth Day." Inform students that the person who first said this is not known. Then ask students what they think this quotation means, and what it tells us about how we should live our lives.

Extra Practice

For more practice, see page 218.

Lesson 60 (student pages 157–158)
Friendly Letters and E-mails

Objectives

- To learn where commas are required in a friendly letter
- To insert commas where needed in a friendly letter
- To rewrite a friendly letter with correct capitalization and punctuation
- To write an e-mail in response to a prompt

English Language Learners

Read aloud the letter and instructions in **Read and Analyze;** also read aloud the rule statement. Point to the first part of the letter. Ask which part of the letter it is. (the heading) Point to the second part and ask which part it is. (the greeting) Have volunteers identify and name the other three parts of the letter. (the body, the closing, the signature) Next, read aloud the letter in **Practice.** Have students work independently to insert commas in the letter.

Next, read aloud the instructions and the heading information in **Apply.** Have students complete the activity independently. Finally, read aloud the instructions for **Reinforce.** Have students read Sections 30 and 32 of the **G.U.M. Handbook.** Distribute a sheet of paper to each student. Have students work in pairs or small groups at computer terminals to complete the assignment.

Speaking and Listening

Have students read aloud their completed e-mails. Afterward, have students vote on the park in their state they would most like to visit.

Extra Practice

For more practice, see page 218.

Unit Review (student pages 159–160)

The **Unit Review** allows you to check students' progress and determine when reteaching is necessary. The review pages may be completed in class or as homework. If a student responds incorrectly to two or more items involving the same skill, you may want to work directly with the student to review the relevant lesson. The lesson number to which each review item relates appears in parentheses on the review pages in the Teacher Edition.

Assign the **Extra Practice** activities (pp. 213–218) to reteach targeted skills in a more focused way.

Spelling Practice (student pages 161–162)

Greek and Latin Roots

Read aloud the example sentence and the directions in **Read and Analyze**. Have students reread the example sentence with you. Ask which word in bold type has a Greek root that means "to measure." (centimeters) Read the rule statement aloud.

Have students work in small groups to complete the **Word Sort** and share their results with the class. For the first **Pattern Practice** activity, read aloud the directions and the words in the word bank. Have student pairs complete items 1–7. Ask them to present their answers to the class. For the second **Pattern Practice** activity, read aloud the directions. Have students work independently to write the word that completes each sentence. Ask students to identify the Greek and Latin roots in the words. (biography—graph, crupt—rupt, portable—port, telescope—tele, dictionary—dict)

Read aloud the directions in **Use the Dictionary**. Have students work independently to write words with the given roots.

English Language Learners

Have students work with a partner who is fluent in English for the spelling activities. English and Spanish share all the Greek and Latin roots in these activities. However, /f/ written with the *ph* consonant digraph in English is written with the letter *f* in Spanish. In addition, the root *ject* is written as **yect** in Spanish. Point out that many words in science, medicine, and mathematics come to both English and Spanish from Greek. Challenge students to keep a list of these words and their origins as they encounter them in science and math studies.

Proofreading (student pages 163–164)

Proofreading Practice

Review the **Proofreading Marks** chart and the examples. Read the first line aloud. Discuss the error (*st* should be *St.*) and how it should be marked. Ask students (in pairs or independently) to correct the remaining errors using proofreading marks. You may wish to have students correct the spelling errors, too.

After students have completed the activity, ask volunteers to read each sentence aloud and to identify the errors. **Note:** Some errors can be corrected in more than one way.

Proofreading Checklist

Ask students to select a recent piece of their own writing and to write the title of that piece at the top of the chart. Ask students to put a check mark next to each item in the checklist after they have checked it in their work. Students might first work independently and then trade papers with a partner to double-check each other's work. You might model, or ask a student to model, using the **G.U.M. Handbook** (beginning on page 239) to clarify a concept or rule.

Suggest that students look at the errors they did not find in the proofreading activity and add them to the checklist. Ask students to think about other kinds of errors they make and to add these to the checklist.

English Language Learners

Have students work with partners who are fluent in English for the proofreading activities.

School Home Connection (student pages 165–166)

These pages provide quick, fun activities that review and reinforce the skills and concepts taught in Unit 5. You might utilize the **School Home Connection** pages in one of the following ways:

- Ask students to take the pages home, choose one or two activities to do, and then ask their parents to sign and return the pages.
- Send the pages home without asking that they be returned.
- Ask students to do one activity at school and then send the pages home.

Notes

GUM

Grammar, Usage, and Mechanics

Conventions of Standard English

ZB **Zaner-Bloser**

Grade Level Consultants

Margaret Bateman
Montgomery, Alabama

Cindy Daniel
Bothell, Washington

Suzanne Klein
Hilliard, Ohio

Nancy Morgan
Sharon, Pennsylvania

Joan Pawloski
Grand Rapids, Michigan

Illustration: Steve Botts, Tracy Greenwalt

ISBN: 978-1-4531-1209-0

Zaner-Bloser, Inc.
1-800-421-3018
www.zaner-bloser.com

Printed in the United States of America
2 3 4 5 6 27950 19 18 17 16 15

ZB Code 16

SUSTAINABLE FORESTRY INITIATIVE

Certified Sourcing
www.sfiprogram.org
SFI-01042

Table of Contents

Unit 1 Sentence Structure

The World Outside: Water

Unit 2 Parts of Speech

Looking Back: United States History

Unit 3 Usage

Unforgettable Folks: Athletes

Unit 4 Grammar

Grab Bag: Cars

Unit 5 Mechanics

Beasts & Critters: Amphibians and Reptiles

Appendix

Unit Pretests

Extra Practice

Unit Posttests

G.U.M. Handbook

Language Index

Water / covers most of Earth's surface.
    a   b

Which part (a or b) of this sentence tells whom or what the sentence is about? __a__ Which part (a or b) tells what happens? __b__

Every sentence has a subject and a predicate. The **complete subject** is made up of a noun or pronoun and words that tell about it. The subject tells whom or what the sentence is about. The **complete predicate** is made up of a verb and words that tell what the subject is, has, or does.

See Handbook Sections 10 and 11

Practice

Underline the complete subject once. Underline the complete predicate twice.

1. The human body is about two-thirds water.

2. A typical American uses almost 100 gallons of water every day.

3. An adult needs about 2½ quarts of water each day.

4. This water comes from food and beverages.

5. A 15-minute shower uses about 75 gallons of water.

6. Many different industries use water.

7. Gasoline production requires water.

8. Agriculture needs large quantities of water, too.

9. The cultivation of wheat for one loaf of bread requires 150 gallons of water.

10. Some farmers use water-saving techniques.

11. The world's oceans contain salt water.

12. Special treatment plants can remove the salt from the water.

Drinking water is tested regularly throughout the United States.

Apply Answers will vary. Accept all reasonable responses.

Create a sentence from each phrase. Add either a subject or a predicate. Underline the complete subject in your sentence.

13. a thirsty person _____

_____

14. a cold, clear stream _____

_____

15. must be watered often _____

_____

16. uses large quantities of water _____

_____

17. rain and snow _____

_____

Reinforce

Write three sentences about your favorite water activity, such as swimming, fishing, boating, or wakeboarding. Circle each complete subject and underline each complete predicate.

18. **Answers will vary.** _____

_____

19. _____

_____

20. _____

_____

(Heat) changes the water in the kettle from a liquid into a gas.
The (steam) from the kettle rises toward the ceiling.

The complete subject in each sentence is in boldfaced type. Circle the most important word in each complete subject. Underline the verb in each sentence that tells what the subject does.

The **simple subject** is the most important word or words in the complete subject. It is a noun or pronoun and tells whom or what the sentence is about. The **simple predicate** is the most important word or words in the complete predicate. It is a verb. The simple predicate may tell what the subject did or what was done to the subject. It may also be a form of the verb *be*.

See Handbook Sections 10 and 11

Practice

Circle the simple subject in each sentence. Draw a line under the simple predicate.

1. (Water) occurs as a liquid, a solid, and a gas.

2. (Steam) is a gaseous form of water.

3. Solid (forms) of water include ice and snow.

4. No other (substance) on Earth exists in all three forms.

5. (Rain) replenishes Earth's water supply.

6. (Moisture) evaporates from Earth's surface.

7. (Vapor) collects in the clouds.

8. One (cloud) contains billions of water molecules.

9. The (molecules) inside the cloud grow heavy.

10. (Water) returns to Earth in the form of rain or snow.

11. All (animals and plants) need water.

12. Some desert (creatures) get water from plants.

Water is the only substance on Earth that is present in three forms: solid, liquid, and gas.

Apply

Write five sentences about water in its solid state. You may use nouns and verbs from the word bank as simple subjects and simple predicates.

hailstones	glisten	snowball	glacier	crashes
icicles	iceberg	melts	whizzes	clatter

13. **Answers will vary.** _____

_____

14. _____

_____

15. _____

_____

16. _____

_____

17. _____

_____

Reinforce

See Handbook **Section 32**

Ask an adult to help you search the Internet for information about winter weather in your area. Then write a brief paragraph describing winter weather where you live. Underline each simple subject in red. Underline each simple predicate in blue.

Answers will vary. _____

_____

_____

_____

_____

__P__   Tides in the ocean rise and fall regularly each day.

__S__   The sun and the moon cause the tides.

Write *S* next to the sentence with two or more subjects. Write *P* next to the sentence with two or more verbs.

> A **compound subject** is two or more subjects joined by the conjunction *and* or *or*. A **compound predicate** is two or more verbs joined by a conjunction.

See Handbook **Sections 10 and 11**

Practice

Circle the two simple subjects that make up each compound subject. Underline the two verbs that make up each compound predicate.

1. (Ports) and (harbors) are helped by tides in many ways.

2. Tides <u>clean</u> the channels and <u>keep</u> them deep enough for ships.

3. Ocean (liners) and cargo (ships) sail through channels at high tide.

4. A high tide <u>can lift</u> a large ship and <u>guide</u> it into port.

5. Tides <u>pick up</u> waste from the shore and <u>carry</u> it far out to the bottom of the sea.

6. Fishing (crews) and (sailors) pay close attention to the tides in their area.

7. The new (moon) and the full (moon) bring spring tides, the highest and lowest tides of each month.

High tide

8. Long ago sailors <u>observed</u> the moon and <u>used</u> a compass.

9. Today fishing boat (crews) and ship (captains) rely on the Internet for information on tides.

10. Tide (charts) and weather (reports) help navigators.

Low tide

Name _____

Apply   Suggested answers appear below. Accept all reasonable responses.

Combine each pair of sentences to form one sentence that has either a compound subject or a compound predicate.

11. Visitors to the beach can swim at high tide. They can dig clams at low tide.

Visitors to the beach can swim at high tide or dig clams at low tide.

_____

12. Sea stars are often left high and dry at low tide. So are sea anemones.

Sea stars and sea anemones are often left high and dry at low tide.

_____

13. Tides contain energy. Waves contain energy, too. **Tides and waves contain energy.**

_____

14. Underwater machines harness tidal power. They convert it into valuable energy.

Underwater machines harness tidal power and convert it into valuable energy.

_____

Reinforce

Unscramble these words. Each word names something found in harbors. All of the words appear on page 11.

15. scanelnh _____**channels**_____

16. sited _____**tides**_____

17. rostp _____**ports**_____

18. iorslas _____**sailors**_____

Now use two of the words to write a sentence with a compound subject or a compound predicate.

Answers will vary.

_____

_____

_____

The **oceans** of **Earth** contain many (plants) and (fish.)

Circle the boldfaced nouns that tell what the oceans contain.

> The **direct object** is the noun or pronoun that receives the action of the verb. Only action verbs can take a direct object. A **compound direct object** occurs when more than one noun or pronoun receives the action of the verb. To find the direct object, say the verb, and then ask "What?" or "Whom?" For example, to find the direct object of *The oceans of Earth contain many plants and fish*, ask "Contain what?" The answer is "plants and fish."

See Handbook | Section 20

Practice

Circle the direct object or compound direct object in each sentence.

1. We use the (ocean) for many purposes.

2. Divers explore its colorful (reefs.)

3. Diners eat its (fish.)

4. Surfers ride its wild (waves.)

5. Workers take (minerals,) (pearls,) (sponges,) and (salt) from it.

6. Boats harvest (seaweed) from the ocean.

7. Manufacturers make (medicines,) (ice cream,) and (cosmetics) from seaweed.

8. Container ships use the (oceans) as superhighways.

9. Luxury liners use the (oceans) as a vast playground.

10. Water purification plants turn (seawater) into drinking water for our thirsty planet.

Coral reefs are home to many colorful species of fish.

Apply Possible answers appear below. Accept all reasonable responses.

Write a direct object or a compound direct object after each action verb. Use words from the word bank and your own words.

| treasures | clouds | ocean | pictures | creatures | plants | rain | coral |

11. People mine the rich _____ **ocean** _____ for valuable minerals.

12. Divers gather precious _____ **treasures** _____ from the ocean bottom.

13. Photographers take beautiful _____ **pictures** _____ of colorful fish.

14. Scientists study strange _____ **creatures and plants** _____ in the ocean's depths.

15. Moisture from the ocean forms _____ **clouds** _____.

16. These clouds eventually bring _____ **rain** _____ to our mountains and valleys.

Reinforce

Draw an underwater scene below or use a computer graphics program to create such a scene. You can use the action words and direct objects in the word bank for ideas. Then write two sentences describing your scene.

| sank | gave | reef | octopus | found | made | fins | cave |

17. **Answers will vary.** _____

_____

18. _____

_____

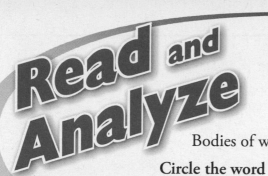

Bodies of water give Earth's (creatures) many gifts.

Circle the word that tells to whom gifts are given.

> An **indirect object** is a noun or pronoun that comes before a direct object. The indirect object tells to whom something has been given, told, or taught. Indirect objects appear only in sentences with direct objects. To test whether a noun or pronoun is an indirect object, try moving it after the direct object and putting the word *to* or *for* in front of it: *Bodies of water give many gifts to Earth's creatures.*

See Handbook | Section 20

Practice

The direct object in each sentence is in boldfaced type. Circle each indirect object.

1. Potholes offer migrating (ducks) resting **places**.

2. Estuaries give (shellfish) a peaceful **habitat**.

3. Bayous offer (alligators) many hiding **places**.

4. Ponds give (frogs) a wet, wonderful **home**.

5. Flooding rivers bring (farmers) rich **silt** for their fields.

6. Rivers also give spawning (salmon) a **nursery** for their young.

7. Hot springs offer (people) with sore muscles **relief** from pain.

8. Creeks offer (hikers) a pleasant, warbling **song**.

9. Waterfalls give (photographers) a magnificent **subject** for a picture.

10. Oceans send the (skies) **water vapor** that eventually returns to Earth as precipitation.

11. Bays provide (boats) a safe **haven** in stormy weather.

12. Sweetwater springs give (hikers) lifesaving drinking **water**.

13. Underground aquifers give (farmers) **water** for irrigation.

14. Lakes offer (boaters) a **place** to have fun.

Alligators move slowly through the shallow, stagnant waters of the bayous.

Apply

Rewrite each sentence so the boldfaced word becomes an indirect object.

Example	Rachel drew a map of the river for her **brother**.

Rachel drew her brother a map of the river.

15. Eddie sold his kayak to **Rachel**. **Eddie sold Rachel his kayak.**

_____

16. Eddie gave two life jackets to **Benvi**. **Eddie gave Benvi two life jackets.**

_____

17. Hobie sang a sea song to the **crew**. **Hobie sang the crew a sea song.**

_____

18. Ernesto wrote a letter about his canoe trip to **Maia**. **Ernesto wrote Maia a letter**

about his canoe trip.

19. Chul told a story about his days as a sailor to **Dexter**. **Chul told Dexter a story about**

his days as a sailor.

Reinforce

Imagine you and three friends are planning a canoe trip. Write three sentences with indirect objects. Each sentence should tell to whom you will give each item in the word bank.

first-aid kit	camera	portable stove

20. **Answers will vary.** _____

_____

21. _____

_____

22. _____

_____

If a snowpack remains frozen for many years, a glacier may form. The many snow crystals become thick (layers.) These layers are very **heavy**.

Circle the boldfaced noun that tells what the subject is or becomes. Underline the boldfaced adjective that describes the subject.

A **linking verb** connects the subject of a sentence to a word or phrase in the predicate that tells about the subject. A **predicate noun** follows a linking verb and renames the subject. A **predicate adjective** follows a linking verb and describes the subject.

See Handbook Section 11

Practice

Draw one line under each boldfaced word that is a predicate noun. Draw two lines under each boldfaced word that is a predicate adjective. Circle the linking verb in each sentence.

1. The layers (become) a **mass** of solid ice.

2. A mass of solid ice (is) a **glacier**.

3. Continental glaciers and valley glaciers (are) two **types** of glaciers.

4. Continental glaciers (are) **sheets** of thick ice.

5. Valley glaciers (are) **long** and **thin**.

6. Alaska's Glacier Bay National Park (is) **home** to bears, wolves, and mountain goats.

7. A glacier's movement (is) quite **slow**.

8. A glacier's surface (is) its hardest **part**.

9. Mountain climbers (become) extremely **cautious** on glaciers.

10. The crevasses in a glacier's surface (are) **dangerous**.

11. Crevasses (are) deep **cracks** in the ice.

Mountain climbers use special equipment to scale glaciers.

Name _____

Apply Suggested answers appear below. Accept all reasonable responses.

Write a predicate noun or a predicate adjective to complete each sentence. You may use words from the word bank if you wish. Use an article (*a, an,* or *the*) if it is needed.

obstacle	iceberg	essential	cause
visible	disastrous	shock	ocean liner

12. A floating chunk of ice from a glacier becomes _____ **an iceberg** _____.

13. Only the very tip of an iceberg is _____ **visible** _____.

14. A collision between a passenger ship and an iceberg can be _____ **disastrous** _____.

15. A life vest for every passenger on board a ship is _____ **essential** _____.

16. The *Titanic* was a large _____ **ocean liner** _____ that sank in 1912.

17. An iceberg was _____ **the cause** _____ of its destruction.

18. The sinking of the "unsinkable" *Titanic* was _____ **a shock** _____ to the world.

Reinforce

See Handbook Sections 31 and 32

Out of 2,200 passengers aboard the *Titanic,* only 705 were rescued. Ask an adult to help you find an article in an online encyclopedia about the sinking of the *Titanic.* Then imagine that you are interviewing a survivor. Write a question and an answer for a "news flash" of April 15, 1912. Use at least one predicate noun or predicate adjective to complete each item.

19. Question: **Answers will vary.** _____

_____

_____

_____

20. Answer: **Answers will vary.** _____

_____

_____

_____

_____

A large lake can affect the weather in nearby areas.

Which words tell where the weather is affected?

in nearby areas

A **prepositional phrase** can tell *how, what kind, when, how much,* or *where.* A prepositional phrase begins with a **preposition**, such as *in, over, of, to,* or *by.* It ends with a noun or pronoun that is the **object of the preposition**. Words between the preposition and the object of the preposition are also part of the prepositional phrase. A prepositional phrase can appear at the beginning, middle, or end of a sentence.

See Handbook Section 19

Practice

Underline each prepositional phrase. Circle the preposition that begins the phrase.

1. A lake absorbs heat ⟨during⟩ the summer.

2. It releases this heat slowly ⟨over⟩ the following months.

3. A lake warms cold winds ⟨in⟩ cooler months.

4. The winds ⟨off⟩ the lake are relatively warm.

5. These temperate winds can extend the growing season ⟨of⟩ an area.

6. The Great Lakes are important ⟨to⟩ Michigan's fruit crops.

7. The lakes help keep the air ⟨around⟩ the orchards warm.

8. Michigan cherries are shipped ⟨to⟩ many American cities.

9. The cherries are harvested ⟨before⟩ the winter frost.

10. Much produce is shipped ⟨by⟩ train.

The Great Lakes and the waterways that connect them are vital to the economies of the United States and Canada.

Apply Suggested answers appear below. Accept all reasonable responses.

Add a prepositional phrase or two to each sentence. Then rewrite each sentence. You may use phrases from the word bank or think of your own.

without their water	to cities and towns	for recreation
during summer months	for irrigation	for manufacturing

11. Lakes are important. **Lakes are important during summer months.**

_____

12. People use them. **People use them for recreation.**

_____

13. Industries use their water. **Industries use their water for manufacturing.**

_____

14. Farmers use their water. **Farmers use their water for irrigation.**

_____

Reinforce

Use the clues to complete the puzzle. Each answer is a preposition.

Across

3. My family visits Lake Michigan ___ the summer months.
4. We drive ___ the state of Michigan.
6. I enjoy going ___ the lake.
8. It takes several days to drive ___ the entire lake.
9. The lake reflects the color of the sky ___ it.

Down

1. We swim in the lake ___ July and August.
2. I wear goggles when I swim ___ the water.
4. I don't like it when fish swim ___ me.
5. We pass factories and orchards ___ our journey.
7. I like diving ___ the cool water.
10. Once I saw a fish swim ___ me.

Crossword grid answers:
- 1 Down: DURING
- 2 Down: UNDER
- 3 Across: IN
- 4 Across: THROUGH
- 4 Down: TOWARD
- 5 Down: ON
- 6 Across: TO
- 7 Down: INTO
- 8 Across: AROUND
- 9 Across: ABOVE
- 10 Down: BY

a. For a hundred years people dreamed of a waterway between the Great Lakes ~~and~~ the Atlantic Ocean.

b. De Witt Clinton planned a canal, ~~but~~ people sneered at his idea.

Cross out the boldfaced conjunction in each sentence.

Which sentence could become two separate sentences? ___b___

A **compound sentence** is two or more closely related simple sentences. A **simple sentence** is also called an independent clause. The two clauses can be joined by a comma and a conjunction (*and, but, or*) or by a semicolon (*;*).

See Handbook Sections 8, 12, and 21

Practice

Write *S* next to each simple sentence and *C* next to each compound sentence. Circle the conjunction or semicolon in each compound sentence.

1. The federal government would not give Clinton any money for his canal, (but) he did not give up. ___C___

2. Clinton asked the New York legislature for money, (and) the State of New York agreed to his request. ___C___

3. The governor of New York named Clinton the head of the canal commission in 1816(;) Clinton became governor of New York the next year. ___C___

4. His crew began construction on July 4, 1817. ___S___

A lock allows a ship to pass from one body of water to another.

5. The Erie Canal grew, (and) the towns along its course became busier. ___C___

6. The canal was not completed until 1825. ___S___

7. Now raw materials from the Great Lakes region could be shipped to the East, (and) manufactured goods from Eastern cities could be shipped to the upper Midwest. ___C___

8. The canal cost over seven million dollars, (but) tolls earned 17 times that by 1882. ___C___

9. Early opponents feared the canal would never pay for itself(;) they were proven wrong. ___C___

Name _____

Apply
Suggested answers appear below. Accept all reasonable responses.

Rewrite each pair of simple sentences as one compound sentence.

10. The *Seneca Chief* made the first journey through the Erie Canal in ten days. De Witt Clinton was one of the happy passengers.

    The <u>Seneca Chief</u> made the first journey through the Erie Canal in ten days, and

    De Witt Clinton was one of the happy passengers.

11. The Erie Canal cost more than seven million dollars. It proved to be a good investment.

    The Erie Canal cost more than seven million dollars, but it proved to be a good

    investment.

12. Barges moved slowly along the canal. They carried heavy loads cheaply and dependably.

    Barges moved slowly along the canal; they carried heavy loads cheaply and dependably.

Reinforce
Suggested answers appear below. Accept all reasonable responses.

Many canals have locks to raise and lower boats. The diagram on page 21 shows what happens when a boat passes through a lock. Put the independent clauses below in order to tell what is happening in the diagram. Then combine the clauses to form three compound sentences.

5 The lock is opened a second time.	2 The lock is opened for the first time.
4 The water in the lock rises.	3 The ship enters the lock.
6 The ship sails out of the lock.	1 The ship sails up to the lock.

13. **The ship sails up to the lock, and the lock is opened for the first time.**

14. **The ship enters the lock; the water in the lock rises.**

15. **The lock is opened a second time, and the ship sails out of the lock.**

As the wind pushes against the water, <u>the wind creates waves</u>.

Look at the two parts of this sentence. Which part makes sense by itself?

    a. the boldfaced part   **ⓑ.** the underlined part

An **independent clause** is a sentence that makes sense by itself. A **dependent clause** has a subject and a verb, but it does not make complete sense by itself. It needs—or is dependent on—an independent clause. A dependent clause often begins with a word such as *although, because, if, as,* or *when.*

See Handbook Sections 12 and 21

Practice

Draw one line under each independent clause. Draw two lines under each dependent clause. Circle the word that begins each dependent clause.

1. ⟨Although⟩ some people think waves are caused by tides, <u>the wind causes most waves</u>.

2. ⟨When⟩ <u>the wind blows for a long time at great speed,</u> <u>the waves grow larger</u>.

3. ⟨Because⟩ <u>waves keep moving even after the winds stop,</u> <u>some waves travel far from where they began</u>.

4. ⟨Although⟩ <u>storms often produce gigantic waves,</u> <u>few huge waves have ever been measured precisely</u>.

5. ⟨When⟩ <u>a ship is in the middle of a storm,</u> <u>its crew members must focus on survival</u>.

The power and repetition of waves can carve steep cliffs.

6. <u>Navigating a ship through a storm is still extremely difficult,</u> ⟨though⟩ <u>modern tracking equipment does provide some help</u>.

7. ⟨If⟩ <u>the crew members are careless,</u> <u>they may be washed overboard by a large wave</u>.

8. <u>A sailor aboard *USS Ramapo* measured a 112-foot wave</u> ⟨when⟩ <u>the ship was caught in a hurricane in 1933</u>.

9. ⟨As⟩ <u>*Weather Reporter* sailed the Atlantic in 1972,</u> <u>its instruments recorded an 86-foot wave</u>.

10. ⟨By⟩ <u>the time they reach the shore,</u> <u>most waves have traveled for many miles</u>.

Name _____

Apply

Draw a line to match each dependent clause on the left with an independent clause on the right. Then write the new sentences you created. Be sure to add a comma in between clauses.

Because waves often hurl 100-pound rocks at it

Although most waves are harmless

When an earthquake struck in Alaska in 1946

Because people had no warning

A giant tsunami hit Waipi'o Valley on the big island of Hawaii.

Many lives were lost.

Tillamook Lighthouse in Oregon has steel bars built around it.

Some huge waves cause damage.

11. **Because waves often hurl 100-pound rocks at it, Tillamook Lighthouse in Oregon has steel bars built around it.**

12. **Although most waves are harmless, some huge waves cause damage.**

13. **When an earthquake struck in Alaska in 1946, a giant tsunami hit Waipi'o Valley on the big island of Hawaii.**

14. **Because people had no warning, many lives were lost.**

Reinforce

Wave warnings often appear near beaches where rough surf is common. Add an independent clause to each dependent clause below to create sentences that warn people of the danger.

| when you walk on the beach | if you use caution |

15. **Answers will vary.** _____

16. _____

<u>Wherever big waves regularly form,</u>

(you will find big wave surfers in search of a thrilling ride.)

Circle the part of the sentence that makes sense by itself.

An **independent clause** has a subject and a verb, and makes sense by itself. A **dependent clause** has a subject and a verb, but it does not make complete sense by itself. Many dependent clauses begin with *although, because, if, when,* or *after.* A **complex sentence** is made up of a dependent clause and an independent clause.

See Handbook Sections 12 and 21

Practice

Write *CX* next to each complex sentence.

1. The native people of Hawaii have ridden waves on boards for hundreds of years. _____

2. In the late 1940s and early 1950s, some surfers gathered at Makaha, where giant waves form in fall and winter. __CX__

3. Makaha is on the west shore of Oahu, the most populous island in Hawaii. _____

4. When the waves at Makaha grew large, those big wave pioneers paddled out to the break line. __CX__

Eddie Aikau is one of the most famous surfers to come from the state of Hawaii.

5. Although they frequently were tossed around or pulled under by the powerful waves, these surfers learned the secrets of big wave riding. __CX__

6. When George Downing developed a special big wave surfboard, it made the rides easier. __CX__

7. In the 1970s Eddie Aikau became the star of big-wave surfing because he was fearless and very skillful. __CX__

8. Hawaii offers five of the best spots for big wave surfing, but there are also famous places in northern California, Mexico, Brazil, Chile, and South Africa. _____

9. If you watch big wave surf events today, you may see Maya Gabeira astride a huge breaker. __CX__

10. In 2009 she won the ESPY Award for Female Sports Athlete of the Year. _____

Apply

Draw a line to match each clause on the left with a clause on the right. Write the new sentences on the lines. Use commas where needed.

When surfers get tossed off a big wave   they may run short of oxygen

Because they have been spun around and pushed so far down   they may be pushed 40 feet under the surface

Unless they swim upward immediately   they at first cannot tell up from down

If surfers take too long on the way up to the surface   they may get pushed back under by the next wave

11. **When surfers get tossed off a big wave, they may be pushed 40 feet under the surface.**

12. **Because they have been spun around and pushed so far down, they at first cannot tell up from down.**

13. **Unless they swim upward immediately, they may run short of oxygen.**

14. **If surfers take too long on the way up to the surface, they may get pushed back under by the next wave.**

Reinforce

Write a paragraph about an exciting sport. Include at least one complex sentence in your paragraph.

Accept reasonable responses.

_____

_____

_____

_____

_____

_____

a. Idaho is a state (where) visitors can travel many miles on rivers through wild country.

b. Captain Elmer Earl is a jet boat pilot (who) has taken thousands of people on rides up the Snake River.

Which sentence has a boldfaced clause that describes a person? __b__ Circle the first word in this clause. Which sentence has a boldfaced clause that tells more about a time, a place, or a reason? __a__ Circle the first word in this clause.

When the pronoun *who, whom, whose, which,* or *that* begins a dependent clause that describes a person, place, or thing, it is called a **relative pronoun**. When the word *when, where,* or *why* begins a dependent clause that tells about a time, a place, or a reason, it is called a **relative adverb**.

See Handbook Sections 16 and 18

Practice

Circle the first word in each boldfaced dependent clause. Write *RP* if it is a relative pronoun. Write *RA* if it is a relative adverb.

1. Elmer Earl's grandparents settled in a place at the bottom of a steep canyon (where) a small **creek flows into the Snake River.** __RA__

2. The Nez Perce Indians, (who) **have lived in the area around the mouth of the Snake River for generations,** were their neighbors. __RP__

3. Only a handful of people live along the long, narrow channel (that) **the Snake River carved for itself.** __RP__

4. In fact, the Snake flows for 100 miles through the deepest, narrowest gorge in North America before it reaches the spot (where) **it empties into the Columbia River.** __RA__

5. During the years (when) **Elmer Earl piloted a boat up the Snake River,** he delivered supplies and mail to the remote ranches in the canyon. __RA__

6. He brought the wool (that) **the ranchers produced** back to the towns near the mouth of the Snake. __RP__

7. No roads will ever reach into the steep, rocky region (where) **Elmer Earl piloted his boat.** __RA__

8. Jet boat passengers see the same kinds of wildlife (that) **Meriwether Lewis, William Clark, and Sacagawea saw two hundred years ago.** __RP__

9. The Luna House Museum in Lewiston, Idaho, displays artifacts from the days (when) **trappers hunted for beaver in the area.** __RA__

10. Toni Earl, Elmer's wife, was one of the people (who) **founded this local museum.** __RP__

Apply

Complete each sentence with the appropriate dependent clause. Then circle the relative pronouns and underline the relative adverbs in the sentences.

> who guides people on river trips   where almost no one lives
>
> which is the West's wildest river   when the snow melts

11. We will visit Stanley, Idaho, in the month <u>**when** the snow melts.</u> _____

12. There we will meet our cousin, (who) guides people on river trips. _____

13. We will kayak with him on the Salmon River, (which) is the West's wildest river. _____

     _____

14. We will spend a week in an area <u>**where** almost no one lives.</u> _____

Reinforce

Unscramble the six words below. Circle the three words that can be used as relative pronouns. Underline the three words that can be used as relative adverbs.

15. ohw _____ (who) _____

16. newh _____ <u>**when**</u> _____

17. hewer _____ <u>**where**</u> _____

18. hatt _____ (that) _____

19. hyw _____ <u>**why**</u> _____

20. chihw _____ (which) _____

Now use three of the words to write three sentences about a river located in or near your community.

_____

_____

_____

_____

_____

a. *Tsunami* is a Japanese word meaning "port wave."

b. A huge wave with enormous power.

c. If people are not warned beforehand.

d. Tsunamis should not be called tidal waves, they are not caused by tides.

Which item is a correct sentence? __a__

Which item has no verb? __b__

Which item is a dependent clause? __c__

Which item is made up of two independent clauses without a conjunction? __d__

A **fragment** does not tell a complete thought. A **run-on sentence** is a compound sentence that is missing a comma and a conjunction. A **comma splice** is a run-on sentence that has a comma but is missing a conjunction. Avoid fragments, run-ons, and comma splices in the final versions of your written work.

See Handbook   Sections 13 and 21

Practice

Circle each fragment. Draw a box around each run-on. Underline each comma splice. (1–6)

(A tsunami, not a single wave but a series of waves sometimes called a wave train.) Tsunamis are dangerous, they are incredibly powerful and travel very fast. Some are caused by earthquakes others are caused by volcanic eruptions. A mighty earthquake occurred under the Indian Ocean on December 26, 2004. (Created a massive tsunami.) Without warning, the tsunami struck Indonesia, Thailand, and other nearby countries. (Caused many deaths and left millions homeless.) Its powerful waves also traveled westward 3,000 miles to the coast of Africa. (Death and destruction there, too.)

One tsunami that struck the Shetland Isles around 4950 B.C. was almost as tall as the Empire State Building.

Apply   Possible answers appear below. Accept all reasonable responses.

Rewrite the incorrect sentences from Practice. Correct all fragments, run-ons, and comma splices. There may be more than one way to correct the errors.

7. **A tsunami is not a single wave but a series of waves sometimes called a wave train.**

   _____

8. **Tsunamis are dangerous because they are incredibly powerful and travel very fast.**

   _____

9. **Some are caused by earthquakes, and others are caused by volcanic eruptions.**

   _____

10. **The earthquake created a massive tsunami.**

   _____

11. **It caused many deaths and left millions homeless.**

   _____

12. **The tsunami caused death and destruction there, too.**

   _____

Reinforce

Read each description of a weather event. Then unscramble the word that names the event.

13. This is a tropical windstorm with heavy rains that starts in the Atlantic Ocean, in the Caribbean Sea, or on the Pacific coast of Mexico. It comes from the Spanish word *huracán*.

    C H R A U N I R E **HURRICANE** _____

14. This is a wind system that produces the dry and wet seasons in India and southern Asia. It comes from the Arabic word *mausim*, which means "season."

    S O N O M O N **MONSOON** _____

15. This is a tropical storm in the western Pacific Ocean or China Sea. It comes from the Cantonese *tai fung*.

    O P O N Y T H **TYPHOON** _____

Review

Subjects and Predicates

Underline the complete subject in each sentence. Draw a circle around the simple subject.

1. ⟨Rain⟩ is one kind of precipitation. **(1,2)**

2. ⟨Regions⟩ with very little rain have few large animals. **(1,2)**

Underline the complete predicate in each sentence. Draw a circle around the simple predicate.

3. Polar regions ⟨get⟩ most of their precipitation in the form of snow. **(1,2)**

4. Winter snowpacks ⟨hold⟩ a great amount of water. **(1,2)**

Draw one line under each compound subject in these sentences. Draw two lines under each compound predicate.

5. Texas and several neighboring states suffered terrible floods during the summer of 2007. **(3)**

6. Thunderstorms flashed and boomed in June and July. **(3)**

7. Creeks and rivers surged over their banks. **(3)**

8. The Brazos River flooded homes and carried away cars. **(3)**

Prepositions

Underline the prepositional phrase in each sentence. Draw a circle around the preposition.

9. Water surged ⟨into⟩ homes. **(7)**

10. Some people climbed ⟨onto⟩ their roofs. **(7)**

11. Volunteers ⟨in⟩ small boats rescued many people. **(7)**

Relative Pronouns and Adverbs

Decide whether the boldfaced word in each sentence is a relative pronoun (RP) or a relative adverb (RA). Write *RP* or *RA* after each sentence to identify the boldfaced word.

12. Warning signs are posted at spots **where** visitors must be especially careful. __RA__ **(11)**

13. Hikers **who** are careful seldom have problems. __RP__ **(11)**

Direct and Indirect Objects, Predicate Nouns, and Predicate Adjectives

Write *DO* (direct object), *IO* (indirect object), *PN* (predicate noun), or *PA* (predicate adjective) to identify the boldfaced word in each sentence.

14. Usually rivers give **people** many benefits. ___IO___ **(5)**

15. In 2007, however, the Brazos River became **dangerous**. ___PA___ **(6)**

16. The raging river was an **enemy**. ___PN___ **(6)**

17. Its surging waters flooded **neighborhoods**. ___DO___ **(4)**

Dependent and Independent Clauses

Circle each sentence that has two independent clauses. Draw a box around each sentence that has one independent clause and one dependent clause.

18. Because the moist air is warm, it rises. **(9)**

19. The upper air is colder, and it cannot hold all the moisture. **(8, 9)**

20. Most water vapor is invisible, but we can see water vapor in the form of clouds. **(8, 9)**

Fragments, Run-ons, and Comma Splices

Identify each item below as a comma splice, a fragment, or a run-on by writing *CS, F,* or *RO*.

21. Deserts in Australia, northern Africa, and the southwestern part of North America. ___F___ **(12)**

22. The driest desert in the world is in South America it is called the Atacama Desert. ___RO___ **(12)**

23. Very little precipitation falls in Antarctica, it is considered a desert. ___CS___ **(12)**

Types of Sentences

Identify each item below as a simple sentence, a compound sentence, or a complex sentence by writing *S, CD,* or *CX*.

24. Large waterfalls are spectacular sights, and Yosemite National Park incudes several of the most dramatic. ___CD___ **(8)**

25. Yosemite Falls, Vernal Fall, Nevada Fall, and Bridalveil Fall are very beautiful in spring. ___S___ **(8)**

26. Hiking near the falls can be dangerous, because spray from the tumbling water makes the rocky trails slippery. ___CX___ **(10)**

Spelling Practice

Read and Analyze

The Amazon flows through the South American **jungle**. It is not a **humble** stream, but a mighty river!

Write the spelling for the /əl/ sound in the words in bold type.

<u>le</u>

Spelling Patterns: Final Schwa with *l*

In an unstressed syllable, the vowel often has the /ə/ sound, which is called **schwa**. The /ə/ sound is like the sound you make when you say "uh" and can be spelled with any vowel. Many words end with the /ə/ sound, which can be spelled *le* as in *battle*, *al* as in *royal*, *el* as in *vowel*, or *il* as in *pupil*.

Word Sort

Use the words below to complete the word sort. **Answers may be in any order.**

| normal | council | angle | civil |
| marvel | general | scramble | panel |

/əl/ spelled *le*	/əl/ spelled *al*
angle	normal
scramble	general

/əl/ spelled *el*	/əl/ spelled *il*
marvel	council
panel	civil

Pattern Practice

rural	fossil	humble
parcel	syllable	loyal

Write each word next to its meaning.

1. a word part _____ **syllable** _____

2. won't brag _____ **humble** _____

3. trustworthy _____ **loyal** _____

4. in the country _____ **rural** _____

5. animal in stone _____ **fossil** _____

6. a package _____ **parcel** _____

Write the word from above that completes each sentence.

7. Kara was _____ **humble** _____ and told no one about her award.

8. Dad received a large _____ **parcel** _____ in the mail.

9. This stone has a _____ **fossil** _____ of an ancient insect.

10. It's nice to have a _____ **loyal** _____ friend I can count on.

11. Josh lives in a _____ **rural** _____ area far from the city.

12. The word *home* has only one _____ **syllable** _____.

Use the Dictionary

Complete each word by adding *le, al, el,* or *il*. Check your spellings in a dictionary.

13. canc____ **el** ____

14. freck____ **le** ____

15. festiv____ **al** ____

16. utens____ **il** ____

Proofreading
Practice

Read this report about wetlands and find the mistakes. Use the proofreading marks below to show how each mistake should be fixed. Use a dictionary to check and correct spellings.

Proofreading Marks

Suggested answers appear below.
Accept all reasonable responses.

Mark	Means	Example
ℐ	take away	Bogs and swamps are are two types of wetlands.
∧	add	Bogs and swamps are two types of wetlands.
≡	make into an uppercase letter	bogs and swamps are two types of wetlands.
/	make into a lowercase letter	Bogs and Swamps are two types of wetlands.
⊙	add a period	Bogs and swamps are two types of wetlands⊙
ⓢⓟ	fix spelling	Boggs and swamps are two types of wetlands.

Wetlands

Wetlands are low-lying areas that are saturated with water for long periods. wetlands are classified according to the tipes of vegetation that grow in them. Swamps are wetlands that have many trees, and marshes are wetlands where mostly grasses grow. Bogs are filled with different types of mosses. All three types are havens for many kinds of wildlife.

Birds throughout the world they depend on wetlands as a place to live and raise their young. Many migrating birds rely on wetlands as a resting place on they're long migrations. The prairie fringed orchid and other rare plants thrive in wet, mossy bogs. Wetlands provide a natural clasroom where scientists can study a wide variety of plant and animal life⊙

Wetlands also teaches us about the past the chemical composition of most bogs is ideal for preserving remains. Scientists have discovered well-preserved animals and other preserved life forms in bogs all over the world. One group of scientists in florida found artifacts of a Native American people who lived 7,000 to 8,000 years ago. The items revealed that this group had advanced weaving and tool-making skills.

Although milliones of acers of wetlands in the United States have been destroyed by pollution or drained for farming or industry, Many groups are working to preserve the wetlands that remain.

Proofreading
Checklist

You can use the list below to help you find and fix mistakes in your own writing. Write the titles of your own stories or reports in the blanks on top of the chart. Then use the questions to check your work. Make a check mark (✓) in each box after you have checked that item. **Answers will vary.**

Titles

Proofreading Checklist for Unit 1

Have I joined compound sentences correctly?				
Does each sentence have both a subject and a predicate?				
Have I avoided run-on sentences, comma splices, and fragments?				
Does each sentence end with the appropriate end punctuation?				

Also Remember…

Does each sentence begin with an uppercase letter?				
Did I use a dictionary to check and correct spellings?				
Have I used commas correctly?				

Your Own List

Use this space to write your own list of things to check in your writing.

In Unit 1 of *Grammar, Usage, and Mechanics,* we are learning about different types of sentences and about the important parts of a sentence. The activities on this page give extra practice with some of the concepts we're learning. You can help your child use the information he or she is learning in school by choosing one or more activities to complete with your child at home.

Sentence Scramble (Complete Subjects and Complete Predicates)

With your child, read the weather forecasts in your local newspaper. Ask your child to copy four sentences from the forecasts onto strips of paper. Have your child underline the complete subject and circle the complete predicate. (The subject is the part of the sentence that tells whom or what the sentence is about. The predicate is the part of the sentence that tells what happens.)

Example   <u>Wednesday</u> will be sunny.

<u>Rain</u> is expected by Friday.

Then snip the strips in half between the subject and predicate, and scramble the parts to make silly new sentences.

Example   <u>Rain</u> will be sunny.

<u>Wednesday</u> is expected by Friday.

Back Then (Simple Subjects and Simple Predicates)

Have your child interview an older relative or friend and ask that person what life was like when he or she was in the fifth grade. Have your child record the conversation or take notes. Afterward, help your child write three sentences about the interview. Ask your child to underline the simple subject and circle the simple predicate in each sentence. (The simple subject is the most important word or phrase in the subject. The simple predicate is the verb that tells what the subject did, or links the subject to descriptive information.)

Example   <u>Grandma</u> rode a trolley car to school.

<u>She</u> worked in her parents' restaurant after school.

Her <u>friend</u> had a pet donkey.

Able to Leap Tall Buildings (Simple and Compound Sentences)

Ask your child to think of some superhuman power he or she would like to have. Then have your child write three compound sentences about how things are now and how they would be different if he or she had that power. (A compound sentence is two separate sentences joined by a comma and *and, or,* or *but*.)

Example   If your child chooses the power to fly, he or she might write, "Now it takes me forty minutes to get to school by bus, but with the power to fly, I could get there in five minutes!"

Work with your child to underline the conjunction *and, or,* or *but* in each sentence.

Find the Shoe (Prepositional Phrases)

You can play this game with the whole family. First, have the other players close their eyes. Then take a shoe and hide it somewhere in the room. Have the other players guess where the shoe is, using prepositional phrases. (A prepositional phrase can tell where something is. Prepositional phrases begin with words such as *in, under, through,* or *beyond*.)

Example   Is it in the refrigerator? Is it under the sink?

When a player asks a question, have him or her identify the prepositional phrase in the question and then go look for the shoe. When the shoe has been found, the finder can then hide the shoe.

What Is Wrong? (Prepositional Phrases)

Ask your child to write three sentences about what is wrong with this picture. Then work with your child to identify any prepositional phrases he or she used. (Prepositional phrases begin with words such as *around, at, by, for, from, in, near, of, off, on, to,* or *with*.)

Example   The cow is floating in the air.

Thanks to the bravery of (Samuel Wilson) the town of (Metonymy) was saved from the British. When the (Revolutionary War) began, Sam was eight years old. He was given the job of drummer boy in his **town**. When he saw the **redcoats** coming, Sam banged his **drum**. He alerted the **townspeople** in time for them to stop the **soldiers**.

Circle the boldfaced words that name particular persons, places, things, or ideas.

A **common noun** names any person, place, thing, or idea. A **proper noun** names a particular person, place, thing, or idea. Proper nouns must be capitalized.

See Handbook Section 14

Practice

Underline each common noun. Circle each proper noun.

1. (Sam Wilson) later started a plant for packing meat in (Troy, New York).

2. Because of his friendliness, (Sam) was called ("Uncle Sam") by his workers.

3. During the (War of 1812,) (Sam) printed (U.S.) on the meat being sent to the army.

4. A curious inspector asked a worker what the letters stood for.

5. The worker didn't know, so he said they might stand for (Uncle Sam.)

6. Soon people all over (America) were saying that things that came from the government were from (Uncle Sam.)

7. (Uncle Sam) has been a national symbol ever since.

8. Illustrators started printing pictures of (Uncle Sam) in newspapers in 1820.

9. The most famous picture of (Uncle Sam) was painted by (James Montgomery Flagg.)

James Flagg's painting of Uncle Sam is still widely used today.

10. This painting was used on recruiting posters for the (U.S. Army) during (World War I.)

11. In striped pants and top hat, (Uncle Sam) is still seen in ads and political cartoons.

Apply

Uncle Sam is a symbol used to represent the United States of America. Write four sentences about other symbols of our nation. Use nouns from the word bank or think of your own. Be sure to capitalize proper nouns.

bald eagle	Old Glory	the Liberty Bell
flag	Stars and Stripes	the White House

12. **Answers will vary.** _____

_____

13. _____

_____

14. _____

_____

15. _____

_____

Reinforce

Circle the eight hidden nouns. Write the proper nouns below. Use proper capitalization.

Proper Nouns

16. _____ **Lincoln** _____

17. _____ **America** _____

18. _____ **Jefferson** _____

19. _____ **Washington** _____

I	J	S	B	F	R	O	P	Q	R
N	E	X	P	L	Q	G	U	G	W
D	F	S	A	S	X	P	K	Y	A
E	F	I	R	E	W	O	R	K	S
P	E	H	A	P	L	Q	U	X	H
E	R	Z	D	H	M	R	V	Y	I
N	S	C	E	I	K	S	W	Z	N
D	O	V	Q	J	O	F	L	A	G
E	N	B	R	K	P	T	M	P	T
N	L	I	N	C	O	L	N	R	O
C	Z	H	Z	D	V	N	A	Z	N
E	A	A	M	E	R	I	C	A	M

Read and Analyze

The **Pilgrims'** first year in Plymouth had been hard. Many had died. But in the fall of 1621, the **survivors** had much to be thankful for.

Circle the part of the word *Pilgrims'* that shows possession.

Circle the part of the word *survivors* that shows it is talking about more than one person.

A **plural noun** names more than one person, place, thing, or idea. Most nouns add *-s* or *-es* to form the plural. Some nouns change spelling instead of adding *-s* or *-es* (*woman, women*). Some nouns have the same singular and plural form (*deer*). Plurals formed in ways other than adding *-s* or *-es* are called **irregular plural nouns**. A **possessive noun** shows ownership. Most plural nouns add an apostrophe after the *-s* to form the possessive (*boys'*). Plurals that don't end in *-s*, such as *men,* add apostrophe and *-s* to show possession (*men's*).

See Handbook Sections 25 and 26

Practice

Draw a box around each noun that is both plural and possessive. For the remaining nouns, underline each plural noun and circle each possessive noun.

1. The colonists' Patuxet friend Squanto had helped them build houses and plant crops.

2. The colony's governor had made peace with Massasoit, chief of the Wampanoag.

3. The settlers' harvest was expected to be good.

4. The colonists planned to invite the Wampanoag to a celebration.

5. Four women and two teenagers cooked food for 147 people.

6. The group's celebration lasted three days.

7. Unfortunately, the next year's harvest was not as good.

8. The settlers did not hold another celebration.

9. Americans did not celebrate Thanksgiving again until 1777.

10. Sarah Josepha Hale tried for more than 30 years to make Thanksgiving a holiday.

11. President Lincoln's proclamation in 1863 made Hale's wish come true.

12. Americans celebrate Thanksgiving on the fourth Thursday of November.

Women ground corn to make bread and biscuits for the first Thanksgiving.

Apply

If the boldfaced noun is singular, write its plural form. If the boldfaced noun is plural, write its plural possessive form.

13. The Wampanoag's **gift** to the feast included five **deer** and, perhaps, popcorn.

    _____gifts_____   _____deer's_____

14. The **celebration** probably began with a blare of **bugles** and a parade.

    _____celebrations_____   _____bugles'_____

15. Everyone feasted on wild **birds**, **pumpkins**, and cranberries.

    _____birds'_____   _____pumpkins'_____

16. For entertainment, the **men** competed in foot races and jumping **matches**.

    _____men's_____   _____matches'_____

17. The **friendship** lasted until 1675, when **war** broke out over land disputes.

    _____friendships_____   _____wars_____

18. Today, **visitors** to Plymouth can tour a village just like the one the **Pilgrims** built.

    _____visitors'_____   _____Pilgrims'_____

Reinforce

See Handbook Section 32

Ask an adult to help you search the Internet to learn more about the first Thanksgiving. Write a paragraph telling what you learned. Use at least one plural noun and one possessive noun.

Answers will vary._____

_____

_____

_____

_____

_____

_____

Each (group) that set out for the West in **wagons** in the 1840s faced **danger** along the trail.

Circle the boldfaced word that names a collection of people. Draw one line under the boldfaced word that names items that could be seen, touched, smelled, heard, or tasted. Draw two lines under the boldfaced word that names an idea.

A **collective noun** names a group of people or things. A **concrete noun** names something you can see, touch, hear, smell, or taste. An **abstract noun** names an idea.

See Handbook | Section 14

Practice

Read each sentence. Circle the boldfaced word that is the type of noun listed in parentheses.

1. One (party) that met disaster on the **trail** west was the Donner Party. (collective noun)

2. In May of 1846, 81 (people) left Independence, Missouri, filled with **hope**. (concrete noun)

3. They decided to follow a route recommended in a **letter** from Lansford W. Hastings, whose (knowledge) of the trail was faulty. (abstract noun)

4. The route would take the Donner party off the main trail, through rugged (mountains) and across the **emptiness** of the Great Salt Lake Desert. (concrete noun)

5. When this (band) of pioneers left the main trail to follow Hastings' cutoff, Tamsen Donner felt **sadness**, for she did not trust Hastings. (collective noun)

6. The trail through the Wasatch Mountains was too steep, rough, and narrow for the party's **wagons**, so on many days they made little (progress). (abstract noun)

7. The weary (bunch) of pioneers did not make it out of the mountains until early September, and food and **supplies** were running short. (collective noun)

8. They crossed the desert in searing heat, with very little (water) to quench their **thirst**. (concrete noun)

9. By the time the Donner Party reached the high Sierra Nevada, **snow** blocked the trail and left them stranded for the (winter) with very little food. (abstract noun)

10. Only 45 of the 81 members of the (group) survived the terrible **ordeal**. (collective noun)

Apply

Write complete sentences to answer these questions. Circle each collective noun you write. Draw a line under each abstract noun you write. **Accept reasonable responses with correct markings.**

11. In addition to bravery, what character trait do you think pioneers needed most?

    _____

    _____

12. Is fearlessness or cautiousness a better trait for a pioneer to possess? Tell why you think so.

    _____

    _____

13. What types of people would you choose as members of a party of pioneers?

    _____

    _____

14. What feelings do you think you would experience as a pioneer on a difficult journey?

    _____

    _____

Reinforce

Many types of animals have special collective nouns to name groups of them. For example, a group of crows can be called a *murder* of crows. Draw lines to connect each collective noun below to the animal it is used with. Then, on the lines below, write a sentence using one of these collective nouns.

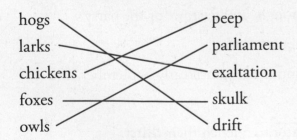

hogs   peep

larks   parliament

chickens   exaltation

foxes   skulk

owls   drift

Accept reasonable responses.

_____

_____

In the early 1890s Katharine Lee Bates, a professor from Massachusetts, visited Colorado. While there, **she** climbed Pikes Peak. The view from the summit was so magnificent that Miss Bates was inspired to write a poem. **Its** first line was "O beautiful for spacious skies."

To whom does the word *she* refer? _____ **Katharine Lee Bates** _____

What word does *Its* stand for? _____ **poem** _____

A **pronoun** can take the place of a noun. Use the **personal pronouns** *I, me, we,* and *us* to speak or write about yourself. Use *she, her, it, he, him, you, they,* and *them* to refer to other people and things. The **possessive pronouns** *his, its, our, her, their, my,* and *your* show ownership. **Remember to use this information when you speak, too.**

See Handbook | Section 16

Practice

Circle each personal pronoun in the sentences below. Underline each possessive pronoun.

1. <u>Her</u> poem was matched with the melody of a hymn called "Materna."

2. (It) had been written by Samuel A. Ward thirteen years earlier.

3. <u>His</u> melody fit perfectly with the verses (she) had written.

4. The result of <u>their</u> creative talents was the song "America the Beautiful."

5. Some of (us) find that song easier to sing than "The Star-Spangled Banner."

6. (We) would prefer to have "America the Beautiful" become <u>our</u> national anthem.

7. (I) am not a good singer, but "The Star-Spangled Banner" is one of <u>my</u> favorite songs.

8. (It) was written by Francis Scott Key during the War of 1812 and quickly became the unofficial national anthem.

9. The sight of the American flag flying after a fierce battle was <u>his</u> inspiration for writing "The Star-Spangled Banner."

10. More than 100 years later, President Herbert Hoover made <u>its</u> status as national anthem official.

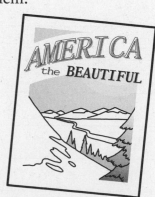

Bates's poem became "America the Beautiful."

Apply Suggested answers appear below. Accept all reasonable responses.

Rewrite each sentence, replacing each underlined word with a pronoun from the box. More than one pronoun may be correct. Remember to capitalize a pronoun that begins a sentence.

they	them	we	us	it	its	she	her	their

11. <u>Katharine Lee Bates</u> would be pleased to know that <u>Katharine Lee Bates's</u> poem remains popular more than a century after <u>the poem</u> was written. **She would be pleased to know that her poem remains popular more than a century after it was written.**

12. Many of <u>the residents of the United States</u> know <u>the song's</u> first verse by heart. **Many of us know its first verse by heart.**

13. <u>School children across America</u> sing <u>this song</u> often. **They sing it often.**

14. <u>Patriotic songs</u> can help people express <u>people's</u> pride in <u>people's</u> country. **They can help people express their pride in their country.**

15. <u>America's national anthem</u> is played at most sports events. **It is played at most sports events.**

Reinforce

Do you think that "America the Beautiful" should become our national anthem? Write two or three sentences to explain how you feel and why. Circle personal and possessive pronouns.

Answers will vary.

_____

_____

_____

_____

_____

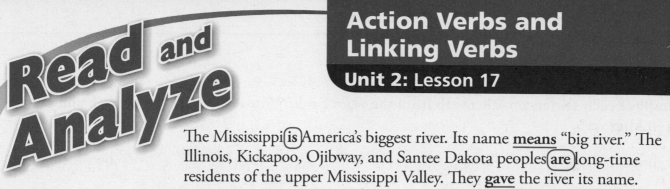

Read and Analyze

The Mississippi (is) America's biggest river. Its name **means** "big river." The Illinois, Kickapoo, Ojibway, and Santee Dakota peoples (are) long-time residents of the upper Mississippi Valley. They **gave** the river its name.

Underline the two boldfaced words that tell about actions. Circle the two boldfaced words that link subjects with words that tell about them.

An **action verb** tells what the subject of a sentence does. (*She shares her books.*) A **linking verb** links the subject with words that tell what the subject is or is like. (*She is friendly.*) Linking verbs include *am, is, are, was, were, become,* and *seem.*

See Handbook Section 17

Practice

Underline each boldfaced word that is an action verb. Circle each boldfaced word that is a linking verb. (1–10)

The first Europeans **traveled** on the Mississippi River in 1541. The river (became) vital to agriculture and industry about 200 years ago.

Today barges constantly **move** important goods up and down the Mississippi. Tugboats **guide** the barges past hazardous areas. Cargoes on southbound barges (are) usually agricultural products. Northbound barges **haul** machinery and fuel.

The lands beside the southern Mississippi River (are) fertile. Spring floods **added** important nutrients to the land for centuries.

New Orleans (is) the southernmost large city on the Mississippi. Workers there **load** cargoes of all kinds onto ships bound for ports all over the world.

Minneapolis/St. Paul

St. Louis

New Orleans

Apply

Complete each sentence with a verb from the word bank. Write *A* if it is an action verb and *L* if it is a linking verb.

contain	flows	is	marks	becomes

11. The Nile River _____**is**_____ the longest river in the world. __**L**__

12. The Colorado river _____**flows**_____ through the southwestern United States and northwest Mexico. __**A**__

13. Most rivers _____**contain**_____ fresh water. __**A**__

14. The Amazon River _____**becomes**_____ several times wider during the wet season. __**L**__

15. The Rhine _____**marks**_____ the border between Germany and France. __**A**__

Reinforce

Suppose you are a captain of a tugboat that hauls barges on the Mississippi River. Write a paragraph about what you typically see and do on a downriver run. Use at least two action verbs and two linking verbs in your descriptive paragraph.

Accept reasonable responses.

_____

_____

_____

_____

_____

_____

_____

_____

_____

_____

Up until late 1953, doctors **could** not **give** leukemia patients any hope for survival. This lesson **will acquaint** you with a researcher responsible for the first effective leukemia treatments.

Circle the more important boldfaced verb in each sentence. Underline the other boldfaced verb.

The **main verb** is the most important verb in a sentence. A **helping verb** may come before the main verb.

See Handbook | Section 17

Practice

In each sentence, circle the main verb and underline the helping verb.

1. Gertrude B. Elion was born in 1918 in New York City.

2. Before her first day of college, Gertrude had chosen a goal.

3. She would find a cure for cancer.

4. She did pursue that goal through the study of chemistry in college.

5. Despite her academic success in college, research labs would not hire Elion as a researcher.

6. Lab directors would give only males jobs as chemists.

7. During World War II, labs could not find enough male chemists.

8. Elion was hired by a pharmaceutical company.

9. Many differences between disease-causing cells and normal cells were identified by Elion and her research partner, George Hitchings.

10. With this knowledge, Elion and Hitchings could create the first drug effective against leukemia.

11. Drugs effective against HIV and gout were also developed by Elion and Hitchings.

12. In 1988 the two were awarded the Nobel Prize in Physiology and Medicine.

Gertrude B. Elion was a Nobel Prize winner.

Name _____

Apply Accept reasonable responses with correct markings.

Write a sentence to answer each question. Underline each helping verb you use.

13. Could you choose a goal for your life in the next few years?

_____

_____

14. What might your goal be?

_____

_____

15. What subjects would you study for your work toward this goal?

_____

_____

16. How else could you prepare yourself for the pursuit of this goal?

_____

_____

Reinforce

The word search puzzle below contains all 23 commonly used helping verbs. Circle each one. Then write them on the lines.

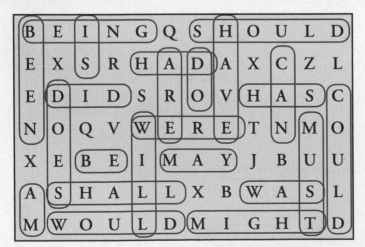

Across: **being, should, had, did, has, were, be, may, shall, was, would, might**

Down: **been, am, does, is, will, are, do, have, can, must, could**

Modal Auxiliaries

Unit 2: Lesson 19

"You **should** join our group," Sidney said to Carlos. "With your help, we (can) create the best history project in the school!"

Circle the boldfaced helping verb which indicates the ability to do something. Underline the boldfaced helping verb which expresses a duty or an obligation.

The helping verbs *may* and *might* can be used to ask or give permission. The helping verbs *can* and *could* can be used to indicate ability. The helping verbs *should* and *must* can be used to communicate a duty or an obligation. The helping verbs *may, might, could, should,* and *will* can be used to indicate possibility—how likely something is to happen. Helping verbs that have these special functions are called **modal auxiliaries**.

See Handbook Section 17

Practice

Circle the modal auxiliary in each sentence. Then underline the word in parentheses that tells about its special function.

1. We (will) create an illustrated timeline of the American Civil War. (<u>possibility</u>/ability)

2. (May) I be in charge of photo research for the project? (obligation/<u>permission</u>)

3. We (should) follow the rules for safe use of the Internet. (<u>obligation</u>/ability)

4. That website (might) show a diagram of the Battle of Gettysburg. (<u>possibility</u>/ability)

5. You (must) reduce photographs to the proper size for the timeline. (permission/<u>obligation</u>)

6. This photograph of General Robert E. Lee on his horse, Traveller, (will) illustrate the entry "Seven Days Before Richmond" in 1862. (possibility/<u>ability</u>)

7. You (should) easily find a photograph of the Sharpsburg Bridge at Antietam. (permission/<u>possibility</u>)

8. The media director says that we (may) use the color printer for reproductions of paintings. (obligation/<u>permission</u>)

9. The writers (might) finish the event cards tomorrow. (<u>possibility</u>/ability)

Robert E. Lee served as the military leader of the Confederacy during the Civil War.

Language Standard(s): L.5.1, L.5.1c

Apply   Answers will vary. Possible responses below.

Use one of the modal auxiliaries in the word bank to complete each sentence.

should	could	will	can	may	must

10. Most Americans _____**can**_____ name the President who was in office during the Civil War.

11. A serious student of the Civil War _____**must**_____ read the Gettysburg Address.

12. With some effort you _____**could**_____ memorize this brief speech.

13. Any history textbook with information about the Civil War _____**will**_____ mention the Battle of Gettysburg.

14. You _____**may**_____ know that President Abraham Lincoln remembered soldiers' heroism in the Battle of Gettysburg when he dedicated a cemetery there on November 19, 1863.

Reinforce

Write five sentences telling a student what she or he can do to learn more about the American Civil War. Use a modal auxiliary in each sentence.

Accept reasonable responses.

_____

_____

_____

_____

_____

_____

_____

_____

_____

_____

_____

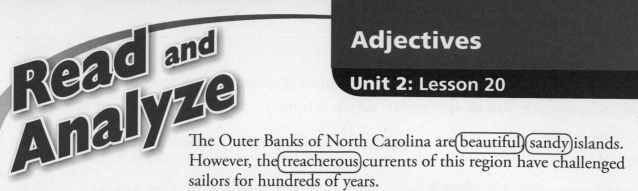

The Outer Banks of North Carolina are (beautiful) (sandy) islands. However, the (treacherous) currents of this region have challenged sailors for hundreds of years.

Circle the two words that tell what the islands are like. Circle one word that tells what the currents are like.

Adjectives describe nouns and pronouns. Some adjectives tell what kind. Others, like *many* and *six*, tell how many. The adjectives *this*, *that*, *these*, and *those* tell which one. These are called *demonstrative adjectives*. The articles *a*, *an*, and *the* are also adjectives.

See Handbook Section 15

Practice

Some adjectives in these sentences appear in boldfaced type. Circle each boldfaced adjective that tells what kind. Underline each boldfaced adjective that tells how many. Draw a box around each boldfaced adjective that tells which one. Underline each boldfaced article (*a, an, the*) twice.

1. One of <u>the</u> United States' most (famous) historical sights was built to warn sailors of the (dangerous) waters of the Outer Banks.

2. <u>Two</u> currents collide near Cape Hatteras, causing (powerful) waves.

3. A (treacherous) reef called Diamond Shoals also lies in <u>the</u> area.

4. This combination has caused many shipwrecks over <u>the</u> centuries.

5. Hurricanes sometimes strike this area as well.

6. For <u>all</u> these reasons, it is known as <u>the</u> Graveyard of <u>the</u> Atlantic.

7. In 1870, <u>a</u> (striped) lighthouse was built on Cape Hatteras to warn ships.

8. At <u>208</u> feet, it is <u>the</u> (tallest) lighthouse in <u>the</u> United States.

9. This (historic) lighthouse still stands today, and it is visited by <u>many</u> tourists each year.

10. <u>the</u> Outer Banks are (beautiful) and (interesting) as well as (dangerous)

11. Tourists come to <u>the</u> Cape Hatteras National Seashore to visit <u>the</u> (gorgeous) beaches.

12. Nearby is Kitty Hawk, where <u>the</u> Wright brothers made their (famous) flight.

The Cape Hatteras Lighthouse is endangered by beach erosion.

Name _____

Apply Possible answers appear below. Accept all reasonable responses.

Complete each sentence with an appropriate adjective from the word bank or use your own word.

| that | ten | brave | modern | few | the | those | heroic |

13. People have made _____**heroic**_____ efforts to help ships near the Outer Banks.

14. In 1899, Rasmus S. Midgett saved _____**ten**_____ men from a sinking ship during a hurricane.

15. _____**Those**_____ men would have died without him.

16. Mr. Midgett was a _____**brave**_____ member of the U.S. Life-Saving Service.

17. _____**That**_____ service joined the Coast Guard in 1915.

18. Today the Coast Guard uses _____**modern**_____ technology to find and help ships in trouble near Cape Hatteras.

19. As a result, _____**few**_____ ships have been wrecked in recent years.

Reinforce

Use these clues to complete the puzzle.

Across

5. A _____ adjective tells which one is being talked about.
6. The word _____ is an article.
7. *This, that, these,* and _____ are demonstrative adjectives.

Down

1. An adjective may _____ a noun.
2. Adjectives such as *two* and *few* tell _____ many.
3. *A* is a special kind of adjective called an _____.
4. Most adjectives come _____ the nouns they tell about.

Crossword:
5 Across: DEMONSTRATIVE
6 Across: THE
7 Across: THOSE
1 Down: DESCRIBE
2 Down: HOW
3 Down: ARTICLE
4 Down: BEFORE

The whaling industry was **very** important to the United States in the early 1800s. During that time, whalers **expertly** hunted thousands of whales each year.

Which boldfaced word tells how people do something? _____**expertly**_____

Which boldfaced word describes an adjective and tells how much? ____**very**____

Adverbs describe verbs or adjectives. They tell how, when, where, or to what extent (how much). Many adverbs end in *-ly*. Other common adverbs are *fast, very, often, again, sometimes, soon, only, however, too, later, first, then, far,* and *now.*

See Handbook | Section 18

Practice

Circle each adverb below.

1. American whalers (first) hunted sperm whales in the 1700s.

2. The oils from sperm whales were (extremely) valuable (then.)

3. These oils were used (chiefly) for lamps.

4. Whaling voyages (sometimes) lasted for four or five years.

5. When the California gold rush started (suddenly) in 1849, many whalers (quickly) abandoned their ships to seek their fortunes on land.

Whalers like this one sailed the high seas in search of whales.

6. The American whaling industry declined (rapidly) after the Civil War.

7. (Soon) (only) a few whaling operations remained in the United States.

8. (However,) the whaling industries of other nations expanded (dramatically) in the late 1800s.

9. New technology helped whalers catch and process whales (efficiently.)

10. (Tragically,) the whalers killed many thousands of whales.

11. Many species were (nearly) made extinct.

12. (Now) commercial whaling is illegal in the United States and most other countries.

13. The population of many whale species has risen (significantly.)

Apply

Circle the adverb that tells more about each underlined word or words. Then tell whether the adverb explains *how, when, where,* or *to what extent*.

14. Humpback whales <u>migrate</u> (yearly) between polar and tropical regions. _____**when**_____

15. Because humpbacks <u>swim</u> (slowly,) they used to be easy prey for whalers. _____**how**_____

16. The commercial whaling of humpbacks (finally) <u>ended</u> in the 1960s. _____**when**_____

17. Many humpbacks (accidentally) <u>become</u> entangled in fishing nets. _____**how**_____

18. If a whale <u>is caught</u> (there) it usually drowns or starves to death. _____**where**_____

19. Whales that <u>struggle</u> (frantically) may tear an expensive net to shreds. _____**how**_____

20. Experts cut a net so that the whale <u>can swim</u> (free) and the net can be fixed. _____**how**_____

Reinforce

Circle five adverbs in the puzzle. Then choose two of the adverbs. Use each in a sentence about whales or whaling.

Q	F	S	X	Y	X	W	Q	J
W	G	O	C	T	C	R	T	K
R	V	M	D	V	V	T	S	L
T	R	E	C	E	N	T	L	Y
Y	J	T	B	R	B	Y	O	N
P	X	I	N	Y	N	D	W	V
S	L	M	Q	R	M	G	L	Y
T	H	E	R	E	S	K	Y	W
D	Z	S	Q	W	D	Z	K	Z

21. **Answers will vary.** _____

_____

22. _____

_____

a. **Many historic** buildings stand near the center of Philadelphia.

b. **Historic many** buildings stand near the center of Philadelphia.

Which sentence has the boldfaced adjectives in an order that sounds natural? __a__

When you use more than one adjective to describe a noun, put the adjectives in an order that sounds natural. This chart can help you put pairs of adjectives in a natural-sounding order:

See Handbook Section 15

how many	what quality	how big	how old	what shape	what color	what material	→ noun
three	*beautiful*	*small*	*new*	*round*	*pink*	*silken*	→ *petals*

Practice

Underline the adjectives in parentheses that are in an order that sounds natural.

1. Philadelphia is (an eastern large/<u>a large eastern</u>) city.

2. It was a (<u>busy young</u>/young busy) city in the mid-1700s.

3. Around 1764, (<u>some successful</u>/successful some) Philadelphians became opposed to English rule.

4. They met with leaders of (<u>other American</u>/American other) colonies to consider independence.

5. In 1776 (colonial brave/<u>brave colonial</u>) leaders signed a document declaring America's independence from England.

6. In 1789 a group of the new nation's leaders wrote a (<u>remarkable new</u>/ new remarkable) document that established our country's legal system.

7. These (<u>two famous</u>/famous two) documents, the Declaration of Independence and the United States Constitution, were both signed in Independence Hall in Philadelphia.

8. Built of (red strong/<u>strong red</u>) bricks, this building still stands in the heart of Philadelphia.

9. This (<u>handsome old</u>/old handsome) building is in Independence National Historic Park.

10. You can also see the (silver large/<u>large silver</u>) bell known as the Liberty Bell, which was sounded when colonial representatives approved the Declaration of Independence.

Both the Declaration of Independence and the United States Constitution were signed in Independence Hall in Philadelphia.

Apply Possible answers appear below. Accept all reasonable responses.

Use two adjectives from the word bank to complete each sentence. Be sure to use each pair of adjectives in a natural-sounding order.

red	colorful	bright	American	national	official	new	early

11. Betsy Ross's family members claimed that she sewed a _____colorful new_____ flag in 1776.

12. According to them, Betsy Ross created this _____early American_____ flag in a house on Arch Street in Philadelphia.

13. On the first version of our American flag, _____bright red_____ stripes alternated with white stripes, and thirteen white stars formed a circle on a field of blue.

14. The stars-and-stripes design was approved by Congress on June 14, 1777, and that day is now an _____official national_____ holiday.

Reinforce

Write a descriptive paragraph about a symbol of America, such as the American flag, the Statue of Liberty, the White House, or the bald eagle. Use a pair of adjectives with one of the nouns you include.

Accept reasonable responses._____

_____

_____

_____

_____

_____

_____

_____

a. Mount Rushmore features enormous carvings of George Washington, Thomas Jefferson, Theodore Roosevelt, and Abraham Lincoln.

b. I recommend seeing it because it is so unusual.

Which word in sentence *a* links several proper nouns? _____**and**_____

Which word in sentence *b* links the first part of the sentence to the second part of the sentence? _____**because**_____

Coordinating conjunctions (*and, but, or*) connect words or groups of words (including independent clauses) that are similar. **Subordinating conjunctions,** such as *although, because, if*, and *before,* show how one clause is related to another clause. Subordinating conjunctions appear at the beginning of dependent clauses.

See Handbook Section 21

Practice

Underline each coordinating conjunction and circle each subordinating conjunction.

1. Doane Robinson had the idea to carve sculptures into Mount Rushmore, <u>but</u> he didn't think of portraying American presidents.

2. His idea was to carve legendary Westerners Kit Carson, Jim Bridger, <u>and</u> John Colter.

The faces of four American presidents stare across the prairies of South Dakota.

3. Gutzon Borglum wanted to make carvings of presidents (because) presidents are important.

4. Borglum was hired (because) he had already carved statues in the sides of mountains.

5. (If) Borglum had not had experience, the project probably would have failed.

6. The peak could be reached only by foot <u>or</u> horseback.

7. Equipment had to be hauled up thousands of feet <u>and</u> then lowered by ropes to work areas.

8. Dynamite <u>and</u> steam drills were used to blast away rock.

9. (Although) Borglum died before the project was finished, his son Lincoln did complete it.

10. It took 14 years <u>and</u> nearly one million dollars to complete the sculpture.

Name _____

Apply   Suggested answers appear below. Accept all reasonable responses.

Complete each sentence with a conjunction from the word bank. Write *C* if it is a coordinating conjunction and *S* if it is a subordinating conjunction.

although	and	or	because	but	before

11. _____**Although**_____ Americans do not often create giant monuments anymore, many still

admire those created in the past. __**S**__

12. Borglum started out as a painter, _____**but**_____ he became a sculptor in later life. __**C**__

13. Visitors to Mount Rushmore are often surprised _____**because**_____ the carved heads are

much paler than the uncarved rock around them. __**S**__

14. The heads are sixty feet high, _____**and**_____ the mouths are eighteen feet wide. __**C**__

15. Almost every visitor to Mount Rushmore takes photographs _____**or**_____ buys postcards of the

huge monument. __**C**__

16. _____**Before**_____ I saw Mount Rushmore, I had no idea of its huge size. __**S**__

Reinforce

Write the name of each president on Mount Rushmore next to the statement that describes him. Then circle the conjunction in each sentence.

17. (Before) he became America's first president, he was a surveyor.

_____**George Washington**_____

18. People may admire him for crafting The Declaration of Independence (and) for bringing the

recipe for ice cream to America. _____**Thomas Jefferson**_____

19. (Since) he once spared a bear cub during a hunting trip, a toy bear was named for him.

_____**Theodore Roosevelt**_____

20. His Gettysburg Address contains only ten sentences, (yet) it is considered one of the greatest

speeches of all time. _____**Abraham Lincoln**_____

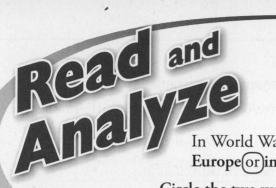

In World War II, most American combat pilots flew missions (either) in Europe (or) in the Pacific region.

Circle the two words that link the boldfaced phrases.

Correlative conjunctions always appear in pairs. They connect words or groups of words and provide more emphasis than coordinating conjunctions. Some common correlative conjunctions are *both . . . and, either . . . or, neither . . . nor, not only . . . but (also),* and *whether . . . or.*

See Handbook Section 21

Practice

Circle the correlative conjunctions and coordinating conjunctions in these sentences. If a sentence contains correlative conjunctions, write *COR.* If the sentence does not contain correlative conjunctions, write *X.*

1. (Neither) the U.S. Army (nor) the U.S. Navy would allow African Americans to fly planes before 1941. ___**COR**___

2. In the 1930s African American leaders argued for training for African American military pilots, (and) a program was established in 1940. ___**X**___

3. Successful candidates were brought to Tuskegee Army Air Field in Alabama, (and) there they were commanded by Captain Benjamin O. Davis. ___**X**___

4. The first group from Tuskegee, which included (both) airmen (and) support personnel, headed for combat in Italy in April of 1943. ___**COR**___

5. The Tuskegee Airmen performed well in Sicily, (and) their unit received a Distinguished Unit Citation. ___**X**___

6. Most of these pilots' missions during the rest of the war involved flying along with bombers (and) protecting them from German planes. ___**X**___

7. The Tuskegee Airmen proved to be (both) courageous (and) skillful as they helped the Allies defeat Adolf Hitler. ___**COR**___

8. (Whether) they received medals for individual acts of bravery (or) just helped with their squadrons' missions, all Tuskegee Airmen earned the right to be called American heroes. ___**COR**___

Name _____

Apply Suggested answers appear below. Accept all reasonable responses.

Rewrite each sentence pair as one sentence using the correlative conjunctions in parentheses.

9. Benjamin O. Davis Jr. was a skillful pilot. He was a natural leader. (not only/but also)

   Benjamin O. Davis Jr. was not only a skillful pilot but also a natural leader.

   _____

10. He fought in World War II. He fought in the Korean War. (both/and)

    He fought in both World War II and the Korean War.

    _____

11. Benjamin O. Davis Jr. always performed excellently in service to America. He was serving as a general in the Air Force. He was leading a government agency. (whether/or)

    Benjamin O. Davis Jr. always performed excellently in service to America, whether he was

    serving as a general in the Air Force or leading a government agency.

Reinforce

Write a paragraph about someone you know or have read about who has performed an important service for our nation. Use at least one pair of correlative conjunctions in your paragraph.

Accept reasonable responses. _____

_____

_____

_____

_____

_____

_____

_____

Review

(Numbers in parentheses identify related lessons.)

Nouns

Write whether the boldfaced word is a proper noun or a common noun. Then circle each boldfaced noun that is plural. Underline each one that is possessive.

1. **America's** first hard-surfaced road was the Lancaster Turnpike in Pennsylvania.

   proper noun (13, 14)

2. Until the automobile became popular, few **roads** in America were paved. **common noun (13, 14)**

Read each sentence. Circle the boldfaced word that is the type of noun listed in parentheses.

3. A **crew** on a steam railroad **train** consisted of a conductor, an engineer, a fireman, and a brakeman. (collective noun) **(15)**

4. When a new railroad line reached a frontier **town**, residents could share news and **gossip** more quickly with relatives in the East. (abstract noun) **(15)**

5. Trains carried **sacks** of mail back and forth between **civilization** and the frontier. (concrete noun) **(15)**

Pronouns

Rewrite each sentence. Use a pronoun in place of each boldfaced word or phrase.

6. In 1820, **Major Stephen Long** said that Nebraska was nearly a desert and that **Nebraska** could not support crops. **In 1820, he said that Nebraska was nearly a desert and that it could not support crops. (16)**

7. **Major Long's** opinion about **Nebraska's** suitability for growing crops was wrong. **His opinion about its suitability for growing crops was wrong. (16)**

8. In Nebraska today, **farmers and ranchers** produce huge amounts of grain and meat for **you and me** to eat. **In Nebraska today, they produce huge amounts of grain and meat for us to eat. (16)**

Verbs

Write *action verb* or *linking verb* to identify the type of each boldfaced verb.

9. The United States **doubled** in size in 1803. _____**action verb (17)**_____

10. Thomas Jefferson **was** President of the United States then. _____**linking verb (17)**_____

Circle the main verb in each sentence. Underline the helping verb.

11. The first official coins of the United States of America <u>were</u> (issued) in 1792. **(18)**

12. The museums of the Smithsonian <u>do</u> not (charge) admission. **(18)**

13. You <u>can</u> (see) hundreds of rare and valuable coins on a visit to the Smithsonian. **(18)**

Circle the modal auxiliary in each sentence. Then underline the word in parentheses that tells about its specific function.

14. (May) I borrow that book about Seattle? (possibility/<u>permission</u>) **(19)**

15. This chapter (might) discuss the construction of the Space Needle. (<u>possibility</u>/obligation) **(19)**

Adjectives and Adverbs

Circle the boldfaced words that are adjectives. Underline the boldfaced words that are adverbs.

16. Boats floated <u>swiftly</u> down the Mississippi River with goods from the (fertile) Ohio Valley. **(20, 21)**

17. The river currents flowed too <u>violently</u> for the boatmen to row upriver <u>safely</u>. **(21)**

18. They <u>wearily</u> rode the (long) way home on horseback along the Natchez Trace. **(20, 21)**

Read each sentence and the adjectives in parentheses. Write those adjectives in the blank in the order that sounds natural.

19. The state of Hawaii includes _____**five main**_____ islands. (main, five) **(22)**

20. The island of Kauai is known for its _____**lush green**_____ valleys. (lush, green) **(22)**

Conjunctions

Draw one line under each coordinating conjunction. Draw two lines under each subordinating conjunction. Circle each correlative conjunction.

21. <u><u>When</u></u> immigrants arrived in America in the late 1800s, they went through an approval process. **(23)**

22. Some immigrants were ill, <u>and</u> they were sent back home. **(23)**

23. Intake centers were maintained on (both) the East Coast (and) the West Coast. **(24)**

Spelling Practice

Read and Analyze

Do you remember how many U.S. presidents first served as governor of their state?

Write the two words in the sentence that end with the /ər/ sound.
remember, governor

Spelling Patterns: Final Schwa + *n*, Final Schwa + *r*

In an unstressed syllable, the vowel often has the /ə/ sound. The /ə/ sound is like the sound you make when you say "uh" and can be spelled with any vowel. Many words end with the /ər/ sound, which can be spelled *er* as in *water* or *or* as in *tractor*. The ending /ən/ sound can be spelled *en* as in *lighten*, *on* as in *onion*, or *ion* as in *million*.

Word Sort

Use the words below to complete the word sort. **Answers may be in any order.**

major	mission	dozen	copper	carbon
senator	motor	thicken	latter	companion

/ən/ sound	/ər/ sound
mission	major
dozen	copper
carbon	senator
thicken	motor
companion	latter

Pattern Practice

common	remember	profession	bother
citizen	major	solution	differ

Write each word next to its synonym.

1. job ___**profession**___

2. recall ___**remember**___

3. important ___**major**___

4. contrast ___**differ**___

5. answer ___**solution**___

6. annoy ___**bother**___

7. usual ___**common**___

8. resident ___**citizen**___

Write the word from sentences 1–8 that completes each sentence.

9. I can't ___**remember**___ the last time we had this much fun!

10. Medicine is a ___**profession**___ that requires years of training.

11. Any ___**citizen**___ of the town can vote on this issue.

12. The robin is a ___**common**___ bird in this state.

13. I would have called, but I didn't want to ___**bother**___ you.

14. The hurricane is the first ___**major**___ storm of the year.

15. How do cats and dogs ___**differ**___ from each other?

16. Please help me find the ___**solution**___ to this math problem.

Use the Dictionary

Complete each word by adding *er, or, en,* or *on.* Check your spellings in a dictionary.

17. mirr___**or**___

18. cinnam___**on**___

19. diamet___**er**___

Proofreading
Practice

Read this report about Route 66 and find the mistakes. Use the proofreading marks below to show how each mistake should be corrected. Use a dictionary to check and correct spellings.

Proofreading Marks

Mark	Means	Example
ꝑ	take away	America is made up ~~up~~ of many cultures.
∧	add	America ^is made up of many cultures.
≡	make into an uppercase letter	america is made up of many cultures.
⊙	add a period	America is made up of many cultures⊙
/	make into a lowercase letter	America is made up of many ₵ultures.
ⓢⓟ	fix spelling	America is maade up of many cultures.

The Main Street of America

Route 66 is **has** been called the "mother road" and the "main street of america." It represents

adventure to many Americans'. The song "Get Your Kicks on Route 66" and a 1960s television

series called "Route 66" are two examples of the role this road has played in popular culture.

Route 66 is one of the most famous roads in the world. When it was completed, it was more

than 2,400 miles long and ran between chicago and Los angeles. Route 66 cross **es** eight states and

three time zones⊙Before the Interstate Highway system was created, Route 66 was one of the most

important roads linking the eastern and western parts of the United States.

In the 1930s, Route 66 carries **d** many families from oklahoma to California. They **ir** farmland had

been ruined by severely droughts in Oklahoma. Oklahomans desperate **ly** needed work and food.

Many of them found work on farms in California. The Oklahomans called Route 66 the "Dust

Bowl Hiway." ⓢⓟ

Today, Interstate 40 has replaced Route 66 as the main Route across America's Southwest. But

Route 66 is still a symbol of adventure, **and** many people are sorry it has been replaced.

Proofreading
Checklist

You can use the list below to help you find and fix mistakes in your own writing. Write the titles of your own stories or reports in the blanks on top of the chart. Then use the questions to check your work. Make a check mark (✓) in each box after you have checked that item. **Answers will vary.**

Titles

Proofreading Checklist for Unit 2

Have I capitalized proper nouns?				
Have I used plural and possessive nouns correctly?				
Have I used adverbs correctly?				
Have I used adjectives correctly?				
Have I used helping verbs correctly?				
Have I used coordinating, subordinating, and correlative conjunctions correctly?				

Also Remember…

Does each sentence begin with an uppercase letter?				
Does each sentence end with the right mark?				
Did I use a dictionary to check and correct spellings?				
Have I used commas correctly?				

Your Own List
Use this space to write your own list of things to check in your writing.

In Unit 2 of *Grammar, Usage, and Mechanics,* students are learning about the different parts of speech, such as nouns, verbs, adjectives, and adverbs. The activities on this page give extra practice with some of the concepts students are learning. You can reinforce the information your child is learning in school by choosing one or more activities to complete with him or her at home.

Survey Says... (Personal and Possessive Pronouns)

Help your child conduct a survey. Together, list the names of family members on a sheet of paper. (Include friends and neighbors if you like.) Have your child ask the people individually whether they think the national anthem should be changed from "The Star-Spangled Banner" to "America the Beautiful" and why they think as they do. Have your child record each person's answer. Then have your child report the results to you, using personal and possessive pronouns in complete sentences. (Personal pronouns include *he, she, her, him, it, you, I, me, we, us, they,* and *them.* Possessive pronouns include *his, her, our, their, your, its,* and *my.*)

Example **My** uncle thinks "America the Beautiful" should be the national anthem. **He** thinks **it** is easier to sing than "The Star-Spangled Banner."

Word Search (Adverbs)

Work with your child to find at least fourteen adverbs in the puzzle below. (Adverbs tell *how, when, where,* and *how much* and often describe actions. Many adverbs end in *-ly,* but some do not. *Slowly, quickly, often, not,* and *never* are adverbs.)

B	F	U	L	G	E	N	E	R	O	U	S	L	Y
E	D	T	R	N	O	U	L	Y	C	P	Q	Q	D
S	S	M	K	O	N	L	Y	U	C	B	C	S	A
P	S	M	O	O	T	H	L	Y	A	P	U	L	N
E	F	F	O	R	T	L	E	S	S	L	Y	O	G
C	X	G	U	Z	L	A	Z	C	I	F	R	W	E
I	O	F	T	E	N	R	X	N	O	T	M	L	R
A	W	S	S	R	A	H	B	W	N	A	O	Y	O
L	M	N	I	H	V	A	L	W	A	Y	S	T	U
L	T	X	D	N	E	V	E	R	L	D	V	R	S
Y	R	A	E	N	I	T	K	U	L	W	S	C	L
L	Y	P	K	W	E	L	L	J	Y	M	O	L	Y

Now invite your child to use each adverb from the puzzle in a sentence.

Example The whale swam **effortlessly** through the water.

River Wild (Action Verbs and Linking Verbs)

Ask your child to recall a river s/he has visited. Have your child write a few short sentences about the visit—two with action verbs and two with linking verbs. Work together to underline each action verb and circle each linking verb.

| Example | The Snake River <u>flows</u> through Colorado. |

The water (is) cold throughout the year.

Mystery Guest (Main Verbs and Helping Verbs)

Ask your child to think of a member of your family or a close friend you both know. Invite your child to write five clue sentences to help you guess the mystery person. Ask your child to reveal one clue at a time, circling the main verb and underlining the helping verb in each clue, until you correctly name the mystery person. Then switch roles.

| Example | The person <u>has</u> (lived) in Wichita for fifty years. |

The person <u>has</u> (visited) New York City many times.

Our Hero (Coordinating and Subordinating Conjunctions)

Work with your child to research an admirable American such as Frederick Douglass, Mother Jones, a past president, or someone else. Have your child write a few short sentences about the person. Work together to see how many pairs of sentences you can combine. Use coordinating conjunctions (*and, but, or*) or subordinating conjunctions (*since, if, because, when, although*).

| Example | George Washington Carver was a scientist. He was an artist. He was an inventor. |

George Washington Carver was a scientist, an artist, **and** an inventor.

| Example | He is responsible for many inventions. He is best known for his work with peanuts. |

Although he is responsible for many inventions, he is best known for his work with peanuts.

Silly Sentences (Plural and Possessive Nouns)

Give each player two index cards. Invite each player to write two nouns. (A noun names a person, place, thing, or idea.) One noun should be singular (*astronaut*) and one should be plural (*pancakes*). Put all the cards into one pile. Form teams of two people and take turns selecting two cards from the pile. Each team has one minute to come up with a sentence that includes both nouns and uses one noun as a possessive. (Possessive nouns, such as *girl's* or *women's*, show ownership.) Encourage the teams to make their sentences as silly as possible. Write all of the sentences on a piece of paper.

| Example | The **crocodile's shoes** were red. |

"Who is your favorite Olympic athlete?" Don asked Angela.
"**They're** all great athletes. **Their** stamina is phenomenal."
"My favorite is Billy Mills, who won the 10,000 meter at the Tokyo Olympic games in 1964," said Don. "I wish I could have been **there!**"

Which boldfaced word means "belonging to them"? _____**their**_____

Which boldfaced word refers to a place? _____**there**_____

Which boldfaced word is a contraction of the words *they* and *are*? _____**they're**_____

The words **their, there,** and **they're** sound alike, but have different spellings and meanings. *Their* is a possessive pronoun meaning "belonging to them." *There* is an adverb that usually means "in that place." *They're* is the contraction made from the words *they are*.

See Handbook Section 28

Practice

Circle the word in parentheses that correctly completes each sentence.

1. "American spectators never thought (**their**/there/they're) countrymate could win," said Don.

2. "No American had ever won the 10,000 meter Olympic race before. (Their/**There**/They're) was an American silver medalist once, but that was back in 1912."

3. "The spectators must have been astounded," said Angela. "Who were (**their**/there/they're) favorites before the race?"

4. "(Their/There/**They're**) not so interesting to me," Don replied, "because those other runners had already won international medals."

5. "Here's how it happened," Don said, getting into the moment. "It's halfway through the race, and a few runners are ahead of the pack. (Their/There/**They're**) chasing Ron Clarke, the leader."

The movie *Running Brave* tells the story of Billy Mills.

6. "As they enter the last few laps, Mohammed Gammoudi pulls ahead. Clarke, then Mills, are right (their/**there**/they're) behind him. Then Mills begins losing ground."

7. "At the last minute, Mills sprints past both Clarke and Gammoudi to cross the finish line! People cannot believe (**their**/there/they're) eyes!"

Apply

Imagine that you are an announcer describing a race. Write three sentences. Use *their* in one, *there* in another, and *they're* in the third.

8. **Answers will vary.** _____

_____

9. _____

_____

10. _____

_____

Reinforce

Write *their, there,* or *they're* in each blank. When you have completed the clues, solve the riddle. (11–19)

_____ **They're** _____ made of valuable material, but _____ **they're** _____

worth more than _____ **their** _____ weight in gold.

_____ **There** _____ are a limited number of them in the world.

They cannot be bought. In fact, _____ **they're** _____ given away.

Every two years _____ **there** _____ is a chance to get one.

_____ **Their** _____ owners hang them around _____ **their** _____ necks

or on _____ **their** _____ walls.

What are they?

They're __O__ __L__ __Y__ __M__ __P__ __I__ __C__ __M__ __E__ __D__ __A__ __L__ __S__ .

It's hard to remain at the top in table tennis. Jan-Ove Waldner has proven himself one of **its** most consistent performers over the past twenty years.

Which boldfaced word means "belonging to something"? _____its_____

Which is a contraction made from the words *it* and *is*? _____It's_____

The words **its** and **it's** sound the same, but they have different spellings and meanings. *Its* is a possessive pronoun that means "belonging to it." *It's* is the contraction made from *it is* or *it has*.

See Handbook Section 28

Practice

Underline the word in parentheses that correctly completes each sentence.

1. To be successful in table tennis, (<u>it's</u>/its) helpful to begin playing at a young age.

2. By the time Jan-Ove Waldner was nine, table tennis had worked (it's/<u>its</u>) charms on him.

3. Jan-Ove studied table tennis in China, where (<u>it's</u>/its) a very popular sport.

4. He began winning championships as a teenager, and continued to win in his 20s and 30s; eventually the world of table tennis honored Jan-Ove as one of (it's/<u>its</u>) greatest champions.

5. Some say that athletic success comes from natural talent, and some say (<u>it's</u>/its) due to practice and desire.

6. Waldner says that to excel at a sport, you must practice (<u>its</u>/it's) skills.

7. He tells table tennis players to work on hitting the ball on (<u>its</u>/it's) way up.

8. He says also to practice hitting the ball at the apex of (<u>its</u>/it's) flight.

9. (Its/<u>It's</u>) important to practice hitting downward-moving balls, too, in his opinion.

10. He says that (its/<u>it's</u>) particularly important to stay relaxed while competing.

Jan-Ove Waldner won two Olympic medals, one silver and one gold.

Name _____

Apply

Write *its* or *it's* to complete each sentence.

11. When table tennis was first invented, _____**its**_____ greatest appeal was that it could be played indoors.

12. Now _____**it's**_____ one of the world's most popular sports, with more than 40 million competitive players worldwide.

13. In 1988 table tennis was awarded _____**its**_____ status as a Summer Olympic sport.

14. Athleticism is a necessity for elite players, but _____**it's**_____ not a requirement for casual players.

15. Children, older people, and disabled people can all play table tennis. _____**It's**_____ recognized as an official sport of the Paralympics.

Reinforce

Write *its* or *it's* in each blank. Remember to capitalize a word if it begins a sentence. Then use the finished clues to solve the riddle. (16–24)

_____**It's**_____ an important part of the game, but _____**it's**_____ not a player.

_____**Its**_____ job is at the table, but _____**it's**_____ not an athlete.

_____**It's**_____ at every game, but _____**it's**_____ not the property of either player.

_____**It's**_____ made of celluloid, the first plastic material.

_____**It's**_____ shaped like an eyeball, and _____**it's**_____ just a little bigger than one.

What is it?

It's a table tennis __B__ __A__ __L__ __L__!

"Who is **your** favorite American figure skater?" Robin asked Simone. "**You're** looking at a poster of her," said Simone, pointing to a huge photo of Michelle Kwan.

Which boldfaced word means "belonging to you"? _____**your**_____

Which boldfaced word is a short form of *you are*? _____**You're**_____

The words **your** and **you're** sound the same, but they have different spellings and meanings. *Your* is a possessive pronoun. It means "belonging to you." *You're* is the contraction of the pronoun *you* and the verb *are*.

See Handbook Section 28

Practice

Underline the word in parentheses that correctly completes each sentence.

1. "I hear that (your/<u>you're</u>) an elegant skater just like Michelle Kwan," Robin said to Simone.

2. "I will never be as elegant as she is, but (your/<u>you're</u>) kind to say that," said Simone.

3. Robin asked, "If (your/<u>you're</u>) going to be here awhile, would you mind watching my routine?"

4. Simone asked, "Do they have (<u>your</u>/you're) music cued up?"

5. Robin nodded and said, "I think (your/<u>you're</u>) going to like it."

6. When Robin finished skating, Simone said, "(<u>Your</u>/You're) form has definitely improved, and the music is great."

7. "(<u>Your</u>/You're) friend Lili says you love Michelle Kwan's autobiography," Robin said.

8. "Oh, (your/<u>you're</u>) talking about *Michelle Kwan: Heart of a Champion*," Simone answered.

9. She continued, "I have a copy signed by Michelle. (Your/<u>You're</u>) welcome to borrow it."

10. "I couldn't take (<u>your</u>/you're) copy; I'll borrow one from the library," Robin replied.

Michelle Kwan was a five-time world figure skating champion.

Apply Possible answers appear below. Accept all reasonable responses.

Imagine you are ice skating, and someone asks you these questions. Write an answer to each one. Use *your* or *you're* in each answer.

11. Is my coach here yet? __Yes, your coach is here._____

_____

12. Am I getting in the way? __No, you're not getting in the way._____

_____

13. Did you find my coat in the dressing area? __Yes, I found your coat in the dressing area.__

_____

14. Am I starting my jump on the correct foot? __No, you're starting your jump on the wrong foot.__

_____

15. Am I the greatest skater you've ever seen? __Yes, you're the greatest skater I've ever seen.__

_____

Reinforce

Imagine you are the coach of a skater or another athlete who is about to compete. What can you say that will help him or her stay calm and perform well? What things should he or she remember? Write a pep talk you could give. Use *your* and *you're*.

__Answers will vary._____

_____

_____

_____

_____

_____

_____

_____

_____

Baseball fans love to argue about whether this star or that star is **better**, and who was the (best) player ever at a position. They also like to debate which of two bad teams is **worse** and which manager is the (worst) of all.

Underline the boldfaced words that compare two people or things. Circle the boldfaced words that compare more than two people or things.

The words **good** and **bad** change form when they're used to compare. Use **better** and **worse** when you compare two people or things. Use **best** and **worst** when you compare three or more people or things. Avoid *gooder, goodest, bestest, more better, worser, worstest, badder,* and *baddest*. These are all nonstandard forms. **Remember to use this information when you speak, too.**

See Handbook | Section 23

Practice
Underline the form of *good* or *bad* that correctly completes each sentence.

1. Many people consider Ichiro Suzuki to be one of the (better/<u>best</u>) hitters of all time.

2. No hitter has ever had a (<u>better</u>/gooder) year than Ichiro had in 2004.

3. His total of 262 hits that year is the (bestest/<u>best</u>) single-year performance in major league history.

4. Ichiro also has the (<u>best</u>/most best) five-year hit total ever.

5. Unfortunately, his team at the time, the Seattle Mariners, had the (worse/<u>worst</u>) record in its division in two of those years.

6. Many players feel it's (<u>worse</u>/worst) to be an all-star on a losing team than to be a decent player on a championship team.

7. Ichiro would have a (<u>worse</u>/worst) batting average than he does if he did not have blazing speed.

8. His time from home plate to first base is (gooder/<u>better</u>) than most players'.

9. Ichiro uses bats of Japanese blue tamo wood, which he believes are (<u>better</u>/more better) than bats made of maple or hickory.

Ichiro Suzuki was the first non-pitcher from Japan to play major league baseball in the United States.

Apply

Write a form of *good* or *bad* from the word bank to complete each sentence.

best	better	worst	worse

10. The owner of the Brooklyn Dodgers, Branch Rickey, wanted only the __**best**__ players of all on his team.

11. He decided that baseball would be a much __**better**__ game with African American players than without them.

12. He signed Jackie Robinson to a contract because he thought Robinson was the __**best**__ person of all for the tough job of integrating the big leagues.

13. Robinson knew that being the first African American major league player would be hard, but his first year on the team was __**worse**__ than he had expected.

14. Prejudiced fans called Robinson the __**worst**__ names you could imagine.

15. Robinson had __**better**__ self-control than many other players, and he never let his anger show.

16. Robinson did the __**best**__ job he could despite the prejudice he faced.

17. Jackie Robinson was one of the very __**best**__ baseball players of his time, and he was certainly one of the bravest.

Reinforce

Compare baseball with another sport. Tell which one you like better and why. Use the words *best, worst, better,* and *worse.*

Answers will vary. _____

_____

_____

_____

_____

_____

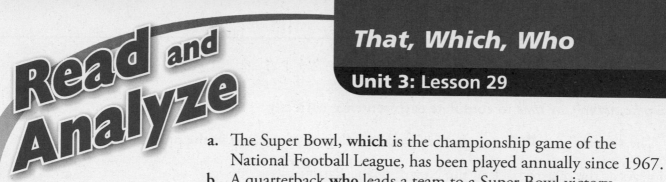

a. The Super Bowl, **which** is the championship game of the National Football League, has been played annually since 1967.

b. A quarterback **who** leads a team to a Super Bowl victory becomes famous for life.

c. Winning two Super Bowl championships is a feat **that** few quarterbacks have accomplished.

In which sentence does the boldfaced pronoun refer to a person? __**b**__

Use **who** to refer to people. Use **which** to refer to things. You may use **that** to refer either to people or to things. Use *that* instead of *which* to begin a clause that is necessary to the meaning of the sentence.
Remember to use this information when you speak, too.

See Handbook Section 27

Practice

Underline the word in parentheses that correctly completes each sentence.

1. Quarterback is a position (who/<u>that</u>) demands leadership as well as athletic talent.

2. Jim Plunkett, (<u>who</u>/which) became a great quarterback, possesses both qualities.

3. Plunkett grew up in a household (who/<u>that</u>) was a bit unusual:

   both his mother and his father were blind.

4. His parents were people (<u>who</u>/which) believed that education

   should be a young person's top priority.

5. They told Jim (<u>that</u>/which) he had to study hard and do well if he

   wanted to play sports.

6. A high school athlete (<u>who</u>/which) competes in football, basketball,

   baseball, track, and wrestling is a rarity.

7. Jim won a football scholarship to Stanford University, (who/<u>which</u>)

   is an outstanding academic school.

8. In his senior year, Jim won the Heisman Trophy, the award

   (who/<u>that</u>) is given to the top college football player each year.

Jim Plunkett led the Oakland Raiders to victory in Super Bowl XV.

Apply

Write *who, which,* or *that* to complete each sentence correctly.

9. The success ____**that**____ Jim enjoyed in college was repeated in the pros during his first five

   years as the quarterback of the New England Patriots.

10. The team never reached the Super Bowl, though, ____**which**____ disappointed Jim.

11. In 1978 Jim Plunkett, ____**who**____ had been let go by his second team, the San Francisco

    49ers, was signed by the Oakland Raiders.

12. Plunkett led the Raiders to the 1981 Super Bowl, ____**which**____ they won by a score of

    27–10 over the Philadelphia Eagles.

13. Three years later Plunkett, ____**who**____ stepped back into the starting role in mid-year, led

    the Raiders to another Super Bowl win!

14. The impressive career ____**that**____ Jim Plunkett had as a quarterback earned him a place in

    sports history.

Reinforce

Complete the clues correctly by writing *who, which,* or *that.* Then answer the riddle. (15–19)

We are the targets ____**that**____ football kickers aim for.

A kick ____**that**____ sails through us adds to the score.

A kicker ____**who**____ sends balls through our uprights is a player who brings joy to

the team's fans!

A conversion, ____**which**____ is worth one point, caps a touchdown.

But we prefer field goals, ____**which**____ are always worth three points!

We are the __G__ __O__ __A__ __L__ __P__ __O__ __S__ __T__ __S__ .

a. Mario Lemieux was **real** young when he began to play hockey.
b. He played on a **very** small rink behind the neighborhood church.
c. Everyone believed that Mario had **real** talent.

In which sentence is the boldfaced word used incorrectly? ____a____

Real is an adjective and must describe a noun or a pronoun. It means "actual." **Very** is an adverb. It means "extremely." Do not use *real* in place of *very*. **Remember to use this information when you speak, too**.

See Handbook Section 27

Practice

Draw *X* through each boldfaced word that is used incorrectly. Write *C* next to each sentence that uses the boldfaced word correctly.

1. In his **very** first season in the National Hockey League, Lemieux was chosen as the most valuable player in the All-Star Game. __C__

2. He became a **real** hero throughout Canada in 1987 when he scored the winning goal in Canada's victory over the Soviet Union in an international championship series. __C__

3. In the 1989–90 NHL season, Lemieux suffered a ~~real~~ painful back injury. _____

4. The next season, Lemieux led his team, the Pittsburgh Penguins, to their first league championship, symbolized by the ~~real~~ famous Stanley Cup. _____

5. In 1992, the Penguins again won the Stanley Cup, a **real** feat. __C__

6. Then Lemieux faced a **real** challenge: he was diagnosed with Hodgkin's disease. __C__

7. He missed a month of the 1992–93 season, but he played ~~real~~ well. _____

8. Later Lemieux missed almost two full seasons due to ~~real~~ serious health problems. _____

9. He surprised almost everyone by having one of his **very** best seasons when he returned. __C__

Mario Lemieux was one of the greatest hockey scorers of all time.

Apply Answers will vary.

Write a sentence about each topic below. Use *very* or *real* in each sentence you write.

10. your favorite sport _____

11. why you like that sport _____

_____

12. your favorite athlete _____

13. why you like that player _____

_____

14. the most exciting sporting event you have seen _____

_____

15. another topic that interests you _____

_____

Reinforce

Complete this poem by writing *very* or *real* in each blank. Then answer the riddle. (16–22)

I'm ____**very**____ small and I'm ____**very**____ fast. If you close your eyes I'll shoot right past!

I live on the ice, where it's ____**very**____ cold. Or at least that's what I've been told.

I myself can't feel at all. I'm not a ____**real**____ player—I'm more like a ball.

Although I don't bounce, I'm perfectly round. I'm ____**very**____ important, though I stay on

the ground.

I'm not ____**very**____ modest, but why should I be? I am hockey's ____**real**____ MVP!

What am I? I'm a __**H**__ __**O**__ __**C**__ __**K**__ __**E**__ __**Y**__ __**P**__ __**U**__ __**C**__ __**K**__ !

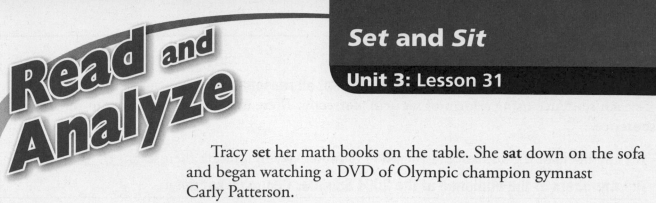

Read and Analyze

Tracy **set** her math books on the table. She **sat** down on the sofa and began watching a DVD of Olympic champion gymnast Carly Patterson.

Which boldfaced verb means "placed something somewhere"? ___**set**___

Which means "moved into a seat"? ___**sat**___

Set and **sit** are different verbs. *Set* takes a direct object and *sit* does not. If you're about to use *set,* ask yourself, "*Set* what?" If you can't answer that question, use *sit*. Also, remember that you can't *sit* anything down—you must *set* it down. The past tense form of *sit* is *sat*. *Set* is spelled the same in the present and past tenses. **Remember to use this information when you speak, too.**

See Handbook Section 27

Practice

Underline the word in parentheses that correctly completes each sentence.

1. Carly (sat/<u>set</u>) her feet firmly on the balance beam.

2. Carly's fans in the bleachers (<u>sat</u>/set) silently and watched.

3. Her coach (sat/<u>set</u>) the clipboard on a chair and stared intently.

4. After she (sat/<u>set</u>) her hands exactly right, Carly slowly raised her body into a perfect handstand.

5. In the bleachers, Carly's fans couldn't (<u>sit</u>/set) still any longer.

6. They held their breath as Carly lowered her legs and (sat/<u>set</u>) her feet back on the balance beam.

7. Throughout Carly's routine, her coach (<u>sat</u>/set) on the sidelines, amazed by her calmness under pressure.

8. Carly (sat/<u>set</u>) her feet perfectly for her final move.

9. After her signature beam dismount, the young athlete (<u>sat</u>/set) down.

10. Carly (<u>sat</u>/set) quietly until the judges scored her performance.

11. In local, regional, and international meets, Carly Patterson has (sat/<u>set</u>) a new standard for gymnastic excellence in the United States.

Carly Patterson says the balance beam is her favorite event.

Apply Possible answers appear below. Accept all reasonable responses.

Rewrite each sentence using a form of *set* or *sit* correctly. There is more than one way to rewrite each sentence.

12. The members of the audience at the 2004 Summer Olympics took their seats. _____

    The members of the audience at the 2004 Summer Olympics sat down.

13. Gymnastic equipment had been carefully arranged in the arena. _____

    Gymnastic equipment had been carefully set up in the arena.

14. Gymnasts from all over the world were in chairs on the sidelines. _____

    Gymnasts from all over the world sat in chairs on the sidelines.

15. Sixteen-year-old Carly Patterson was with the U.S. women's gymnastics team. _____

    Sixteen-year-old Carly Patterson sat with the U.S. women's gymnastics team.

16. She always placed her feet perfectly in position on the balance beam. _____

    She always set her feet perfectly on the balance beam.

17. By the end of the competition, Carly Patterson had a gold medal in the Women's Individual

    All-Around to deposit in her trophy case. **By the end of the competition, Carly Patterson**

    had a gold medal in the Women's Individual All-Around to set in her trophy case.

Reinforce Answers will vary.

List three things you might set on a table. Then write three places you might sit down.

Things I Might *Set* Down	Places Where I Might *Sit* Down
_____	_____
_____	_____
_____	_____

Briana Scurry's parents **taught** her that she could succeed, but Briana **learned** for herself that success requires overcoming obstacles.

Which boldfaced word means "gained knowledge"? **learned**

Which means "gave knowledge"? **taught**

Both **learn** and **teach** are related to knowledge, so they are often confused. *Learn* means "to get knowledge" and *teach* means "to give knowledge." **Remember to use this information when you speak, too.**

Present	Past	With *have, has,* or *had*
learn(s)	learned	learned
teach(es)	taught	taught

See Handbook Section 27

Practice

Underline the word in parentheses that correctly completes each sentence.

1. At twelve years old, Briana (<u>learned</u>/taught) that there were no girls' soccer leagues in the Minneapolis area, so she joined a boys' league.

2. The coach (learned/<u>taught</u>) Briana to be a goalkeeper because he thought that was the safest position.

3. He soon (<u>learned</u>/taught) that Briana could take care of herself; the next three years she played in the field.

4. Then Briana became goalie again because she had (<u>learned</u>/taught) that she could control the game from there.

5. Briana (<u>learned</u>/taught) a lot in high school, where she played both soccer and basketball.

6. At the University of Massachusetts, coach Jim Rudy (learned/<u>taught</u>) her the fine points of goaltending.

7. After she graduated, she (<u>learned</u>/taught) that the U.S. Women's National Team wanted her.

8. From 1994 to 1999, Scurry started 95 international matches and posted 54 shutouts; she (learned/<u>taught</u>) the world how to be a great goalie.

Briana Scurry was a member of the gold medal-winning 2004 Olympic soccer team.

Apply Answers will vary.

Answer each question. Use the boldfaced word in your answer.

9. What do you want to **learn** in high school? _____

_____

10. What important skill would you like to **teach** to a younger family member or friend?

_____

_____

11. What is the most important thing you have **learned** in the past year? _____

_____

_____

12. Think of a sport or hobby you like. What is the first thing a beginner should be **taught**

about this sport or hobby? _____

_____

_____

Reinforce

Write a paragraph about something you learned from an important person in your life. Use *learn* **and** *teach* **correctly.**

Answers will vary. _____

_____

_____

_____

_____

_____

_____

_____

Keilani Ricketts has led her team **to** victory in a college softball championship and has sparked teams to victory in two international competitions, **too.**

Circle the boldfaced word that means "also." Underline the boldfaced word that means "toward." Draw a box around the boldfaced word that means "one plus one."

Two, to, and *too* sound the same, but they have different spellings and meanings. *Two* is a number. *Too* means "also" or "more than enough." *To* often means "toward."

See Handbook Section 28

Practice

Circle the correct word in parentheses in each sentence. (1–10)

Keilani Ricketts experienced the best possible finish (to/two/too) her college softball career. She led her Oklahoma Sooners team (to/two/too) the NCAA national championship. Ricketts drove in all four of her team's runs to lead them to a 4–0 victory over the University of Tennessee in game (to/two/too) of the finals.

Ricketts had starred in game one of the finals, (to/two/too). She had pitched all 12 innings in Oklahoma's initial triumph over Tennessee. The national championship was number (to/two/too) for the Sooner women. They won the NCAA softball championship in 2000, (to/two/too).

Keilani Ricketts was named 2013 Player of the Year in NCAA women's softball.

In addition (to/two/too) her four years as an all-star at the University of Oklahoma, Ricketts has excelled in international competition, (to/two/too). In 2011 she led her USA Softball team (to/two/too) victory in the Pan American Games. In 2012, she pitched and won (to/two/too) games for USA Softball as they won the World Cup of Softball.

Apply

Write *two*, *to*, or *too* to complete each sentence correctly.

11. Can a family have ____**too**____ much athletic talent?

12. Keilani Ricketts has ____**two**____ sisters, Samantha and Stephanie.

13. They are outstanding softball players, ____**too**____.

14. Like Keilani, Samantha went ____**to**____ the University of Oklahoma.

15. She was an All-American softball player there, ____**too**____!

16. Stephanie went ____**to**____ the University of Hawaii and played on their softball team.

17. Keilani's brother Richard won entrance ____**to**____ the United States Air Force Academy.

18. He played varsity sports, ____**too**____, but his sport was football.

Reinforce

Write a paragraph about a sport or an athlete. Use *two*, *to*, and *too* as many times as you can. Be sure to use each of these words correctly.

Accept reasonable responses.

_____

_____

_____

_____

_____

_____

_____

_____

_____

_____

Maritza Correia **growed** up near the ocean, so she (**knew**) how to stay safe at the beach.

Circle the boldfaced verb that is correct. Write the correct form of the other boldfaced word. ___grew___

Know and **grow** are **irregular verbs**. You cannot make the past tense of these verbs by adding -*ed*. These verbs have different forms.

📢 **Remember to use this information when you speak, too.**

Present	Past	With *have, has,* or *had*
know(s)	knew	known
grow(s)	grew	grown

See Handbook | Section 17

Practice

Underline the verb in parentheses that correctly completes each sentence.

1. When Maritza Correia was 6, doctors discovered that her spine had (grew/<u>grown</u>) curved.

2. If her parents had (knew/<u>known</u>) about her condition earlier, they probably would have acted sooner to correct it.

3. Correia's doctor (<u>knew</u>/known) that swimming could help, so Correia started to swim.

4. Her back condition improved, and she also (<u>grew</u>/growed) to be a strong swimmer.

5. Her skills (<u>grew</u>/grown), winning her medals at the World Championships in 2001, 2003, and 2004.

6. When Correia made the Olympic team in 2004, she (<u>knew</u>/knowed) she had made history.

7. Did you (<u>know</u>/known) that Correia was the first African American woman on a U.S. Olympic swim team?

8. Her reputation (<u>grew</u>/grown) when she won a silver medal at the 2004 Olympics.

Maritza Correia overcame a physical challenge to become a champion swimmer.

9. She has swum so well that she has become (knowed/<u>known</u>) as "Relay Woman."

Apply   Answers will vary.

Write sentences to answer the following questions. Use a form of *know* or *grow* in each sentence.

10. When did you first know you liked the sport or hobby that is now your favorite?

_____

_____

11. How does someone grow more and more skilled at that sport or hobby? _____

_____

_____

12. How much have you grown in the last year? _____

_____

13. How long have you known your best friend? _____

_____

Reinforce

Use the correct forms of *know* or *grow* to complete the puzzle.

Across

2. "That girl has ___ to be a fine athlete," said her coach.
3. "I always ___ she would," said her mother.
4. "I have always ___ that I wanted to be a swimmer," said the girl.

Down

1. "I want to get better as I ___ older," she added.
2. She ___ more confident as she won more and more competitions.
3. "I ___ you will achieve your goals," said her coach.

a. I bought **myself** a video about free throw technique. According to the instructor, **anyone** can learn to shoot free throws accurately.

b. I bought **me** a video about free throw technique. According to the instructor, **any one** can learn to shoot free throws accurately.

Look at the boldfaced words in each pair of sentences. Circle the letter by the sentences that are written correctly.

Myself, yourself, and *ourselves* are **reflexive pronouns**. A reflexive pronoun refers back to the subject of a sentence. *Anyone, nobody,* and *someone* are **indefinite pronouns**. An indefinite pronoun refers to one or more people or things not identified as individuals.

See Handbook Section 16

Practice

Read each sentence. Circle the word in parentheses that is the correct form of the pronoun.

1. My sister has taught (her self/**herself**) to relax before shooting a free throw.

2. She showed (**me**/myself) a video clip of Maya Moore, the WNBA all-star.

3. (No body/**Nobody**) looks more comfortable than she does at the free throw line.

4. (Every one/**Everyone**) else on my team made a higher percentage of free throws than I did last year.

5. I made (me/**myself**) a promise that I would work hard and improve.

6. The instructor on the video taught (**himself**/hisself) to shoot free throws after watching tapes of Steve Nash.

7. (Any one/**Anyone**) who is a real NBA fan knows that Steve Nash is the best free throw shooter in history.

8. My sister and I consider (us/**ourselves**) lucky.

9. Our family lives near a schoolyard with basketball courts, and there is almost always (some one/**someone**) to play with.

10. You can make (you/**yourself**) a more valuable player by working on your free throw technique.

Maya Moore is now among the best free throw shooters in women's pro basketball.

Apply

Choose a word from the word bank to complete each sentence. Use correct capitalization.

anyone	yourself	ourselves
nobody	myself	themselves

11. You can help _____**yourself**_____ improve as a basketball player by working on

    your defense.

12. _____**Anyone**_____ who wants to play good defense must keep a hand in the air

    at all times.

13. Players must remind _____**themselves**_____ to communicate with their

    teammates constantly.

14. _____**Nobody**_____ who stands flat-footed can move quickly enough to stop a dribbler.

15. I constantly remind _____**myself**_____ to stay between the player I am guarding

    and the basket.

16. We should always think of _____**ourselves**_____ as team players!

Reinforce

Unscramble each pronoun below. Then write whether it is a reflexive pronoun or an indefinite pronoun.

slymef _____**myself**_____ _____**reflexive pronoun**_____

boomsedy _____**somebody**_____ _____**indefinite pronoun**_____

shelfer _____**herself**_____ _____**reflexive pronoun**_____

eyonever _____**everyone**_____ _____**indefinite pronoun**_____

shelmevest _____**themselves**_____ _____**reflexive pronoun**_____

Write two sentences using at least two of the reflexive pronouns and indefinite pronouns above.

_____

_____

_____

Pronoun-Antecedent Agreement
Unit 3: Lesson 36

(Bob Coomber) is a record-setting wheelchair hiker. **He** has scaled White Mountain. At 14,246 feet, **it** is California's third-highest peak.

Circle the words that the pronoun *he* replaces. Draw a line under the words that *it* replaces.

An **antecedent** is the word or words a pronoun refers to. The antecedent is usually a noun. Sometimes it also includes words that modify the noun. When you write a pronoun, be sure its antecedent is clear. Pronouns must also **agree** with their antecedents. An antecedent and a pronoun agree when they have the same number (singular or plural) and gender (male or female).

See Handbook Section 16

Practice

Circle the antecedent for each boldfaced pronoun.

1. (Bob Coomber's wheelchair) is light and sturdy. With his strong arms, he can power **it** up rocky trails.

2. (4WheelBob,) as **he** is known, also hikes on smoother, more level trails.

3. He and (his wife) spend time outdoors almost every weekend. **She** walks on two legs, and he rolls on four wheels.

4. (Bob) began using a wheelchair when **his** legs became too fragile to walk on as the result of complications from diabetes.

5. 4WheelBob writes a newspaper column for (mobility device users.) He tells **them** about trails they can move along easily.

6. In addition to White Mountain, Bob has climbed (Mount Diablo,) (North Peak,) and (Mission Peak.) **They** are three of the highest peaks in the San Francisco Bay Area.

4WheelBob Coomber climbs mountains in his wheelchair.

7. 4WheelBob refuses to believe in limits, and he inspires (others with disabilities) to increase **their** participation in outdoor activities.

8. Bob Coomber received the President's Council on Physical Fitness Community Leadership Award in 2008. **It** was given to only 27 Americans in that year.

Name _____

Apply

Write the pronoun that could stand for the boldfaced word or words in each sentence. Use correct capitalization.

9. **White Mountain** is located in eastern California. _____It_____ is near the town of Bishop.

10. **4WheelBob** had tried to climb that mountain before _____he_____ made his successful ascent, but altitude sickness had forced him to turn back.

11. To prevent a recurrence of the problem, **Coomber** camped for five days at 8,500 feet. This stay gave _____his_____ heart and lungs the chance to adjust to high altitude.

12. **Four friends** accompanied Coomber on his push to the summit. _____They_____ brought him water and supplies.

13. **Hikers** must bring water with _____them_____, because there is no water or shade on the trail to the summit.

14. Coomber needed three days to hike 5½ miles to the top of **White Mountain**. On _____its_____ slopes, Coomber saw a herd of bighorn sheep.

15. From the summit of White Mountain, **Coomber** could look out across 200 miles of Nevada desert. To the north _____he_____ could see 100 miles of snowy peaks.

Reinforce

Write a pair of sentences about someone you know who enjoys an outdoor activity. Use and circle two personal pronouns. Draw an arrow from each pronoun to the word or words it replaces.

Accept reasonable responses.

_____

_____

_____

_____

_____

_____

Review

(Numbers in parentheses identify related lessons.)

Usage

Underline the word in parentheses that correctly completes each sentence.

1. The exhausted surfers stuck (<u>their</u>/there/they're) surfboards in the sand. **(25)**

2. Then they sat down to catch (<u>their</u>/there/they're) breath. **(25)**

3. "That was the (bestest/<u>best</u>) surfing I've done in weeks," said Alyssa. **(28)**

4. "Not I," said Gustavo. "I did (gooder/<u>better</u>) yesterday." **(28)**

5. "Look at that wave over (their/<u>there</u>/they're)!" Lani exclaimed. **(25)**

6. "(<u>It's</u>/Its) at least twenty feet high!" **(26)**

7. "A yacht would fit in (it's/<u>its</u>) curl!" she cried. **(26)**

8. "Aren't you glad (<u>you're</u>/your) not out there?" Gustavo asked. **(27)**

9. "Look at the lifeguards! (Their/There/<u>They're</u>) calling everyone in to shore," he continued. **(25)**

10. "I (<u>knew</u>/knowed) it was a good time to quit," said Lani. **(34)**

Write *who*, *which*, or *that* on the line to complete each sentence correctly.

11. Edson Arantes do Nascimento may be the greatest soccer player _____who (29)_____ has ever lived.

12. You may be more familiar with this star's nickname, _____which (29)_____ is Pelé.

13. It was Pelé's exploits as a member of the Brazilian national team _____that (29)_____ made him famous.

14. Soccer, _____which (29)_____ is popular throughout the world, is especially popular in Brazil.

Underline the word in parentheses that correctly completes each sentence.

15. If you want to learn to ski well, (<u>you're</u>/your) going to have to train hard. **(27)**

16. First you must find a coach who will (learn/<u>teach</u>) you the right techniques. **(32)**

17. It is also (real/<u>very</u>) important to eat a healthy diet. **(30)**

18. Your training schedule won't leave you much time to (set/<u>sit</u>) on the sofa watching TV. **(31)**

19. When your coach sees that you have (growed/<u>grown</u>) stronger and have developed good technique, you'll be allowed to compete in more challenging events. **(34)**

20. Slalom racing is a (real/<u>very</u>) difficult event. **(30)**

21. Slalom skiers are (know/<u>known</u>) for their strength, agility, and speed. **(34)**

22. Bowling is a (<u>very</u>/real) popular sport. **(30)**

23. Since bowlers spend much of their time (setting/<u>sitting</u>) down and waiting for their turns, this sport usually does not provide aerobic exercise. **(31)**

24. My uncle wants to (learn/<u>teach</u>) me how to deliver a bowling ball correctly. **(32)**

25. He (<u>taught</u>/learned) me to keep my eyes on the pins when I roll the ball. **(32)**

26. (<u>Two</u>/To/Too) fun board sports are gaining popularity. **(33)**

27. A wakeboarder holds tight (two/<u>to</u>/too) a tow rope and does tricks behind a boat. **(33)**

28. A wake surfer uses a towrope, (two/to/<u>too</u>), but then drops the rope and rides the curl of the boat's wake. **(33)**

29. Have you seen (<u>anyone</u>/any one) wakeboard or wake surf? **(35)**

30. Wake surfers must keep (theirselves/<u>themselves</u>) balanced. **(35)**

31. I might buy (me/<u>myself</u>) a wakeboard if I can save enough money. **(35)**

**Write the pronoun that could stand for the boldfaced word or words in each sentence.
Use correct capitalization.**

32. **My sister** is an excellent gymnast. _____**She**_____ does amazing moves on the balance beam. **(36)**

33. **Her coaches** film her routines. _____**They**_____ post the clips on the team's website. **(36)**

34. **My sister** watches the clips on _____**her**_____ computer. **(36)**

Read and Analyze

The tennis champion has a (quicker) serve than his opponent. He is also the (calmest) person in the league. There's no (denying) that he's the one to beat!

Circle each word that ends with the suffix -*er*, -*est*, or -*ing*.

Adding Suffixes: -*er*, -*est*, -*ed*, -*ing*

The suffixes **-er**, **-est**, **-ed**, and **-ing** can be added to base words to form new words. There are rules to follow when adding these suffixes. If the word ends in a consonant and silent e, drop the e and add the ending (*late*, *later*). If the word ends in a consonant and *y*, change the *y* to *i* and add the ending (*funny*, *funniest*). In most cases, if the word ends in a vowel and one consonant, double the final consonant before adding the ending (*grin*, *grinned*).

Word Sort

Use the words below to complete the word sort. **Answers may be in any order.**

removing	wiser	happiest	denied
trimmed	grayest	interesting	sunnier

Base word + -*er*	Base word + -*est*
wiser	happiest
sunnier	grayest

Base word + -*ed*	Base word + -*ing*
denied	removing
trimmed	interesting

Pattern Practice

Add *-er, -est, -ed,* or *-ing* to each base word and write the new word.

1. wise + est _____**wisest**_____

2. slim + er _____**slimmer**_____

3. supply + ed _____**supplied**_____

4. laugh + ing _____**laughing**_____

5. safe + est _____**safest**_____

6. wide + er _____**wider**_____

7. borrow + ed _____**borrowed**_____

Add *-er, -est, -ed,* or *-ing* to the base word in parentheses to make it fit in the sentence. Write the new word.

8. Spain is the _____**sunniest**_____ place in Europe. (sunny)

9. Aiden is _____**trimming**_____ the bushes in the front yard. (trim)

10. Mr. Slone _____**removed**_____ the leaves from the pool. (remove)

11. Emma is _____**kinder**_____ than her older sister. (kind)

12. Brian _____**admitted**_____ that he had forgotten to meet me. (admit)

13. My family _____**traveled**_____ to Egypt to see the pyramids. (travel)

14. Mrs. Kirk needed help _____**carrying**_____ her groceries. (carry)

Use the
Dictionary

Write the base word for each word. Check your spellings in a dictionary.

15. excelling _____**excel**_____

16. fluffier _____**fluffy**_____

17. directed _____**direct**_____

18. denied _____**deny**_____

Proofreading
Practice

Read this passage about bike tours and find the mistakes. Use the proofreading marks below to show how each mistake should be fixed. Use a dictionary to check and correct spellings.

Proofreading Marks

Suggested answers appear below. Accept all reasonable responses.

Mark	Means	Example
و	take away	Riders climbs France's highest peaks.
∧	add	Riders ∧climb France's highest peaks.
≡	make into an uppercase letter	Riders climb france's highest peaks.
/	make into a lowercase letter	Riders Climb France's highest peaks.
⊙	add a period	Riders climb France's highest peaks⊙
sp	fix spelling	Riders climb France's hiest peaks.

Tour de France? Sure!

Nelson wasn't a professional cyclist. He was, like a regular cycling enthusiast who happened to be sixty-one years old. Still, Nelson had just completed six days of the Tour de France bicling route. **sp**

Just hours ahead of the real Tour de France, nelson's tour group had cycled the same steep roads ∧**that** the professional riders would cycle later in the day. His tour group was made up of amateur cyclists which ∧**who** wanted to experience the challenges of the Tour de France.

The tour guides provided the hotels, meals, transportation, and medical support. The tour members even had they're ∧**their** own van following them, ready with food, advice, doctors, and, you know, a comfortable place to set ∧**sit** down and catch a breath.

Do you think you'll ever want to ride in you're ∧**your** own Tour de France? By joining a group like this, nearly anyone can⊙Anyone, that is, which ∧**who** can cycle a grooling **sp** 50 miles or more in a day, up and down mountains that are real **very** steep. Do you think you might be interested? Then its ∧**it's** time to start training!

Proofreading
Checklist

You can use the list below to help you find and fix mistakes in your own writing. Write the titles of your own stories or reports on the blanks on top of the chart. Then use the questions to check your work. Make a check mark (✓) in each box after you have checked that item. **Answers will vary.**

Titles

Proofreading Checklist for Unit 3

Have I used *your* and *you're* correctly?				
Have I used *its* and *it's* correctly?				
Have I used *their, there,* and *they're* correctly?				
Have I used *good* and *bad* correctly?				
Have I used *very* and *real* correctly?				
Have I used *sit* and *set* correctly?				
Have I used past tense forms of irregular verbs correctly?				

Also Remember…

Does each sentence begin with an uppercase letter?				
Does each sentence end with the correct end mark?				
Did I use a dictionary to check and correct spellings?				
Have I used commas correctly?				

Your Own List

Use this space to write your own list of things to check in your writing.

In Unit 3 of *Grammar, Usage, and Mechanics,* students are learning how to use words that are often confused in writing, such as *its* and *it's*. The activities on these pages give extra practice with some of the concepts they are learning. You can help reinforce this information by choosing one or more activities to complete with your child at home.

Crossword Puzzle (Irregular Verbs: *Know* and *Grow*)

Work with your child to complete this crossword puzzle. Each missing word is a form of the word *know* or *grow*.

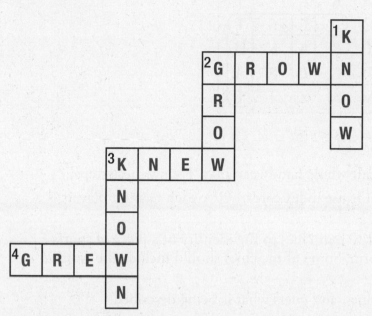

Across

2. Eli has ___ stronger by doing exercises.

3. Even before yesterday's victory, I ___ we'd win.

4. I ___ more and more excited each time we scored.

Down

1. I ___ it's not easy to become a professional soccer player.

2. When I ___ up, I want to keep playing soccer on weekends.

3. I've ___ for a long time that soccer is my favorite sport.

They're Over There with Their Sister (*Their, There, They're*)

With your child, write some sentences that describe family photos. Use the words *their, there,* and *they're* in your sentences. Have your child make sure each of these words is used correctly.

Example   This photo shows Rosie and Eileen. **They're** my aunts.

In this photo, our family is posing with the Ortiz family and **their** dog.

Grab Bag (*Its* and *It's; Their, There, They're; Your* and *You're; Too, Two, To*)

You can play this game with several family members. Write these words on slips of paper: *its, it's, their, there, they're, your, you're, two, too,* and *to*. Put the slips into a paper sack. Take turns drawing a word and using it in a sentence. Ask listeners to decide which spelling of each word is being used in the sentence and how they know.

Word Search (Comparing with *Good* or *Bad*; *That, Which, Who*; *Real* and *Very*; *Set* and *Sit*)

There are 13 words hidden in the puzzle. Work with your child to find them all. Then ask your child to use each word in a sentence.

V	W	H	O	S	S	R	V	W
X	O	K	B	E	T	T	E	R
N	R	P	T	T	Q	C	R	P
R	S	Q	G	R	R	W	Y	S
G	E	W	O	R	S	T	Z	Q
K	M	Q	O	Z	K	R	P	J
F	B	A	D	Q	B	E	S	T
A	L	S	K	L	K	A	K	H
W	H	I	C	H	G	L	X	A
P	S	T	X	M	N	Z	J	T

Guessing Game (*Its* and *It's*)

Work with your child to create a guessing game your whole family can play. Follow these steps:

1. Cut thick paper into six 3" x 5" cards. (Or use index cards.) Give each team of players two cards.

2. On each card, team members should write four clues to the identity of a piece of sports equipment or one part of a sports uniform. Some of the clues should include the word *its* or *it's*.

3. Ask teams to exchange cards, read the clues, and guess what is being described.

> 1. It's made of wood or metal.
> 2. It's long and thin.
> 3. Its surface is smooth.
> 4. It's a little thicker at one end than it is at the other.
>
> **(a baseball bat)**

You might enjoy making up more categories, such as *animals, birds,* or *food.*

Auto racing fans admire the sleek cars before the race. **They** watch **them** closely during the warm-up period.

Which boldfaced word replaces the phrase *auto racing fans*? **They**

Which boldfaced word replaces the phrase *the sleek cars*? **them**

Which boldfaced word is the subject of the sentence? **They**

A pronoun can be the subject or the object in a sentence. **Subject pronouns** include *I, he, she, we,* and *they*. **Object pronouns** can be used after an action verb or a preposition. Object pronouns include *me, him, her, us,* and *them*. The pronouns *it* and *you* can be either subjects or objects. **Remember to use this information when you speak, too.**

See Handbook Section 16

Practice

Circle each boldfaced word that is a subject pronoun. Underline each boldfaced word that is an object pronoun.

1. My friends and (I) watch the Indy 500 every year on TV.

2. The speed, the noise, and the excitement thrill <u>us</u>.

3. (You) might know that only three drivers have four Indy victories to their credit.

4. Can (you) name <u>them</u>?

5. (They) are A.J. Foyt, Jr., Al Unser, Sr., and Rick Mears.

6. (I) have an autographed photo of Al Unser and

   his brother Bobby, another Indy winner.

7. My aunt Dinah gave <u>it</u> to <u>me</u>.

8. (I) keep <u>it</u> next to a photograph of Janet Guthrie.

Race cars are custom built for stability and speed.

9. Many fans remember <u>her</u> because (she) was the first woman to race at Indy.

10. Today more women are competing at Indy, and (they) are well prepared.

11. Indy competitor Sarah Fisher started racing a quarter-midget car when (she) was five.

Apply

Rewrite each sentence. Replace each boldfaced phrase with a pronoun.

12. **Janet Guthrie** had to quit **the 1977 race** after 27 laps because of mechanical problems.

    She had to quit it after 27 laps because of mechanical problems. _____

    _____

13. Sometimes **a driver's crew** can solve **mechanical problems** during a race.

    Sometimes they can solve them during a race. _____

    _____

14. **The crew** must often change **two or more tires** in just a few seconds. **They must often**

    change them in just a few seconds. _____

15. **The driver** watches for **colored flag signals.** **He/She watches for them.** _____

    _____

16. **Safety** must be strictly maintained to prevent **accidents.** **It must be strictly maintained**

    to prevent them. _____

Reinforce

Imagine that you were at an Indy 500 car race. Write two or three sentences about what you saw, heard, and felt at the racetrack. Use subject and object pronouns in your sentences.

Answers will vary. _____

_____

_____

_____

_____

_____

_____

a. Tyrin and me went to the drag races last weekend.
b. My cousin Phil introduced Tyrin and me to his racing partner, Betty.

If you remove "Tyrin and" from each sentence, which sentence sounds correct? _____**b**_____

Use the pronouns *I, you, we, he, she, it,* and *they* as **subjects** in sentences. Use the pronouns *me, you, us, him, her, it,* and *them* as **objects** in sentences. **Remember to use this information when you speak, too.**

See Handbook Sections 16 and 27

Practice

Circle the correct pronoun in each pair. Write *S* if you chose a subject pronoun and *O* if you chose an object pronoun.

1. Betty and (he/him) take turns driving their dragster. _____**S**_____

2. They showed Tyrin and (I/me) a picture of a dragster with an open parachute behind it. _____**O**_____

3. Tyrin asked (they/them) why the parachute was there. _____**O**_____

4. (She/Her) and Phil explained that parachutes help the dragsters stop after they cross the finish line. _____**S**_____

5. Betty took Tyrin and (I/me) to the drag strip. _____**O**_____

6. Phil took a picture of (she/her) and me standing in front of the dragster. _____**O**_____

7. Then Tyrin and I watched Phil and (her/she) on their practice runs. _____**O**_____

8. Phil told Tyrin and (I/me) that race car drivers need great concentration. _____**O**_____

9. Now Tyrin and (I/me) want to learn how to drive a dragster. _____**S**_____

10. (He/Him) and I will begin by reading more about drag racing. _____**S**_____

11. Phil gave Tyrin and (I/me) a book about drag racing. _____**O**_____

12. Tyrin and (I/me) can't wait to read it. _____**S**_____

Some dragsters can travel over 300 miles per hour.

Name _____

Apply

Rewrite the sentences. Substitute a pronoun for each boldfaced noun.

13. **Betty** and **Phil** drive a "funny car." **She and he drive a "funny car."** _____

_____

14. A mechanic helped **Betty** and **Phil** build the car and perfect its engine. **A mechanic helped her and him build the car and perfect its engine.**

15. **Tyrin** and **Lorene** laughed when they heard the name of the car, <u>Betty, Set, Go!</u> **He and she laughed when they heard the name of the car, <u>Betty, Set, Go!</u>**

16. Then Phil told **Lorene** and **Tyrin** that the car goes 200 miles per hour! **Then Phil told her and him that the car goes 200 miles per hour!**

17. Tyrin told **Phil** and **Betty** he wouldn't laugh anymore. **Tyrin told him and her he wouldn't laugh anymore.**

Reinforce

Decide to whom each pronoun refers. (The answers appear in the sentences above.) Use the names to complete the puzzle.

Across

2. **She** drives a "funny car."
3. Tyrin told **him** he wouldn't laugh anymore.
5. Phil told **him** that the car goes 200 miles per hour.
6. **She** laughed at the name of the car.

Down

1. **He** helped Betty and Phil improve the car.
4. **He** laughed at the name of the car.

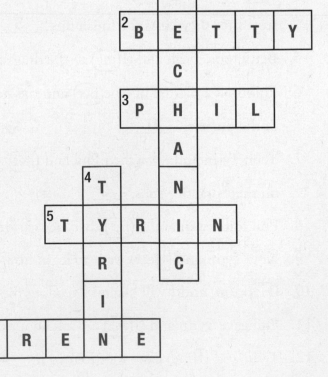

A ☐pack of growling ⟨autos⟩ approaches the village at top speed.

Draw a box around the boldfaced noun that is the simple subject. Circle the boldfaced noun that is the object of the preposition *of*. Is the subject singular or plural? **singular** Now underline the verb.

The **subject** and its **verb must agree**. Add *-s* or *-es* to a regular verb in the present tense when the subject is a singular noun or *he, she,* or *it*. Do not add *-s* or *-es* to a regular verb in the present tense when the subject is a plural noun or *I, you, we,* or *they*. Be sure that the verb agrees with its subject and not with the object of a preposition that comes before the verb. **Remember to use this information when you speak, too.**

See Handbook Section 17

Practice

Circle the simple subject in each sentence. Underline the correct verb in parentheses.

1. Many ⟨types⟩ of race cars (<u>compete</u>/competes) in races today.

2. Most ⟨experts⟩ (<u>say</u>/says) that Formula One cars are the costliest to build and race.

3. ⟨Engineers⟩ (<u>create</u>/creates) Formula One cars using some principles of airplane design.

4. A long, tubelike ⟨body⟩ and ⟨tires⟩ without fenders (<u>make</u>/makes) these cars easy to recognize.

5. Two ⟨pairs⟩ of wings attached to the car's body (<u>keep</u>/keeps) the car on the ground.

6. The ⟨downforce⟩ from the wings (enable/<u>enables</u>) the car to go fast around turns.

7. The ⟨engine⟩ (release/<u>releases</u>) much power to make the car move fast.

8. The ⟨engines⟩ (<u>make</u>/makes) a deafening roar.

9. ⟨People⟩ close to the track often (<u>cover</u>/covers) their ears.

10. ⟨Fans⟩ worldwide (<u>follow</u>/follows) Formula One racing.

11. Many ⟨fans⟩ (<u>believe</u>/believes) that Formula One competitions are more exciting than any other form of racing.

Some Formula One races are still held on roads and highways.

Name _____

Apply Possible answers appear below. Accept all reasonable responses.

Write a verb to complete each sentence correctly. You may use words from the word bank.

reach	earn	range	compete	win
reaches	earns	ranges	competes	wins

12. Formula One cars _____**compete**_____ in a series called the Grand Prix.

13. Grand Prix races _____**range**_____ from about 150 to about 200 miles long.

14. The leader in a typical race _____**reaches**_____ speeds above 200 mph.

15. The top eight drivers to finish a Grand Prix race _____**earn**_____ points.

16. At the end of the year, the driver with the most points _____**wins**_____ the World
Drivers' Championship.

Reinforce

Use the clues to complete the puzzle. Each answer is a verb that appears in this lesson.

```
1 C  O  V  E  R
  O
  M        2 W
  P          I
3 E  A  R  N  S
  T
4 R  E  L  E  A  S  5 E
  S              N
           6 M  A  K  E
              B
              L
           7 R  E  A  C  H  E  S
```

Across

1. When the cars race by, I _____ my ears.
3. A boy in my class _____ money washing cars.
4. The driver of the car must _____ the parking brake before driving.
6. Winning this race will _____ him a champion.
7. The car in that showroom _____ speeds of 200 miles per hour.

Down

1. The woman in these pictures _____ in auto races.
2. Will the man in that car _____ the race?
5. A victory in this race will _____ him to enter the finals.

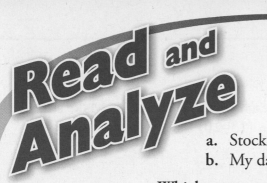

Forms of *Be*

a. Stock car races **are** very popular in the United States.

b. My dad (is) happy to go to the Southern 500 this year.

Which sentence has a singular subject? ___**b**___ Circle the boldfaced verb in that sentence.

Which has a plural subject? ___**a**___ Underline the verb in that sentence.

Am, is, was, are, and *were* are forms of the verb *be.* Use *am* after the pronoun *I.* Use *is* or *was* after a **singular subject** or after the pronouns *he, she,* or *it.* Use *are* or *were* after a **plural subject** or after the pronouns *we, you,* or *they.* **Remember to use this information when you speak, too.**

See Handbook Sections 17 and 27

Practice

Underline the correct form of *be* in each sentence.

1. Stock car racing (<u>was</u>/were) first popular in the southern United States.

2. NASCAR (<u>is</u>/are) the association that governs stock car racing in the United States.

3. Once, only American cars (was/<u>were</u>) contestants in NASCAR races.

4. Today, cars of other nations (is/<u>are</u>) among the cars that compete.

5. Stock cars (is/<u>are</u>) similar in appearance to regular passenger cars.

6. Regular car engines (is/<u>are</u>) required in NASCAR autos.

7. However, a stock car (<u>is</u>/are) different from an ordinary car in many ways.

8. The car's engine (<u>is</u>/are) modified to make it more powerful.

9. The inside of the car (<u>is</u>/are) empty, except for the driver's seat and the controls.

10. Because stock cars have regular steel bodies, they (is/<u>are</u>) much heavier than most race cars.

11. The first NASCAR race (<u>was</u>/were) on a beach in Daytona, Florida, in 1948.

12. Today, the Daytona 500 (<u>is</u>/are) a famous stock car race.

The banked corners of a stock car track help cars go around curves at over 200 mph.

Apply

Write a form of the verb *be* from the word bank to complete each sentence correctly. Make sure the first word in each sentence begins with an uppercase letter. (13–20)

am	is	was	were	are

____**Were**____ you at the NASCAR races last Saturday? I ____**was**____ there with my family.

My sisters and I ____**are**____ big fans of car racing. My parents ____**are**____ fans, too. We ____**were**____

in the front row.

I ____**am**____ also a fan of drag racing. The races ____**are**____ very exciting! What ____**is**____

your favorite kind of car race?

Reinforce

Imagine that you and a friend are auto racers. Write five sentences about yourselves. Use a form of the verb *be* in each sentence.

21. **Answers will vary.** _____

_____

22. _____

_____

23. _____

_____

24. _____

_____

25. _____

_____

Drivers first **competed** in the 24 Hours of Daytona in 1966. The drivers in this race **cover** as many miles as they can in 24 hours. Who **will win** this race next year?

Circle the boldfaced verb that tells about something that will happen in the future. Underline the boldfaced verb that tells about something that already has happened. Draw a box around the boldfaced verb that tells about something that happens regularly or is true now.

A **present tense verb** is used to indicate that something happens regularly or is true now. A **past tense verb** tells about something that has already happened. A **future tense verb** tells what is going to happen.

See Handbook Section 17

Practice

The verb in each sentence appears in bold type. Draw a box around each present tense verb. Underline each past tense verb. Circle each future tense verb.

1. Until the 1960s, Ferraris **were** among the fastest race cars in the world.

2. In the late 1960s, Porsches **won** race after race.

3. Ferraris and Porsches still **compete** in auto races.

4. In 1970, Ferrari engineers **produced** an improved car.

5. A superior car **will win** a race only if it has an excellent driver.

6. The Ferrari team **chose** Mario Andretti as their driver.

7. Even today Andretti **is** famous for his driving ability.

8. Andretti **put** the new Ferrari to the test at Daytona.

9. To begin an auto race, the starter **waves** a green flag.

10. Perhaps someday you **will see** the green flag at Daytona.

11. Sixty-five cars **started** the race that year.

12. Spectators still **recall** Andretti's skillful handling of his Ferrari.

13. A Porsche **covered** more distance, though.

14. In 1972, Mario Andretti finally **drove** his Ferrari to victory at Daytona.

Name _____

Apply

Rewrite the following sentences to indicate that the events took place in 1970.

15. Cars race around the track for 24 hours. **Cars raced around the track for 24 hours.** _____

    _____

16. Pedro Rodriguez drives the winning Porsche. **Pedro Rodriguez drove the winning Porsche.**

    _____

17. Andretti finishes third in a Ferrari. **Andretti finished third in a Ferrari.** _____

    _____

The Porsche retained its racing crown at Daytona in 1970.

Reinforce

Write three sentences using the characters and verbs below. Use a different verb tense in each sentence. Check to make sure the verb tenses are correct. **Answers will vary.**

Characters	Action Verb	Tense/Time
Laura, Polly	race	future
Zeon	watch	present
Ira	win	past

18. _____

    _____

19. _____

    _____

20. _____

    _____

Read and Analyze

Vera and I **are going** to a demolition derby. We **will be seeing** dozens of collisions. Yesterday she and I **were watching** video clips of last year's derby.

Circle the boldfaced verb phrase that tells about an action that is going on now. **Underline** the boldfaced verb phrase that tells about an action that was happening for a while in the past. **Draw a box** around the verb phrase that tells about an action that will happen in the future.

Progressive forms of verbs show continuing action. To form a **present progressive** verb, add *am, is,* or *are* to the present participle of a verb (usually the present form + *-ing*): *is snoring.* To form a **past progressive** verb, add *was* or *were* to the present participle: *was playing.* To form a **future progressive** verb, add *will be* to the present participle: *will be ringing.*

See Handbook Section 17

Practice

Look at the boldfaced verb in each sentence. Circle each boldfaced verb that is a present progressive form. Underline each verb that is a past progressive form. Draw a box around each verb that is a future progressive form.

1. At half past twelve, the drivers **were starting** their beat-up vehicles.

2. Even now I **am remembering** the deafening noise and the pungent fumes!

3. "Which car **will** still **be running** at the end of the day?" Vera wondered.

4. Suddenly the announcer **was screaming** into his microphone.

5. "This derby **will be starting** in thirty seconds!" he hollered.

6. Vera **was explaining** that all parts which could injure drivers had been removed from the cars.

7. Within seconds after the starting gun, cars **were crashing** into each other!

8. "Some drivers **are going** backward!" I hollered to Vera.

9. "By ramming other cars with their rear bumpers, drivers **are protecting** their engines," she added.

10. "That blue Dodge **will be entering** the winner's circle," I predicted, and my prediction turned out to be correct!

Apply

Use one or two helping verbs from the word bank plus a form of the verb in parentheses to complete each sentence. Each verb you write should be a progressive form.

am	are	was	will	be

11. Tomorrow at this time Betty and Phil _____ **will be watching** _____

motorcycles at the raceway. (watch)

12. Betty and Phil _____ **are expecting** _____ speeds in excess of 150 mph! (expect)

13. Last year my cousin _____ **was studying** _____ auto mechanics. (study)

14. I _____ **am guessing** _____ that she would enjoy watching motorcycles race. (guess)

Reinforce

Answer each question in a complete sentence. Use at least one progressive verb form in each answer. **Accept reasonable responses.**

15. What were you studying in school at this time last year?

_____

_____

16. What are you studying in school now?

_____

_____

17. What do you expect to study at this time next year?

_____

_____

18. What activities do you hope to participate in next year?

_____

_____

Today **is** February 12, 1908. Six teams (**have come**) here to New York City for the greatest auto race in history!

Circle the boldfaced verb that tells about an action that began in the past and continues into the present.

The **present perfect tense** indicates action that started in the past and may still be happening. To form the present perfect tense, add the helping verb *has* or *have* to the past participle of a verb. The **past participle** of regular verbs is formed by adding *-ed* (*work/have worked*). Irregular verbs change their spelling when they form past participles (*build/have built*).

See Handbook Section 17

Practice

Circle each verb in the present perfect tense. Be sure to include the helping verb. If the verb is not in present perfect tense, don't mark anything.

1. This New York-to-Paris auto race (has attracted) worldwide interest.

2. Organizers (have planned) this race as a test of automobiles.

3. Perhaps it will be more of a test of drivers.

4. The first leg of this race (has begun!)

5. Drivers will race westward all the way across the United States, a distance of 3,000 miles.

6. Several days (have passed) since our last report.

7. Two French teams (have quit) the race.

8. They ran out of money.

9. All the remaining teams (have become) famous.

10. The American team is driving their car on the tracks of the transcontinental railroad!

11. The car's tires (have popped) from the rough ride.

12. The American, German, and Italian teams (have crossed) the Continental Divide.

The 1908 race took drivers across three continents and 22,000 miles.

Apply

Write the present perfect form (*has* or *have* plus the past participle) of the verb in parentheses to complete each sentence correctly.

13. The German car _____**has had**_____ a breakdown here in Utah! (have)

14. The team _____**has arranged**_____ for the car to be shipped to Seattle by train. (arrange)

15. They _____**have broken**_____ a race rule, and they may pay for this error later! (break)

16. The other teams _____**have reached**_____ San Francisco and are now headed north. (reach)

17. The race organizers _____**have changed**_____ the plan for how the cars will reach Russia. (change)

18. Instead of having the race cars drive across ice to go from Alaska, the organizers _____**have decided**_____ that the cars will go by ship. (decide)

19. We are now in Paris, and the German team _____**has crossed**_____ the finish line! (cross)

20. The judges have penalized the Germans for breaking a race rule, and _____**have declared**_____ the American team the winners. (declare)

Reinforce

Imagine you are a sports commentator posting live updates to the Internet on an exciting car race. On a separate sheet of paper, write a paragraph detailing the activity leading up to the big finish. Use the present perfect tense options from the word bank below. **Answers will vary.**

has/have crossed	has/have passed	has/have charged
has/have switched	has/have sped	has/have won

Read and Analyze

By the time she finished high school, Elaine Larsen **had performed** as a cheerleader in front of crowds many times. As an adult she **has excited** audiences in quite a different way. In less than five minutes you will have learned what she does to thrill spectators.

Underline the boldfaced verb phrase that tells about an action that was completed by a certain time in the past. Draw a box around the boldfaced verb phrase that tells about an action that will be completed before a certain time in the future.

The **past perfect** tense (*had understood*) shows action that was completed by a certain time in the past. To form the past perfect tense, use *had* with the past participle of a verb. The **future perfect** tense (*will have affected*) shows action that will be completed by a certain time in the future. To form the future perfect tense, use *will have* with the past participle of a verb.

See Handbook | **Section 17**

Practice

Underline each boldfaced verb that is in the past perfect tense. Draw a box around each boldfaced verb that is in the future perfect tense.

1. Shirley Muldowney and Janet Guthrie **had proven** that women could be excellent drag racers before Elaine Larsen began her racing career.

2. By the time she was 25, Elaine Larsen **had received** her dragster license.

3. Her husband Chris **had become** an expert welder and mechanic by then, and he later built a jet dragster for Elaine to drive.

4. Perhaps by the end of this year Elaine Larsen will have set a speed record.

5. If she is successful, she will have used all 6,000 horsepower generated by her dragster's powerful engine.

6. Until 2009 Elaine Larsen **had been** the only woman to drive one of Larsen Motorsports's jet dragsters.

7. Prior to that year, a young woman named Marisha Falk **had assisted** Elaine Larsen in a number of ways.

8. Thanks to Elaine Larsen, Marisha Falk **had earned** her dragster license by the time she was 26.

9. Maybe in a year or two Marisha Falk will have exceeded 300 mph in a jet dragster.

10. By the time Elaine Larsen and Marisha Falk have completed their driving careers, they almost certainly will have attracted other women to the world of jet drag racing.

Apply

Write the past perfect form (*had* + past participle) or the future perfect form (*will have* + past participle) of the verb in parentheses to complete each sentence.

11. Before I watched videos of jet drag racers, I _____**had planned**_____ a career as an Indy car driver. (plan)

12. If I reach my goal, I _____**will have earned**_____ my dragster license by 2024. (earn)

13. Before the beginning of this year I _____**had thought**_____ that aerodynamics would be too difficult for me to understand. (think)

14. By this weekend I _____**will have read**_____ my third book about the aerodynamics of race cars. (read)

15. I _____**will have completed**_____ my science fair project about wind resistance by March 16, two weeks before the deadline! (complete)

Reinforce

Write a sentence about a goal you had chosen before you started school this year. Use a past perfect tense verb in the sentence. Then write a sentence about a time by which you will have achieved this goal (or will have set a different goal). Use a future perfect verb in the sentence.

Accept reasonable responses.

_____

_____

_____

_____

_____

_____

_____

_____

_____

a. John wanted to know how to get involved in auto racing, so he sends an expert an e-mail asking for advice.

b. The expert responded to John's e-mail quickly and offered several positive suggestions.

Which sentence contains a verb that shifts the time frame in a way that doesn't make sense? ____**a**____ How should this sentence be rewritten so it stays in the time frame it established?
The verb _sends_ should be changed to _sent_.

Choose **verb tenses** carefully so that the verb forms you use work together to indicate time accurately and consistently. When you describe events that happen in the same time frame, do not shift tenses. When you describe events that happen at different times, use verbs in different tenses to indicate the order in which the events happened.

See Handbook Section 17

Practice

Read each sentence. If the sentence contains a time shift that doesn't make sense, mark an _X_ through the verb that makes the inappropriate tense shift. Then write the correct form of that verb on the line.

1. The expert writes an advice column for an auto magazine, and every month he ~~chose~~ a letter to answer. ____**chooses**____

2. He answered John's letter in the May issue and ~~tells~~ John that the most important thing for him was to stay in school. ____**told**____

3. The expert told John to study auto mechanics, because everyone needs to know how cars work. _____

4. The expert has driven race cars for many years, and he has won many awards. _____

5. The expert recommended that John go to auto races, and he ~~advises~~ John to buy a pit pass. ____**advised**____

6. According to the expert, drivers and mechanics will answer polite questions when they ~~were~~ not too busy. ____**are**____

7. The expert also told John to consider becoming a go-kart racer and explained that racing stars such as Jeff Gordon and Tony Stewart drove go-karts when they were young. _____

8. John read the suggestions with great excitement, and he immediately ~~writes~~ a thank-you message to the expert. ____**wrote**____

Go-kart organizations teach young drivers how to race safely.

Apply

Rewrite the paragraph below to correct the inappropriate tense shifts.

From my seat I could see the mechanics working on the race car's engine. One mechanic holds a wrench and turned a bolt very slowly. The noise level was incredible! Then the crew chief suddenly gave a wave, all the mechanics jumped back, and the car roars back onto the track.

From my seat I could see the mechanics working on the race car's engine. One mechanic held a wrench and turned a bolt very slowly. The noise level was incredible! Then the crew chief suddenly gave a wave, all the mechanics jumped back, and the car roared back onto the track.

Reinforce

On the lines below, write a paragraph about the most exciting moment you've experienced at a sporting event. Start your paragraph with a description of that exciting moment. Then tell about what led up to that moment. Finally, tell what happened after the event. Choose verb tenses carefully so that the verb forms you use work together to indicate time accurately and consistently.

Answers will vary.

_____X_____ Piero Taruffi hadn't never won the famous Mille Miglia.

_____ The Silver Fox didn't stop trying, however.

Write X in front of the sentence that has two negative words.

A **negative** is a word that means "no" or "not." The words *no, not, nothing, none, never, nowhere,* and *nobody* are negatives. The negative word *not* is often found in contractions like *don't* or *wasn't.* Use only one negative word in a sentence to express a negative idea. **Remember to use this information when you speak, too.**

See Handbook | Section 22

Practice

Write *X* next to each sentence with two negative expressions.

1. Taruffi wouldn't never have another chance to win this race. ___**X**___

2. After 1957, the race wouldn't ever be run no more. ___**X**___

3. Racing experts thought Taruffi had almost no chance of beating the great British driver Stirling Moss. _____

4. Moss wasn't no threat after his brake pedal broke. ___**X**___

5. He wasn't in the race no more. ___**X**___

6. Late in the race, a young English driver named Collins held a large lead, but Taruffi would not give up. _____

7. Taruffi didn't never believe he would finally win the race. ___**X**___

8. "It wouldn't be so bad to come in second," he thought. _____

9. Collins had pushed his Ferrari too hard earlier, and it wasn't running well no more. ___**X**___

10. Taruffi flew past; he didn't have nobody in front of him. ___**X**___

11. There wasn't no one happier than the Silver Fox when he finally won the Mille Miglia after trying for so long. ___**X**___

12. His family and friends couldn't have been happier for him. _____

Brescia

Rome

Mille Miglia means "thousand miles" in Italian.

Apply   Possible answers appear below. Accept all reasonable responses.

Rewrite these sentences correctly. There is more than one way to correct each sentence.

13. After 1957, the Mille Miglia wasn't held no more. **After 1957, the Mille Miglia wasn't held anymore.**

14. Fans along the racing route wouldn't never see the race cars zooming through their towns again. **Fans along the racing route would never see the race cars zooming through their towns again.**

15. Italian authorities had complained that there weren't no safety precautions. **Italian authorities had complained that there were no safety precautions.**

16. They didn't want no fans to get hurt. **They didn't want any fans to get hurt.**

17. Anyone who saw the final race wouldn't never forget it. **Anyone who saw the final race wouldn't ever forget it.**

Reinforce

Circle the hidden negatives and write them on the lines.
Add apostrophes where they belong. **Note: Answers can be in any order.**

D	N	O	T	D	Q	P
O	D	B	Y	W	B	N
N	O	W	H	E	R	E
T	E	C	X	R	G	V
B	S	T	K	E	B	E
G	N	V	H	N	Q	R
D	T	B	Q	T	Z	K
Y	N	I	S	N	T	Y

18. _____ **NOT** _____

19. _____ **NOWHERE** _____

20. _____ **ISN'T** _____

21. _____ **DON'T** _____

22. _____ **DOESN'T** _____

23. _____ **WEREN'T** _____

24. _____ **NEVER** _____

Lou was determined to create the fastest soap box racer in all of St. Louis this year. He needed to find a more effective type of axle grease than the one he had been using.

Circle the boldfaced adjective that compares something with one other thing. Draw a box around the boldfaced adjective that compares something with more than one other thing.

The **comparative form** of an adjective compares two people, places, or things. It is often followed by the word *than*. Add *-er* to short adjectives to create the comparative form. Use the word *more* before long adjectives to create this form. The **superlative form** of an adjective compares three or more people, places, or things. The superlative form usually follows the article *the*. Add *-est* to short adjectives to create the superlative. Use the word *most* before long adjectives to create this form. **Remember to use this information when you speak, too.**

See Handbook Sections 15 and 23

Practice

Think about how many things are being compared in each sentence. Then underline the correct form of the adjective in parentheses.

1. Last year, Lou had worked to make his car the (more beautiful/<u>most beautiful</u>) in the race.

2. He had used the (brighter/<u>brightest</u>) paints he could find.

3. He had used (<u>brighter</u>/brightest) colors for the sides than the top because a racer's sides are more visible than its top is.

4. When Lou and his friend Bill had compared their racers, Bill had admitted that Lou's was definitely (<u>more colorful</u>/the most colorful).

5. But Lou's pride faded when his car proved to be (slower/<u>the slowest</u>) of all the racers.

6. Lou knew he would have to work (<u>harder</u>/hardest) this year to build a better racer.

7. "Use (<u>lighter</u>/lightest) building materials than you used last year," said Lou's mom.

8. Lou decided to use a(n) (efficienter/<u>more efficient</u>) design for his new racer.

9. He was determined to build the (more streamlined/<u>most streamlined</u>) racer in the derby.

Apply

On the blank, write the correct form of the adjective in parentheses. You will need to add *more*, *most*, *-er*, or *-est* to each adjective.

10. Soap box racers have no engine, so Lou had looked in hundreds of books to find the

_____**most efficient**_____ design. (efficient)

11. He had bought lightweight materials to make sure the new car would

be _____**faster**_____ than last year's model. (fast)

12. Today he would test his new car against Bill's car, the

_____**swiftest**_____ soap box racer in the

neighborhood. (swift)

Soap box races start on a downhill ramp.

13. He thought his racer was the _____**sleekest**_____ car in the world. (sleek)

14. For Lou, driving his newly designed racer was _____**more exciting**_____ than beating Bill.

(exciting)

Reinforce

Circle six hidden adjectives. If an adjective is a comparative, write its superlative form. If an adjective is a superlative, write its comparative form. **Note: Answers can be in any order.**

M	C	N	X	Q	C	S	S	C	H
L	D	G	J	T	B	O	J	P	I
S	N	T	K	X	D	F	K	M	G
W	I	L	D	E	S	T	N	G	H
V	R	O	C	R	H	E	L	K	E
N	Z	W	Q	B	S	R	D	B	S
J	K	E	A	R	L	I	E	S	T
X	S	S	P	K	N	L	J	P	G
P	T	T	F	A	S	T	E	R	K

15. _____**WILDER**_____

16. _____**EARLIER**_____

17. _____**FASTEST**_____

18. _____**LOWER**_____

19. _____**SOFTEST**_____

20. _____**HIGHER**_____

The racers drove their midget race cars (**more carefully**) when it started to rain. Hank drove the **most carefully** of all the racers.

Circle the boldfaced adverb that compares two actions. Draw a box around the boldfaced adverb that compares three or more actions.

The **comparative form** of an adverb compares two actions. Adverbs that end in *-ly* are preceded by *more* for the comparative form (*more carefully*) and are often followed by the word *than*. The **superlative form** of an adverb compares three or more actions. Adverbs that end in *-ly* are preceded by *most* for the superlative form (*most carefully*). Some adverbs add *-er* for the comparative form (*faster*) and *-est* for the superlative form (*fastest*).

See Handbook Sections 18 and 23

Practice

Underline the correct form of the adverb.

1. After skidding on the first turn, Adrian approached the next corner

   (more cautiously/most cautiously).

2. Jayne drove the last lap (faster/fastest) than the first.

3. Kesara drove the last lap (more quickly/most quickly) than anyone else.

4. When Kesara crossed the finish line, her sister cheered (louder/loudest) of all.

5. Reza's midget car moved (more quickly/most quickly) than Anthony's car.

6. Tuan's engine ran (more smoothly/most smoothly) in the first race than in any other race.

7. Vera took the turns (more swiftly/most swiftly) than Reza.

8. Reza drives (most carefully/more carefully) than Vera.

9. Adrian drives (more cautiously/most cautiously) than Kesara.

10. Out of all the racers, Vera drives the

    (most boldly/more boldly).

11. Vera wins (more often/most often) than Reza.

Midget cars are very small race cars with very powerful engines.

Apply

Complete each sentence by writing the correct form of the adverb in parentheses. You will need to add *more, most, -er,* or *-est* to each adverb.

12. Vito's bright yellow car ran the _____**most smoothly**_____ of all the midget

    race cars. (smoothly)

13. Kathy had thought she would be bored, but she ended up cheering ___**more enthusiastically**___

    than any of her friends. (enthusiastically)

14. Now she is thinking that she could drive a midget car _____**more skillfully**_____

    than any driver on the track. (skillfully)

15. "After all, I ride my mountain bike downhill the _____**fastest**_____ of all," she said to

    herself. (fast)

16. She watched the drivers _____**more closely**_____ during the second race than she

    did during the first. (closely)

Reinforce

Write four sentences comparing the contestants in a competition you have recently seen. Use comparative and superlative adjectives and adverbs in your comparison.

17. **Answers will vary.** _____

    _____

18. _____

    _____

19. _____

    _____

20. _____

    _____

Review

(Numbers in parentheses identify related lessons.)

Pronouns

Circle each boldfaced word that is a subject pronoun. Underline each boldfaced word that is an object pronoun. (1–4)

Barney Oldfield brought speed to racing. (He)**(37)** was the first person to drive a car one mile per minute. In 1902 Henry Ford built a race car for **him.(37)** Oldfield drove **it(37)** in Detroit and won his first race in that car. In 1910 (he)**(37)** set a world speed record of 131 mph.

Circle the correct pronoun or pronouns in parentheses.

5. Last weekend Grandma and Grandpa took my sister and (I, (me)) to the drag races. **(37, 38)**

6. They told ((her and me)/me and her) how they first became interested in drag racing. **(37, 38)**

7. She and ((he)/him) went to see Shirley "Cha-Cha" Muldowney race in 1969. **(37, 38)**

Verbs

Circle the correct form of each verb in parentheses.

8. "Shirley Muldowney ((was)/were) one of the first female race car drivers," Grandpa added. **(40)**

9. "Many people (was/(were)) fans of Shirley," Grandma said. **(40)**

10. "I still (has/(have)) articles about her performance at the 1971 Hot Rod Nationals in my scrapbook," Grandma said. **(41)**

11. In the past I (collect/(collected)) toy race cars. **(41)**

12. Now I frequently ((sketch)/sketched) race cars of my own design. **(41)**

13. Tomorrow at this time I (was meeting/(will be meeting)) a race car driver. **(42)**

14. This driver ((was driving)/is driving) a Porsche in races last year. **(42)**

15. Right now she ((is planning)/was planning) to join a different racing team. **(42)**

16. Before last Sunday I never (have expected/(had expected)) such a wonderful opportunity. **(43)**

17. By next Sunday I (have talked/(will have talked)) with one of the most skillful race drivers in the world! **(43)**

In each sentence, mark an *X* through the verb that makes an inappropriate time shift. Write the correct form of that verb on the line.

18. My brother writes a blog about auto racing, and every Friday he ~~presented~~ a summary of

recent race results. _____**presents (45)**_____

19. Last week I gathered information for my brother, and he ~~uses~~ it in the blog.

_____**used (45)**_____

Negatives **Possible answers appear below. Accept all reasonable responses.**

Rewrite each sentence so it has only one negative term.

20. Great race car drivers never do nothing foolish. **Great race car drivers never do anything foolish. (46)**

21. None of them would never drive no unsafe car in a race. **None of them would ever drive an unsafe car in a race. (46)**

22. On freeways, many drivers don't pay no attention to what they're doing. **On freeways, many drivers don't pay any attention to what they're doing. (46)**

Adjectives and Adverbs

Complete each sentence by writing the correct form of the adjective or adverb in parentheses.

23. A person who has a new car drives the _____**most carefully (48)**_____ of

all. (carefully)

24. Bruce's hot rod is _____**noisier (47)**_____ than his brother's sedan. (noisy)

25. After reading about different models, Gord decided that the new Remarka was the

_____**safest (47)**_____ car of all. (safe)

26. Gord believes the Remarka is _____**prettier (47)**_____ than the Afforda. (pretty)

27. He was surprised to learn that the Remarka handles _____**more precisely (48)**_____

than the Afforda. (precisely)

28. Dan's car is the _____**quietest (47)**_____ of all. (quiet)

Spelling Practice

a. It is a good idea to have the brakes of your car inspected.

b. You don't want to be stuck on the road if something breaks.

Which sentence has a boldfaced word that means "stops working properly"? **b**

Which sentence has a boldfaced word that means "parts that cause a machine to stop"? **a**

Homophones

Homophones are words that sound the same but have different spellings and meanings, such as *waist* and *waste*. Homophones can be confusing. You will need to pay attention to the context of the sentence or use a dictionary to choose the correct spelling when writing homophones.

Words in Context

Write the word that best completes each sentence. Use a dictionary if you need help.

capitol	principal	coarse	vein
capital	course	principle	vain

1. The _____**principal**_____ makes the school announcements each morning.

2. This scientific theory is based on one simple _____**principle**_____.

3. The _____**coarse**_____ fabric of this shirt is uncomfortable.

4. It was a nice day to be playing on the golf _____**course**_____.

5. I could see the blue _____**vein**_____ in her wrist.

6. A _____**vain**_____ person is very concerned with his or her looks.

7. The state's _____**capitol**_____ building has a dome.

8. Topeka is the _____**capital**_____ of Kansas.

Name _____

Pattern Practice

Circle the homophone in parentheses that best completes each sentence.

9. My cat has gained too much (wait/**weight**) and needs to go on a diet.

10. Sara brushed her horse and put on its (**bridle**/bridal.)

11. Are you (aloud/**allowed**) to come to the movies with us?

12. Matt couldn't believe he forgot to put the (flower/**flour**) in the cake.

Write each homophone next to its meaning. Use a dictionary if you need help.

colonel	kernel	pedal	naval
through	peddle	threw	navel

13. ride a bike _____**pedal**_____

14. sell something _____**peddle**_____

15. related to sailing _____**naval**_____

16. a physical feature on the stomach _____**navel**_____

17. a military rank _____**colonel**_____

18. a grain of corn _____**kernel**_____

19. tossed something _____**threw**_____

20. finished _____**through**_____

Use the Dictionary

Complete each homophone pair. Check your spellings in a dictionary.

21. c___**y**___mb___**a**___l, a musical instrument

    s___**y**___mb___**o**___l, something that stands for something else

22. v___**e**___ry, really

    v___**a**___ry, to change

Proofreading
Practice

Read this report about race car driver Kelly Sutton and find the mistakes. Use the proofreading marks below to show how each mistake should be fixed. Use a dictionary to check and correct spellings. **Suggested answers appear below. Accept all reasonable responses.**

Proofreading Marks

Mark	Means	Example
⊙	add a period	Kelly Sutton is a NASCAR driver⊙
/	make into a lowercase letter	Kelly Sutton is a NASCAR D̸river.
ꝰ	take away	Kelly Sutton s̶h̶e̶ is a NASCAR driver.
∧	add	Kelly Sutton ∧^is a NASCAR driver.
ⓢⓟ	fix spelling	Kelly Sutton is a NASCAR dryver.⁽ˢᵖ⁾

Kelly Sutton: NASCAR Driver

Kelly Sutton grew up wanting to be a race car driver, ̷Like her grandfather and her father. When
Kelly **was** is̶ sixteen, doctors gave her father and s̶h̶e̶ **her** some bad news. They said Kelly had multiple
sclerosis, or MS. That disease attacks the nervous system m̶o̶s̶t̶ **more** vigorously than many other
illnesses do. People with MS may have trouble controlling their movements. The disease can get
b̶a̶d̶d̶e̶r̶ **worse** over time. Some people with MS must use wheelchairs⊙

Kelly Sutton was determined to pursue her goals. She would not let n̶o̶t̶h̶i̶n̶g̶ **anything** keep her down. She
told her father she still wanted to drive a race car. She b̶e̶g̶i̶n̶s̶ **began** racing when she was nineteen years old.
She proved herself to be a skillful driver, and she worked hard to get even better. Her determanation ⁽ˢᵖ⁾
paid off. She became a NASCAR racer, just as h̶e̶r̶ **she** had hoped. Sometimes she has to take time off
because of her illness. As soon as she can, tho,⁽ˢᵖ⁾ she returns to the track.

When she isn't busy racing, Kelly helps other people with MS. She tells t̶h̶e̶y̶ **them** about treatment
options. She and t̶h̶e̶m̶ **they** share experiences. Kelly wan̶t̶ **wants** people with MS to know that they can make
their dreams come true. M̶e̶ ̶a̶n̶d̶ ̶y̶o̶u̶ **You and I** can learn much from this inspiring person.

Proofreading
Checklist

You can use the list below to help you find and fix mistakes in your own writing. Write the titles of your own stories or reports in the blanks on top of the chart. Then use the questions to check your work. Make a check mark (✓) in each box after you have checked that item. **Answers will vary.**

Proofreading Checklist for Unit 4

	Titles			
Have I used subject pronouns correctly? (*I, you, he, she, it, we, they*)				
Have I used object pronouns correctly? (*me, you, him, her, it, us, them*)				
Have I used progressive and present perfect tenses correctly?				
Do the subject and verb agree in every sentence?				
Have I used comparative and superlative forms of adverbs and adjectives correctly?				
Have I avoided extra negatives?				

Also Remember…

Does each sentence begin with an uppercase letter?				
Does each sentence end with the right mark?				
Did I use a dictionary to check and correct spellings?				
Have I used commas correctly?				

Your Own List

Use this space to write your own list of things to check in your writing.

School 🔔🏠 Home Connection

In Unit 4 of *Grammar, Usage, and Mechanics,* students are learning how different kinds of words are used in sentences. The activities on these pages give extra practice with some of the concepts they are learning. You can help reinforce the information your child is learning in school by choosing one or more activities to complete at home.

Guess What? (Subject and Object Pronouns)

Have your child think of an object that is familiar to both of you. Then have your child write three sentences about that object using pronouns; ask him or her not to tell what the object is.

> **Example** Aunt Sarah gave **it** to **you. You** wear **it** on your wrist. **It** ticks.

Read the sentences and guess what the secret object is. After you have guessed, work with your child to circle each pronoun he or she used.

Capture the Caption (Forms of *Be*)

With your child, flip through old magazines or a family photo album. Have your child select three or four pictures and write captions for them using forms of the verb *be,* such as *am, is, are, was,* or *were.*

> **Example** Grandma **is** in front of the piano. All the kids **are** in the kitchen.

Interview (Pronouns in Pairs)

Have your child interview you (or another adult) about what you did with your best friend when you were in the fifth grade. Encourage your child to take notes during the interview. Then have your child write four sentences describing what you and your friend did, using pronouns in some of the sentences.

> **Example** Mom and Greta were best friends.
>
> **She and Mom** used to play on the soccer team together.

Read the completed sentences together to make sure the pronouns have been used correctly.

Silly Sentences (Subject-Verb Agreement)

Work with your child to think of three subjects, three verbs, and three locations. (Or, use the list below.) Write these in three columns, like this:

A bright red apple	roll	the sky
Three blue bikes	skid	the barn
The gray clouds	twist	the aisle

Then have your child choose one word or phrase from each column and write a sentence.

Example   A bright red apple rolls down the aisle.

What's Wrong with These Pictures? (Negatives)

Look at these pictures with your child. Talk together about what is wrong with each picture. Then have your child use negatives to write one sentence about each picture. Make sure each sentence has only one negative word. Negatives include *no, not, nothing, none, never, nowhere,* and *nobody*.

Example   The car has no tires.

Compare/Contrast (Comparative and Superlative Adjectives)

Have your child think of something that both of you have, such as a jacket, a closet, a hairbrush, or a bicycle. Then have your child write three sentences comparing the two things.

Example   Your closet is <u>bigger</u> than mine. My closet is <u>messier</u> than yours.

In each sentence, have your child underline the word that compares.

Read and Analyze

What is the largest turtle alive today? It is the leatherback turtle. Look at this picture of a leatherback. Wow, the caption says some leatherbacks weigh 1,400 pounds!

Which sentence gives a command? Draw a line under its end punctuation.

Which sentence shows excitement? Circle its end punctuation.

Which sentence asks a question? Draw a box around its end punctuation.

Which sentence makes a statement? Draw two lines under its end punctuation.

Begin every **sentence** with an uppercase letter. A **declarative** sentence makes a statement and ends with a **period**. An **interrogative** sentence asks a question and ends with a **question mark**. An **imperative** sentence gives a command and ends with a **period** or an **exclamation point**. An **exclamatory** sentence shows excitement and ends with an **exclamation point**.

See Handbook Section 9

Practice Suggested answers appear below. Accept all reasonable responses.

Correct each capitalization or punctuation error. Then label each sentence *declarative, interrogative, imperative,* or *exclamatory*.

1. Tell me all about leatherback turtles. _____imperative_____

2. Leatherbacks range over an extremely wide area. _____declarative_____

3. they can live in icy seas as well as tropical waters. _____declarative_____

4. Why are they called leatherbacks? _____interrogative_____

5. These huge turtles do not have a hard shell! _____exclamatory_____

6. How big is a leatherback's shell? _____interrogative_____

7. some shells are about six feet long. _____declarative_____

8. do you know another way leatherbacks are unusual? _____interrogative_____

9. a leatherback can't pull its head into its shell. _____declarative_____

10. Don't try to eat the leatherback's favorite food, the man-of-war. _____imperative_____

11. These jellyfish are deadly to humans. _____declarative_____

12. Wow, the leatherback in that photograph is huge! _____exclamatory_____

Apply Answers will vary.

Look at the picture below. Write four sentences about it, one of each kind.

13. Imperative: _____

_____

_____

_____

Leatherbacks have been found as far north as Norway and as far south as Australia.

14. Interrogative: _____

_____

15. Declarative: _____

_____

16. Exclamatory: _____

_____

Reinforce

Add end punctuation to each clue. Then solve the riddle.

17. I am round and smooth**.**

18. Female sea turtles bury me on the beach**.**

19. Please don't break me **. or !**

20. I can't wait until a tiny turtle comes out of me **. or !**

21. What am I**?**

Answer: I am an ___E___ ___G___ ___G___.

The babies were scaly and rough. The zoologists at the (Bronx Zoo) in (New York City) thought they were adorable, however.

Circle the words that name specific people, places, or organizations.

A common noun names a person, place, or thing. A **proper noun** names a specific person, place, or thing. All the important words in proper nouns are capitalized. The names of months and days of the week are proper nouns. **Proper adjectives** are descriptive words formed from proper nouns. They must be capitalized. A **title of respect** is used before a person's name. Titles of respect include *Chairperson* and *Mr.* They are also capitalized.

See Handbook Sections 1, 14, and 15

Practice

Circle lowercase letters that should be uppercase letters. Draw a line through uppercase letters that should be lowercase letters.

1. In the early 1980s, roughly 500 chinese alligators lived in the wild in china.

2. The Alligators' natural habitat in the Anhui province of china was being destroyed.

3. An american zoologist named doctor John L. behler wanted to help.

4. He brought chinese alligators to the bronx Zoo to create a breeding program.

5. On august 21, 1984, the Zoologist's effort finally paid off.

6. Four baby chinese alligators hatched from their shells.

7. The Zoo became the leader in captive breeding of Chinese alligators in the united states.

8. Another american reptile specialist, doctor myrna Watanabe, studied the alligators in China.

9. chinese officials and scientists worked hard to study and protect the Alligators, too.

10. Today there are about 10,000 Chinese alligators at a Research Center in anhui.

11. In april 2003, the bronx zoo sent three alligators to Shanghai to introduce into protected wetlands.

12. researchers were heartened when the Animals survived and one female had hatchlings.

Apply

Rewrite these sentences to correct the errors.

13. The rockefeller Wildlife Refuge in louisiana is also working to protect chinese alligators.

    The Rockefeller Wildlife Refuge in Louisiana is also working to protect Chinese alligators.

    _____

14. Parts of louisiana are like the alligators' home in the yangtze river in china.

    Parts of Louisiana are like the alligators' home in the Yangtze River in China.

    _____

15. Researchers in new york and louisiana work together to determine how captive-bred chinese alligators can be introduced into the wild.

    Researchers in New York and Louisiana work together to determine how captive-bred Chinese alligators can be introduced into the wild.

Reinforce

Circle eight proper nouns, proper adjectives, or titles of respect. (All the hidden words appear in this lesson.) Write a sentence using two words you found. Use correct capitalization.

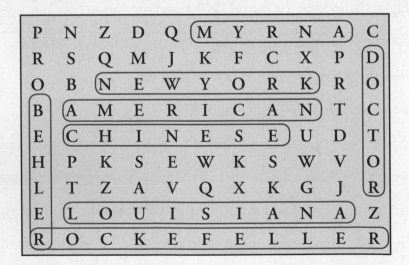

16. **Answers will vary.** _____

    _____

Read and Analyze

Our teacher, <u>Mr.</u> Miles, sent ⬚Dr.⬚ Marilyn C. Winters an invitation to talk to our class about snakes next Friday. ⬚Dr.⬚ Winters wrote herself a note that read, "Fri., Jan. 12—talk to class."

Underline a short way to write *Mister*. Draw a square around a short way to write *Doctor*. Circle short ways to write *Friday* and *January*. Underline a single letter that stands for a name.

An **abbreviation** is a shortened form of a word. **Titles of respect** are usually abbreviated. So are words in **addresses** like *Street* (*St.*) and *Avenue* (*Ave.*). Days, most months, and kinds of businesses are often abbreviated in e-mail and informal notes. Abbreviations usually begin with an uppercase letter and end with a period. An **initial** takes the place of a name. It is written as an uppercase letter followed by a period.

See Handbook **Section 2**

Practice

In the sentences below, circle each lowercase letter that should be an uppercase letter. Draw a line through each uppercase letter that should be a lowercase letter. Add periods where they are needed.

1. Mr. Miles gave dr. Winters directions to u s Grant Middle School.

2. He told her to drive east on Elm Blvd. and make a right on Oak st.

3. Dr. Winters owns the most unusual business on Franklin ave.

4. Her company, Snakes inc., supplies snakes for films.

5. She showed us the feeding schedule for the boa constrictors.

   It read, "Feb. Feeding Schedule: Feed boas every wed."

Boa constrictors use powerful muscles to squeeze and kill their prey.

6. Dr. Winters explained that she sometimes orders the food from Hungry Reptile corp.

7. She also feeds the boas mice from mrs. Joy g. Wong's pet store on Maple blvd.

8. Dr. Winters said that boa constrictors do not lay eggs. Their babies are born live.

9. Mrs. wong's assistant, ms. Brown, had a big surprise last week.

10. When she got to the office on Franklin Ave., she found fifty newborn boas.

11. She told mrs. Wong, "I hope you have plenty of mice because we're going to need them!"

Apply

Rewrite the items below. Use abbreviations and initials where you can.

12. Mister Michael Edward Cleveland _____ **Mr. M. E. Cleveland** _____

13. Reverend Marcia Ann Fong _____ **Rev. M. A. Fong** _____

14. 1055 West Lincoln Boulevard _____ **1055 W. Lincoln Blvd.** _____

15. Reptile Research Incorporated _____ **Reptile Research Inc.** _____

16. Tuesday, January 3 _____ **Tues., Jan. 3** _____

17. Doctor Duane Estaris _____ **Dr. D. Estaris** _____

18. today's date (include the day of the week) _____ **Answers will vary.** ___

19. your date of birth _____ **Answers will vary.** _____

Reinforce

Imagine you are addressing an envelope to your teacher. Write your teacher's name and the name and the address of your school. Then write your name and address in the top left corner. Check the capitalization and punctuation of the abbreviations you use in each address.

Answers will vary.

Answers will vary.

You can find wild mustangs on the range in **Nevada** and **Utah**. You can find **Ford Mustangs** in an auto showroom run by the **Ford Motor Company**.

Underline the boldfaced words that are the names of places. Circle the boldfaced words that are the name of a product. Draw a box around the boldfaced words that are the name of a company.

Proper nouns are the names of particular people, places, or things. Capitalize each important word in geographic names, important events, holidays, companies, and products.

See Handbook | **Sections 1 and 14**

Practice

Circle each word that should begin with an uppercase letter.

1. Many auto companies in the united states have chosen animal names for their models.

2. The ford motor company, which has headquarters in dearborn, michigan, favors equine names.

3. In addition to the highly successful ford mustang, this company also has produced the ford bronco and the ford pinto.

4. Ford also manufactures mercurys, several of which have had feline names.

5. Have you heard of the mercury cougar, the mercury bobcat, or the mercury lynx?

6. These and other models of the mercury have been assembled in edison, new jersey, and wayne, michigan, as well as in canada and mexico.

7. Many years ago the hudson motor company produced cars with insect names.

8. The hudson hornet was one of the best cars of its day for both racing and everyday driving.

9. You can see both hudson hornets and hudson wasps at hostetler's hudson auto museum in shipshewana, indiana.

10. The museum is open tuesday through saturday most of the year, but it is closed from new year's day to april fool's day.

Apply Accept reasonable responses. Check for correct capitalization.

Think of a proper noun to complete each sentence. Write it in the blank. Capitalize each important word.

11. _____ is a company I might want to work for someday.

12. I'm also interested in working at _____.

13. One city I would like to visit is _____.

14. That city is in the state of _____.

15. One product our family uses and likes is _____.

16. The best holiday on which to visit our community is _____.

Reinforce

Write a paragraph about a type of store you would like to manage. Tell where it would be located and what products it would sell. Also tell when the store would be open and what holidays it would celebrate with special sales.

Accept reasonable responses. _____

_____

_____

_____

_____

_____

_____

_____

_____

_____

_____

_____

Don't waste your money on the movie (Temple of the Turtles.)
The short story "Froggy's Fandango" is quite funny.
I used The Reptile Encyclopedia when I wrote my science report.

Circle the movie title. Draw a box around the story title. Tell how they are written differently. The movie title is underlined. The story title is in quotation marks.

Underline **book titles** and **movie titles** in handwritten work. Italicize book titles and movie titles when you write with a word processor. Use quotation marks around the titles of **songs, stories, and poems**. Capitalize the first word and last word in every title you write. Capitalize all other words except articles, prepositions, and conjunctions. Remember to capitalize forms of the verb *be,* such as *is* and *are*.

See Handbook Sections 1 and 3

Practice

Circle each lowercase letter that should be an uppercase letter. Draw a line through uppercase letters that should be lowercase letters. Underline or add quotation marks to the titles.

1. Sagit lent Jorge a book called cobra capers.

2. Sagit thought "spitting mad" was the best story in the book.

3. Lu loved the movie the ghosts of rattlesnake ranch.

4. The movie's theme song is called "spurs are jingling. "

5. Mark Twain wrote a short story called "the celebrated jumping frog of calaveras county. "

6. After reading that story, Tran got the book teaching your frog to leap farther.

7. Nola wrote a poem called "notes to a newt."

8. Brad set the poem to music, and he called the song "amphibian rhapsody."

9. Joelle read the book the adventures of Leroy the lizard three times.

10. After dinner, Anya read us a poem from the book Odes to Toads.

11. The poem was titled "a toad is a beautiful thing."

12. Then I read my poem titled "A frog makes a Better pet than A hog."

Apply

Read the titles below. Then write a title to answer each item. Be sure to write each title correctly.

13. Which book would tell you how to treat a snake bite? **First Aid**

    _____

14. Make up a title for a short story that might appear in <u>Reptile Tales</u>. **Answers will vary**

    but should be in quotation marks.

15. Which movie is likely to be a horror film? **The Monster of Gila Bend**

    _____

16. Which book might give you information about painted turtles? **Turtle Territory**

    _____

Reinforce

Draw a line to match each title in the first column with the item that best describes it in the second column.

17. "Ferdinand Frog's Life at the Plaza"   a movie about the life cycle of a turtle

18. <u>Larry Lizard's Loud Act</u>   a poem about a snake shedding its skin

19. "Marvin's Miraculous Molting"   a short story about a frog that lives in a fancy hotel

20. "Dot, the Silly Salamander"   a book about a singing lizard

21. <u>The Life and Times of Tommy Turtle</u>   a song about a spotted salamander

Most **amphibians'** lives are spent partly in water and partly on land. **They're** descendants of the first vertebrates that crawled on land long ago.

Which boldfaced word shows ownership? _____ **amphibians'** _____

Which boldfaced word combines two words? _____ **They're** _____

To form the **possessive** of a singular noun, add an **apostrophe** and -*s* (*snake's fangs*). For plural nouns that end in -*s,* add an apostrophe. For plural nouns that do not end in -*s,* add an apostrophe and -*s* (the *children's snake*). Apostrophes are also used in **contractions,** two words that have been shortened and combined.

See Handbook **Sections 7, 24, and 26**

Practice

Underline the correct word in parentheses. If the answer is a possessive, write *P*. If the answer is a contraction, write *C*.

1. (Ive/<u>I've</u>) read that amphibians stay the same temperature as their surroundings. __C__

2. (<u>That's</u>/Thats') why we say they are "cold-blooded." __C__

3. An (<u>amphibian's</u>/amphibians') body tells a lot about how it lives and moves. __P__

4. Sticky disks on a tree (frogs'/<u>frog's</u>) fingers and toes help it grip and climb. __P__

5. The spade-like shape of an African (bullfrogs'/<u>bullfrog's</u>) feet help it burrow into the ground. __P__

6. Water (<u>dwellers'</u>/dweller's) webbed feet help them swim. __P__

7. Some amphibians are colored to match their surroundings so that predators (<u>won't</u>/wo'nt) see them. __C__

8. An (<u>amphibian's</u>/amphibians') color may help it stay warm or cool. __P__

9. A (<u>tadpole's</u>/tadpoles') form changes as it grows into a frog. __P__

10. Tadpoles (<u>don't</u>/do'nt) breathe air. __C__

11. They (cant/<u>can't</u>) live out of water until they have changed form and become frogs. __C__

12. Frogs (<u>don't</u>/dont) flip out their tongues at their prey unless the prey is moving. __C__

Most amphibians absorb much of the water they need through their skin.

Apply

Rewrite the sentences below. Replace the boldfaced words with possessives or contractions.

13. The **gills of some salamanders** let them breathe underwater. <u>Some salamanders' gills let them breathe underwater.</u>

14. **Do not** expect a short-legged frog to make long jumps. <u>Don't expect a short-legged frog to make long jumps.</u>

15. The **skin color of a poison-dart frog** warns other creatures to stay away. <u>The poison-dart frog's skin color warns other creatures to stay away.</u>

16. **It is** a little known fact that some amphibians have no legs. <u>It's a little known fact that some amphibians have no legs.</u>

17. **They are** called caecilians, and they look like worms. <u>They're called caecilians, and they look like worms.</u>

Reinforce

Circle the five hidden words in the puzzle. Then write the possessive form of each noun and the contraction of the negative expression. (Hint: Two of the nouns are plural.)

Note: Answers can be in any order.

Y	D	L	T	A	D	P	O	L	E
W	C	K	X	G	M	B	S	K	F
S	A	L	A	M	A	N	D	E	R
Q	N	B	J	M	K	Q	F	B	O
X	N	G	U	S	S	E	R	P	G
Z	O	X	K	J	G	N	V	R	S
V	T	O	N	G	U	E	S	D	B

18. _____ **TADPOLE'S** _____

19. _____ **SALAMANDER'S** _____

20. _____ **TONGUES'** _____

21. _____ **FROGS'** _____

22. _____ **CAN'T** _____

Salamanders may look like (lizards,) (geckos,) or even (snakes.)

In the sentence above, circle three items in a series. What punctuation mark follows each of the first two items? _____**a comma**_____

(Well,) salamanders are not related to any of those creatures.

In the sentence above, circle the introductory word that expresses an emotion and is not part of the independent clause that follows it. What punctuation mark separates the word from the rest of the sentence?
_____**a comma**_____

A **series** is a list of three or more words or phrases. **Commas** are used to separate the items in a series. The last comma in a series goes before the conjunction *and* or *or*. A comma is also used to separate a mild **interjection** at the beginning of a sentence from the rest of the sentence.

See Handbook | Section 8

Practice

Add commas where they are needed below. Cross out commas that should not appear. Circle each interjection.

1. (Hey,) salamanders are actually related to frogs, toads, and other amphibians.

2. An adult spotted salamander has~~,~~ four legs, a tail, black skin, and yellow spots.

3. Spotted salamanders~~,~~ hatch, mate, and lay eggs underwater.

4. A female lays her eggs, attaches them to a stick, covers them with a jelly-like substance, and~~,~~ leaves them.

5. Grubs, mold, or acid rain~~,~~ can kill the salamander eggs.

6. The spotted salamander larvae~~,~~ eat fleas, shrimps, and grubs.

7. Beetles, salamanders, or giant water bugs might eat~~,~~ the larvae.

8. As adults, the spotted salamanders leave the pool, crawl on land, and find hiding places.

9. Adult spotted salamanders live under rocks, in holes, or~~,~~ in rotten logs.

10. (Oh,) I just found a salamander's hiding place!

The life cycle of the spotted salamander

Apply Possible answers appear below. Accept all reasonable responses.

Use what you read on page 147 to write a sentence to respond to each item. Include items in a series in each answer.

11. List three creatures that spotted salamander larvae eat.

    Spotted salamander larvae eat fleas, shrimps, and grubs. _____

    _____

12. List three places where you might find a spotted salamander.

    You might find a spotted salamander under rocks, in holes, or in rotten logs. ____

    _____

13. List three dangers for spotted salamander eggs and larvae.

    Three dangers for spotted salamander eggs and larvae are grubs, mold, and acid rain. ____

    _____

Reinforce Answers will vary.

Imagine that you have discovered a new species of salamander. Complete the sentences below to describe your salamander. Use at least three adjectives in each answer. (Use words from the word bank or your own words.) Be sure to use commas correctly. Also, add an interjection to one of your sentences. Then draw your salamander.

| green | long | striped | bumpy | spotted | wrinkled |
| red | smooth | slimy | yellow | shiny | short |

14. Its body is _____

15. Its tail is _____

16. Its legs are _____

Yes, we decided to have a frog jumping contest. Ms. Li helped us catch the bullfrogs, but she said that we'd have to let them go later. "Celia, I asked you to handle your frog carefully, didn't I?" said Ms. Li.

Find the word that introduces the first sentence. What punctuation mark follows it? __comma__

Find the conjunction that joins the two parts of the second sentence. What punctuation mark comes before it? __comma__

Find the name of the person being spoken to in the third sentence. What punctuation mark comes after it? __comma__

Find the question that is tagged onto the end of the sentence in quotation marks. What punctuation mark comes before it? __comma__

Commas tell a reader where to pause. A comma is also used to separate an **introductory word** such as *yes* or *no*, an **introductory element**, a **noun of direct address**, or a **tag question** from the rest of a sentence. A comma is also used to separate the **independent clauses** in a compound sentence.

See Handbook Sections 8 and 21

Practice

A comma is missing from each sentence. Add the missing comma. Then decide why each comma is needed. Write *I* for introductory word or element, *D* for direct address, *T* for tag question, or *C* for compound sentence.

1. "Ms. Li, what species of frog is the best jumper?" asked Ken. __D__

2. "Ken, the African sharp-nosed frog can jump 65 times its body length," she said. __D__

3. "Its legs are really long, aren't they?" asked Ray. __T__

4. Ms. Li said, "Yes, frogs' powerful legs make them good jumpers." __I__

5. "Do you know another way frogs use their legs, Ali?" Ms. Li asked. __D__

6. "Yes, they use them to swim," Ali answered. __I__

7. "Many frogs have webbed feet, and that helps them swim faster." __C__

8. Because we were studying frogs, we had a frog race. __I__

9. "Follow that frog, will you?" Jenny shouted at Raj. __T__

10. Ms. Li gave the signal, and we urged our frogs to jump. __C__

Bullfrogs can jump up to nine times the length of their bodies.

Name _____

Apply

Rewrite the sentences so they include the word or words in parentheses. Be sure to use commas correctly.

11. Some frogs live near water. (and) Others are tree dwellers. **Some frogs live near water, and others are tree dwellers.**

12. Many frogs capture insects with their long, sticky tongues. (but) Others gulp food directly into their mouths.
Many frogs capture insects with their long, sticky tongues, but others gulp food directly into their mouths.

13. Put your frog back in the pond. (James) **Put your frog back in the pond, James.**

14. The frog will be happier there. (won't it) **The frog will be happier there, won't it?**

Reinforce

Amphibians can live on land or in water. The words *amphibian* and *amphibious* come from two Greek roots: *amphi,* meaning "both," and *bios,* meaning "life." Write a paragraph explaining how amphibians live a double life. Use commas to separate elements in your sentences.

Accept reasonable responses.

_____

_____

_____

_____

_____

_____

_____

_____

a. The chameleon crouched on a branch; an unsuspecting butterfly landed nearby.

b. Chameleons don't like each other, they must be kept in separate enclosures.

In which sentence do you think the two clauses are separated correctly? _____a_____

A **semicolon** can be used instead of a comma and a conjunction to separate the independent clauses in a compound sentence.

See Handbook Section 8

Practice

Write a semicolon to separate the clauses in each sentence.

1. The chameleon is a very quiet lizard;it sits perfectly still.

2. The chameleon's name comes from two Greek words;the words mean "dwarf lion."

3. Some chameleons have horns on their heads;they use the horns for fighting.

4. Chameleons are adapted for living in trees;they can grasp branches with their tails.

5. Chameleons' feet are shaped like hands;they have thumbs and fingers.

6. A chameleon's eyes move independently;they can focus on two different objects at once.

7. Some chameleons eat insects;others eat grasses.

8. Chameleons also change colors;a chameleon can make itself gray, black, green, or brown.

9. A chameleon doesn't change color to match its background;it can change color as its mood changes.

10. A chameleon that's won a fight for territory might turn bright green;the loser might turn gray.

11. Sometimes temperature affects a chameleon's color;a chameleon might turn pale when it gets cold.

12. Chameleons aren't the only lizards that change color;many lizards have this ability.

A chameleon's powerful tongue can grow as long as its body.

Apply

Each sentence on the left can be matched with a sentence on the right to make a compound sentence. Draw a line to connect each pair of sentences that have related information. Then rewrite each pair of sentences as one sentence. Use a semicolon to separate the independent clauses.

Chameleons are usually green or brown.　　Insects get trapped on the end of it.

Chameleons move very slowly when hunting.　　It can shoot out far and fast.

A chameleon's tongue is long and powerful.　　They are hard to see against the leaves.

A chameleon's tongue is also very sticky.　　They lift one foot at a time.

13. **Chameleons are usually green or brown; they are hard to see against the leaves.**
_____

14. **Chameleons move very slowly when hunting; they lift one foot at a time.**
_____

15. **A chameleon's tongue is long and powerful; it can shoot out far and fast.**
_____

16. **A chameleon's tongue is also very sticky; insects get trapped on the end of it.**
_____

Reinforce

Use what you have read about chameleons to answer the questions below. Each answer should include two independent clauses separated by a semicolon. **Answers will vary.**

17. What are two interesting features of a chameleon's appearance? _____

_____

18. How does a chameleon move? _____

_____

19. How does a chameleon eat? _____

_____

Tony asked, "How will we know where the rattlesnakes are?"
Joe explained that he knew where to look for timber rattlers.

Which sentence shows a speaker's exact words? Underline it.

Circle the marks that begin and end the quotation. Then circle the first letter of the quotation.

A **direct quotation**, or direct speech, is a speaker's exact words. Use **quotation marks** around the beginning and end of a direct quotation. Use a comma to separate the speaker's exact words from the rest of the sentence. Begin a direct quotation with an uppercase letter, and add end punctuation before the last quotation mark. An **indirect quotation** retells a speaker's words. Do not use quotation marks when the words *that* or *whether* come before a speaker's words.

See Handbook Section 4

Practice

Write *I* after each indirect quotation and *D* after each direct quotation. Add quotation marks, commas, and end punctuation to direct quotations. Circle lowercase letters that should be capitalized.

1. Nico asked whether timber rattlesnakes are easy to find. __I__

2. "They spend more than half the year hibernating in holes and rock cracks," Joe said. __D__

3. Joe commented that snakes are cold-blooded and need the sun to warm them. __I__

4. "Timber rattlers warm up on sunny rocks for a few days every spring," Joe said. __D__

5. "That's the best time to see them," he added. __D__

6. Joe said that rattlesnakes hibernate in groups and return to the same spot each year. __I__

7. He said, "this is an area where I saw snakes sunning themselves last year." __D__

8. "What's that buzzing sound?" Tony asked nervously. __D__

9. "Look! It's a rattlesnake," Nico shouted. __D__

10. Joe said that we should stay calm and stand back. __I__

11. "These snakes are poisonous," he warned. __D__

12. Tony said, "look at that one's beautiful stripes." __D__

Timber rattlesnakes are found in the forests of the eastern United States.

Apply Possible answers appear below. Accept all reasonable responses.

Rewrite each indirect quotation as a direct quotation. Rewrite each direct quotation as an indirect quotation. There is more than one right way to rewrite each one. Be sure to use punctuation marks correctly.

13. "Joe, how does a rattlesnake make its rattling sound?" Nico asked.

    Nico asked Joe how a rattlesnake makes its rattling sound.

14. Joe said that a rattlesnake sheds its skin a few times every year.

    Joe said, "A rattlesnake sheds its skin a few times every year."

15. "Each time the snake sheds its skin, a loose, hardened piece of skin stays on the end of its tail,"

    Joe explained.

    Joe explained that each time the snake sheds its skin, a loose, hardened piece of skin stays

    on the end of its tail.

16. He said that these hardened pieces click together when the snake shakes its tail.

    He said, "These hardened pieces click together when the snake shakes its tail."

Reinforce

Will Joe, Nico, and Tony meet more rattlers? Draw pictures in these boxes to show what will happen to these characters next. Under each box write a direct quotation to tell what a character is saying.

Answers will vary.   Answers will vary.

"Nature is not easy to live with," wrote the essayist Wendell Berry. "It is hard to have rain on your cut hay, or floodwater over your cropland, or coyotes in your sheep. It is hard when nature does not respect your intentions."

Circle each punctuation mark that tells the reader that the writer is using a quotation from a text.

You can make a report more interesting and informative by including a **quotation from a text** by an expert on the subject you are writing about. Use **quotation marks** at the beginning and end of a direct quotation. Use a comma to separate the speaker's exact words from the rest of the sentence. Begin a direct quotation with an uppercase letter. Add end punctuation (period, question mark, exclamation point, or comma in place of a period) before the last quotation mark.

See Handbook Sections 4 and 8

Practice

Add quotation marks and commas so that each direct quotation below is written correctly.

1. The ancient Greek poet Theocritus seemingly yearned for a simpler life. He wrote, "Oh, to be a frog, my lords, and live aloof from care."

2. Marie Curie, winner of Nobel Prizes in physics and chemistry, said, "All my life through, the new sights of nature made me rejoice like a child."

3. The ancient Greek philosopher and scientist Aristotle was also inspired by the natural world. He wrote, "In all things of nature there is something of the marvelous."

4. The American poet Robert Frost believed that nature is a great teacher. He wrote, "How many times it thundered before Franklin took the hint! How many apples fell on Newton's head before he took the hint. Nature is always hinting at us. It hints over and over again. And suddenly we take the hint."

5. The English poet William Wordsworth seems to agree with Frost. Wordsworth wrote, "Let Nature be your teacher."

Apply

Complete each sentence using one of the direct quotations below. Be sure to add the correct punctuation marks.

He that plants trees loves others besides himself.   The earth is what we all have in common.

—Thomas Fuller   —Wendell Berry

When one tugs at a single thing in nature, he finds it attached to the rest of the world.

—John Muir

6. I've always been inspired by Thomas Fuller's quote, **"He that plants trees loves others besides**

    himself."_____

7. Wendell Berry was correct when he noted, **"The earth is what we all have in common."**

    _____

8. How true is John Muir's quote, **"When one tugs at a single thing in nature, he finds it attached**

    to the rest of the world."_____

Reinforce

Write a short paragraph about a type of animal you believe is important to protect or treat well. Tell why you feel this way. Include a quotation from a text in your paragraph.

Accept reasonable responses. Check for correct use of quotation marks and commas.

_____

_____

_____

_____

_____

_____

_____

Camp Iguana
Box B-755
Yuma, AZ 85364
August 10, 20__

Dear Miguel,

Today is the hottest day of the year so far! Tomorrow morning we're supposed to go on a nature hike in the Yuma Desert. If tomorrow is as hot as today, I'll bet the hike will be cancelled. Write soon!

Your buddy,
Ron

Circle the commas in the heading of this letter. Underline the comma in the greeting. Draw a box around the comma in the closing.

A **friendly letter** has five parts: the heading, the greeting, the body, the closing, and the signature. In the heading, use a comma between the city and the state abbreviation, and between the date and the year. Capitalize all important words. Use commas also at the end of the greeting and the closing. A **formal e-mail** is similar to a letter, but it usually has only four parts: the greeting, the body, the closing, and the signature.

See Handbook Sections 8, 29, and 30

Practice

Add commas where they are needed in the letter below.

116 Hope St.
Baltimore,MD 21210
August 15,20__

Dear Ron,

Nestor and I visited the Taylor Natural History Museum this morning. The snake keeper let me hold a humongous boa constrictor. I was very surprised: its body felt cool and dry, not hot and slimy as I had expected.

Did you ever get to take that desert hike? If you did, maybe you have a snake story to tell, too! Well, that's all for now.

Your pal,
Miguel

Name _____

Apply

Rewrite this friendly letter on the lines below. Use correct capitalization and punctuation.

camp livingston 1100 pitcher road ross springs OH 43210 July 10 20__ dear sandra today at camp we caught tadpoles for the aquarium. I'll write to tell you when they grow into frogs. Your friend denise

Camp Livingston

1100 Pitcher Road

Ross Springs, OH 43210

July 10, 20__

Dear Sandra,

Today at camp we caught tadpoles for the aquarium. I'll write to tell you when they grow into frogs.

Your friend,

Denise

Reinforce

See Handbook Section 32

Ask an adult to help you use the Internet to research a state or national park you would like to visit. Then write a formal e-mail to the park in which you request information. For example, you might ask whether the park offers tours or what wildlife might be seen at a particular time of year. Write a draft of your email below.

Accept reasonable responses. Check for correct form.

_____

_____

_____

_____

_____

_____

_____

_____

Review

(Numbers in parentheses identify related lessons.)

Quotation Marks and Apostrophes

Write *D* after each direct quotation and *I* after each indirect quotation. Add quotation marks and other punctuation marks to direct quotations. Draw three lines (≡) under letters that should be capitalized.

1. Mr. Chi said that we were going to see a movie about how lizards defend themselves. __I__ **(58)**

2. Trinh shouted, "the skink broke off its own tail and got away!" __D__ **(58)**

3. Mr. Chi told us that this is an unusual kind of defense. __I__ **(58)**

4. Biologist Barry Commoner wrote, "The proper use of science is not to conquer nature but to live with it." **(59)**

5. The essayist Ralph Waldo Emerson wrote, "Adopt the pace of nature: her secret is patience." **(59)**

Underline the correct word in each pair. Write *C* if the answer is a contraction. Write *P* if the answer is a possessive.

6. Many people (<u>can't</u>/cant') tell the difference between salamanders and lizards. __C__ **(54)**

7. (<u>Salamanders'</u>/Salamander's) bodies look like the bodies of lizards. __P__ **(54)**

8. A (lizards'/<u>lizard's</u>) skin is dry and scaly, but salamanders have moist skin. __P__ **(54)**

Commas and Semicolons

Add commas and semicolons where they are needed. Cross out commas that are not needed.

9. "Some of the largest lizards can be found in Africa, India, and Australia," said Ms. Kaplan. **(55)**

10. "Which lizard is the biggest, Ms. Kaplan?" Katie asked. **(56)**

11. "Well, the world's largest lizard is the Komodo dragon," said Ms. Kaplan. **(55, 56)**

12. These lizards hatch from small eggs, but they grow to be over ten feet long. **(56)**

13. Komodo dragons are very rare; they live only on a few islands in Indonesia. **(57)**

14. The zoo had a special display of Komodo dragons; I saw it. **(57)**

15. I watched Komodo dragons eat, walk, and sleep. **(55)**

Punctuation and Capitalization

Use proofreading marks to correct each capitalization or punctuation error. Then label each sentence *declarative, interrogative, imperative,* or *exclamatory.*

16. did you know that some snakes are called "flying snakes"?   **interrogative (49)**

17. Look at the snake in this picture.   **imperative (49)**

18. It can glide through the air for short distances.   **declarative (49)**

19. wow, that's amazing!   **exclamatory (49)**

20. Its belly scales act like a parachute.   **declarative (49)**

Use proofreading marks to correct each capitalization or punctuation error. Add underlines and quotation marks where they are needed.

21. professor starsky said that japanese giant salamanders can grow to be over five feet long. **(50)**

22. These huge amphibians live only on the island of honshu in japan. **(52)**

23. mr. f.b. Baker's Enterprise Productions inc. is making a movie about giant salamanders. **(50, 51, 52)**

24. His studio is on Main st. near the shoe factory. **(50)**

25. The movie will be called salamanders are super. **(53)**

26. It is based on a book titled the japanese giant salamander. **(53)**

27. The movie's theme song will be "dance of the amphibians." **(53)**

28. I like the poem "salamander soup." **(53)**

29. I just bought a pair of froggy flyers; they are a brand of athletic shoes. **(52)**

Note: Students may refer to the list of proofreading marks on page 163.

Letters

Rewrite this friendly letter correctly on a separate sheet of paper.

30. Camp Komodo markland NJ 07902 June 22 20__ dear Matt I can't wait for your visit. We're going to have a great time! Wait until you see my pet salamander. I'll see you next week. your friend Daniel

**Camp Komodo
Markland, NJ 07902
June 22, 20__**

Dear Matt,
        I can't wait for your visit. We're going to have a great time! Wait until you see my pet salamander. I'll see you next week.

**Your friend,
Daniel   (60)**

Spelling Practice

Read and Analyze

Liz took a **photograph** of a lizard that was ten (centimeters) long.

Circle the word in bold type that has a Greek root that means "to measure."

Greek and Latin Roots

Many words in English have major parts, or **roots**, that come from the ancient Greek and Roman languages. For example, *telephone*, *photocopy*, *graphics*, and *millimeter* contain the Greek roots *tele* ("distant"), *photo* ("light"), *graph* ("written"), and *meter* ("measure"). *Inspect*, *describe*, *disrupt*, *export*, *eject*, and *dictate* contain the Latin roots spec ("see"), *scrib* ("write"), *rupt* ("break apart"), *port* ("carry"), *ject* ("throw"), and *dict* ("speak").

Word Sort

Use the words below to complete the word sort. Answers may be in any order.

predict	prescribe	telecast	photocopy	thermometer
prospect	reject	erupt	import	photograph

Greek roots (*tele, photo, graph, meter*)	Latin roots (*spec, scrib, rupt, port, ject, dict*)
telecast	predict
photocopy	prescribe
thermometer	prospect
photograph	reject
	erupt
	import

Pattern Practice

dictionary	telescope	biography	portable
inspector	photocopy	erupt	

Write the word that answers each question.

1. Which word has a Greek root that means "light"? _____**photocopy**_____

2. Which word has a Latin root that means "break apart"? _____**erupt**_____

3. Which word has a Latin root that means "speak"? _____**dictionary**_____

4. Which word has a Greek root that means "written"? _____**biography**_____

5. Which word has a Latin root that means "see"? _____**inspector**_____

6. Which word has a Greek root that means "distant"? _____**telescope**_____

7. Which word has a Latin root that means "carry"? _____**portable**_____

Write the word from above that best completes each sentence.

8. You should read this _____**biography**_____ about Ben Franklin's life.

9. It is hard to tell when the volcano will _____**erupt**_____ again.

10. Because the speakers are _____**portable**_____, I can take them anywhere.

11. Lily tracks the movement of the stars with her _____**telescope**_____.

12. Use a _____**dictionary**_____ to check the word's meaning.

Use the Dictionary

Write a word that begins with each Greek or Latin root. Use a dictionary to find words and check spellings. **Suggested answers appear below. Accept all reasonable responses.**

13. photo _____**photography**_____

14. spec _____**spectator**_____

15. tele _____**telephone**_____

Proofreading
Practice

Find the mistakes in the letter below. Use proofreading marks to show how to fix each mistake. Use a dictionary to check and correct spellings.

Suggested answers appear below.
Accept all reasonable responses.

Proofreading Marks

Mark	Means	Example
∧	add	Iguanas have long tails.
≡	make into an uppercase letter	iguanas have long tails.
/	make into a lowercase letter	Iguanas Have long tails.
⊙	add a period	Iguanas have long tails⊙
∧	add a comma	Yes‸ iguanas have long tails.
⌄" ⌄"	add quotation marks	"Iguanas have long tails," he said.
ⓢⓟ	fix spelling	Igwanas have long tails.
⌄'	add an apostrophe	Iguanas' tails are long.

224 Hummingbird st⊙
Los Angeles, CA 90012
May 11, 2012

dear Max,

Last weekend my dad and I drove into the mojave Desert, I was looking for lizards. I borrowed my mom's binoculars. I also brought along a book, the story of reptiles, by dr. R. J. Jackson.

We hiked into a canyon. All of a sudden, Dad shouted, "Kevin, look there!" A lizard skittered by, but I got a good look at it. I found a picture of the lizard in my book, it was a chuckwalla.

Chuckwallas store water in sacs under their skin, they are able to survive in temperatures of up to 113° F. The chuckwalla is a species of iguana.

I've learned some amazing facts about iguanas. Most iguanas eat fruit, leafs, or insecs. One species in South america can run across the surface of a pool of water without sinking. Another one in Fiji turns from bright green to black when it's frightened. I wrote a poem called "i want to be an iguana."

Would you like to visit next month, we could look for lizards in my yard.

Your friend,
Kevin

Proofreading
Checklist

You can use the list below to help you find and fix mistakes in your own writing. Write the titles of your own stories or reports in the blanks on top of the chart. Then use the questions to check your work. Make a check mark (✓) in each box after you have checked that item. **Answers will vary.**

Titles

Proofreading Checklist for Unit 5

Have I capitalized proper nouns, proper adjectives, and all the important words in titles?				
Have I placed quotation marks around direct quotations?				
Have I used commas to separate items in a series?				
Have I joined each compound sentence with a comma followed by a conjunction or with a semicolon?				

Also Remember…

Does each sentence begin with an uppercase letter and end with the right end mark?				
Do all abbreviations begin with an uppercase letter and end with a period?				
Did I use a dictionary to check and correct spellings?				
Have I used contractions correctly?				

Your Own List

Use this space to write your own list of things to check in your writing.

School 🔔🏠 Home Connection

In Unit 5 of *Grammar, Usage, and Mechanics,* students are learning which letters to capitalize and how to use punctuation marks such as periods, apostrophes, commas, and quotation marks. The activities on this page give extra practice with some of the concepts in this unit. You can help your child use the information he or she is learning in school by choosing one or more activities to complete with him or her at home.

Word Search (Apostrophes)

Work with your child to find the eleven words hidden in the word search. Then ask your child to write as many contractions as possible by combining these words in different ways.

Example   The word *don't* is formed by combining *do* and *not*.

Postcard (Proper Nouns and Proper Adjectives; Initials and Abbreviations)

Help your child use a 4" × 6" blank card to design his or her own postcard. First have your child draw a picture on one side of the card. Then have him or her draw a line down the middle of the back of the card and write a message on the left side of the line. Help your child write the address of a friend or family member on the right side. Encourage your child to capitalize proper nouns and use abbreviations (*St., Ave.*).

Thumbs Up/Thumbs Down (Titles)

Ask your child to write a short review of a favorite book, movie, or song. Then ask him or her to write a review of a book, movie, or song he or she did not enjoy. Invite your child to be specific about what he or she liked or disliked. Remind your child to capitalize all important words in any title. He or she should underline the titles of books and movies and use quotation marks around titles of songs.

The Envelope, Please (Titles)

Ask each member of your family to write the title of a favorite movie, book, and story on a slip of paper. Put all the slips in a hat or bag. Then work with your child to use the slips and create a poster of these favorites. Make sure your child underlines movie titles and book titles and puts quotation marks around story titles. Decorate the poster and give it to another family you know.

Favorite Movie
<u>Ratatouille</u>

Best Book
<u>George Washington's Teeth</u>

Greatest Story
"The Gold Coin"

Traveling Game (Apostrophes; Commas in a Series)

Play a game with your child in which you plan an imaginary trip. Have your child write a list of objects he or she will borrow to bring on the trip. Encourage your child to use apostrophes to show possession (*Lucia's, students'*) and to separate the items in his or her list with commas.

 I'm going on a trip to Africa, and I will borrow my **sister's** tent, my **teacher's** map, **Alex's** cowboy boots, and my **grandparents'** camera.

Pen Pal (Friendly Letters and E-mails)

Encourage your child to begin writing to a pen pal. Help him or her find a pen pal through an organization such as KidsCom (www.kidscom.com). If your child uses e-mail to correspond, remind him or her to include a greeting, body, closing, and signature. If your child writes a friendly letter, remind him or her to include all five parts of a letter.

The Show Must Go On! (Commas)

Invite your child to write a very short play. Suggest that he or she use introductory elements (such as *Yes, No,* and *Well*) and direct address (for example, *Carl, come here!*) in the dialogue. Make sure your child uses commas to separate these elements from the rest of a sentence. Then read the play out loud with your child. Point out to him or her the way commas make a reader pause.

 SCENE ONE

Ballet Dancer: Ouch, my ankle!

Stage Hand: Hurry, we have to find a doctor!

SCENE TWO

Ballet Dancer: Will I ever dance again, Dr. Woo?

Doctor: Well, you've had a bad sprain, but with some rest you'll be fine.

Appendix Table of Contents

TEST TIP: Read all four answer choices carefully before choosing and marking the answer you think is correct.

(Numbers in parentheses identify related lessons.)

Read each item carefully. Fill in the circle next to the best answer.

1. Read this sentence.

   > Farm ponds attract wildlife of many kinds.

   What is the complete subject of this sentence? **(1)**

   (A) ponds   (C) ponds attract
   (B) farm ponds   (D) wildlife

2. Read this sentence.

   > Some farmers make their ponds attractive to wildlife.

   What are the simple subject and simple predicate of this sentence? **(2)**

   (A) some; farmers   (C) make; ponds
   (B) ponds; attractive   (D) farmers; make

3. Which of the following sentences has a compound predicate? **(3)**

   (A) Some farmers build sediment traps and ponds.
   (B) The traps and ponds receive irrigation water.
   (C) Irrigation water carries fertilizer and pesticides.
   (D) The traps absorb the water and remove chemicals.

4. Read this sentence.

   > Farm ponds provide a habitat for frogs.

   What is the direct object in this sentence? **(4)**

   (A) farm   (C) habitat
   (B) provide   (D) frogs

5. Read this sentence.

   > Frogs give farmers <u>help</u> with pest control.

   The direct object in this sentence is underlined. What is the indirect object? **(5)**

   (A) frogs   (C) pest
   (B) farmers   (D) control

6. Read these sentences.

   > Frogs are hungry creatures.
   > Flies are yummy to frogs.

   Which statement tells about the sentences? **(6)**

   (A) The first sentence contains a predicate noun, and the second contains a predicate adjective.
   (B) The first sentence contains a predicate adjective, and the second contains a predicate noun.
   (C) Both sentences contain predicate nouns.
   (D) Both sentences contain predicate adjectives.

7. Which sentence has a prepositional phrase underlined? **(7)**

   (A) <u>Hawks and owls</u> may hunt near a farm pond.
   (B) An egret <u>or a heron</u> may take up residence.
   (C) Native grasses <u>provide cover</u> for birds.
   (D) Helpful insects can thrive <u>in grassy areas</u>.

Read each item carefully. Fill in the circle next to the best answer.

8. **Which sentence is a compound sentence? (8)**

   (A) Flocks of migratory birds stop and rest at farm ponds.

   (B) Toads and reptiles make their homes near these ponds.

   (C) Birds, frogs, toads, and reptiles can be helpful because they eat insect pests.

   (D) Fewer pests mean healthier crops, and healthier crops mean more money for the farmer.

9. **Read this sentence.**

   > Although farm ponds take up space, they can make farms more productive.

   What is the dependent clause in this sentence? (9)

   (A) although farm ponds take up space

   (B) farm ponds take up space

   (C) they can make farms more productive

   (D) make farms more productive

10. **Which sentence is a complex sentence? (10)**

   (A) My aunt and uncle built a different kind of pond on their farm.

   (B) They call it a pond, but it is more like a small lake.

   (C) Water skiers come from miles around and ski on this pond.

   (D) Whenever I visit their farm, I practice my jumps and turns.

11. **Read this sentence.**

   > My sister and I enjoy chores that help us learn about farming.

   Which word in this sentence is a relative pronoun? (11)

   (A) my

   (B) I

   (C) that

   (D) us

12. **Read this item.**

   > Students help with some farm pond projects, they plant wild shrubs and grasses.

   How should this sentence be rewritten? (12)

   (A) Change *Students help* to *Students, they help*.

   (B) Insert the word *although* after the comma.

   (C) Change the comma to a period, and capitalize the word *they*.

   (D) It should not be rewritten. It is written correctly.

13. **Read this sentence.**

   > Some giant bluefin tuna live for thirty years.

   What is the complete subject of this sentence? (1)

   (A) some giant bluefin tuna

   (B) bluefin tuna

   (C) tuna live

   (D) for thirty years

Read each item carefully. Fill in the circle next to the best answer.

14. Read this sentence.

> These huge fish range from Arctic waters to tropical regions.

What are the simple subject and simple predicate of this sentence? **(2)**

(A) huge; fish
(B) fish; range
(C) range; from
(D) Arctic; waters

15. Which of the following sentences has a compound predicate? **(3)**

(A) The meat of this fish is prized for its texture and its taste.
(B) Ancient peoples caught bluefin and painted pictures of them on cave walls.
(C) Today fishing crews search for bluefin tuna with high-tech equipment.
(D) Large numbers of bluefin have been caught, and these fish are now rare in many areas.

16. Read this sentence.

> Fishing crews chase bluefin at high speeds.

What is the direct object in this sentence? **(4)**

(A) crews
(B) chase
(C) bluefin
(D) speeds

17. Read this sentence.

> A large catch of bluefin brings a crew a huge <u>profit</u>.

The direct object in this sentence is underlined. What is the indirect object? **(5)**

(A) bluefin
(B) brings
(C) crew
(D) huge

18. Read these sentences.

> Bluefin tuna are swift swimmers.
> Adults are very large.

Which statement tells about the sentences? **(6)**

(A) The first sentence contains a predicate noun, and the second contains a predicate adjective.
(B) The first sentence contains a predicate adjective, and the second contains a predicate noun.
(C) Both sentences contain predicate nouns.
(D) Both sentences contain predicate adjectives.

19. Which sentence has a prepositional phrase underlined? **(7)**

(A) Bluefin tuna are <u>warm-blooded fish</u>.
(B) They live in icy waters and can <u>dive deeply</u>.
(C) These fish once were numerous <u>in the Mediterranean Sea</u>.
(D) Overfishing <u>has greatly reduced</u> the number of bluefin tuna there.

Read each item carefully. Fill in the circle next to the best answer.

20. **Which sentence is a compound sentence? (8)**

   Ⓐ Bluefin are protected by laws in some areas, but not all fishing crews obey the laws.

   Ⓑ Scientists count bluefin populations and study their behavior.

   Ⓒ The extinction of this remarkable and valuable fish seems a possibility.

   Ⓓ Protection of this species requires international cooperation and greater enforcement of laws.

21. **Read this sentence.**

> Giant bluefin still flourish near Alaska because that state effectively manages fishing there.

   What is the dependent clause in this sentence? (9)

   Ⓐ giant bluefin still flourish near Alaska

   Ⓑ still flourish near Alaska

   Ⓒ that state effectively manages fishing there

   Ⓓ because that state effectively manages fishing there

22. **Which sentence is a complex sentence? (10)**

   Ⓐ New Zealand protects its bluefin tuna population, and Iceland does, too.

   Ⓑ The establishment of protected areas does not keep bluefin tuna safe, however.

   Ⓒ When these fish migrate through unprotected areas, they can be caught.

   Ⓓ The United States belongs to tuna protection groups, but these groups have not been effective.

23. **Read this sentence.**

> Yellowfin tuna that is caught off U.S. shores is an ocean-friendly choice.

   Which word in this sentence is a relative pronoun? (11)

   Ⓐ that

   Ⓑ off

   Ⓒ is

   Ⓓ choice

24. **Read this sentence.**

> Another ocean-friendly choice is albacore tuna caught by the troll pole method in waters where these fish are plentiful.

   Which word in this sentence is a relative adverb? (11)

   Ⓐ is

   Ⓑ by

   Ⓒ in

   Ⓓ where

25. **Read this sentence.**

> You can find information on the Internet about ocean-friendly fishing, the Monterey Bay Aquarium Seafood Watch is an informative website.

   How should this sentence be rewritten? (12)

   Ⓐ Insert a comma between *Watch* and *is*.

   Ⓑ Make it into two sentences by changing the comma to a period and capitalizing *the*.

   Ⓒ Remove the comma between *fishing* and *the*.

   Ⓓ Add the word *although* after the comma and before *the*.

TEST TIP: Don't spend too much time on one question.

(Numbers in parentheses identify related lessons.)

Read each item carefully. Fill in the circle next to the best answer.

1. **Which of the following sentences has a proper noun underlined? (13)**

   Ⓐ Let me show you this <u>timeline</u>.
   Ⓑ It shows the dates of early voyages to our <u>continent</u>.
   Ⓒ Not all dates are <u>exact</u>.
   Ⓓ No one knows exactly when <u>Leif Ericson</u> sailed to North America.

2. **Which of the following sentences has a possessive noun in it? (14)**

   Ⓐ Christopher Columbus moved to Lisbon, Portugal, at the age of 25.
   Ⓑ In that city he learned to read and write.
   Ⓒ Christopher Columbus's brother taught him mapmaking skills.
   Ⓓ These skills helped him prepare for his historic voyage.

3. **Read this sentence.**

   In the colonial period, some settlers built cabins out of whole logs.

   Which of these nouns is an abstract noun? (15)

   Ⓐ period   Ⓒ cabins
   Ⓑ settlers   Ⓓ logs

4. **Read this sentence.**

   Many New England colonists built their homes out of logs.

   Which word in the sentence is a possessive pronoun? (16)

   Ⓐ many   Ⓒ their
   Ⓑ New England   Ⓓ of

5. **Which of the following sentences has a linking verb in boldfaced type? (17)**

   Ⓐ Sara **collects** commemorative American stamps.
   Ⓑ This stamp **depicts** the first flight by the Wright Brothers.
   Ⓒ I **like** stamps with scenes from the American Revolution.
   Ⓓ This stamp **is** the oldest one in my collection.

6. **Read this sentence.**

   Our family has visited Paul Revere's house in Boston, Massachusetts.

   What is the main verb in this sentence? (18)

   Ⓐ family   Ⓒ visited
   Ⓑ has   Ⓓ house

7. **Read this sentence.**

   Yes, you **may** borrow my American history book this weekend.

   What is the special function of the modal auxiliary in boldfaced type? (19)

   Ⓐ to indicate ability
   Ⓑ to communicate an obligation
   Ⓒ to indicate possibility
   Ⓓ to give permission

Read each item carefully. Fill in the circle next to the best answer.

8. Read this sentence.

> Travelers in colonial America generally depended on horses for transportation.

Which of these words is an adjective in the sentence? **(20)**

Ⓐ colonial
Ⓑ generally
Ⓒ depended
Ⓓ for

9. Read this sentence.

> On a trip from Boston to New York in 1704, Sarah Knight narrowly avoided a tragic fall into a river.

Which of these words is an adverb in the sentence? **(21)**

Ⓐ from
Ⓑ 1704
Ⓒ narrowly
Ⓓ tragic

10. Read this sentence.

> We live in a large rectangular state famous for its blue clear skies.

How should this sentence be rewritten? **(22)**

Ⓐ Change *large rectangular* to *rectangular large*.
Ⓑ Change *blue clear* to *clear blue*.
Ⓒ Change *large rectangular* to *rectangular large* and *blue clear* to *clear blue*.
Ⓓ Make no change. The sentence is correct as written.

11. Which of the following sentences has a subordinating conjunction in it? **(20)**

Ⓐ Benjamin Franklin traveled to Philadelphia at age 17.
Ⓑ He worked as a printer, but he also invented devices.
Ⓒ One of his inventions was the lightning rod.
Ⓓ Before he invented this device, lightning caused many house fires.

12. Which sentence has a pair of correlative conjunctions? **(24)**

Ⓐ Most roads in the American colonies were just dirt paths.
Ⓑ These roads were either muddy or dusty most of the year.
Ⓒ Rocks littered main roads, and fallen trees sometimes blocked them.
Ⓓ Steep hills caused problems for horses with heavily loaded wagons.

13. Which of the following sentences has a proper noun underlined? **(13)**

Ⓐ Where can we go to see <u>totem poles</u>?
Ⓑ The Indians of the <u>Northwest Coast</u> carved them.
Ⓒ That totem pole commemorates an important <u>event</u> in a person's life.
Ⓓ A few Northwest Indian <u>artists</u> still carve these poles today.

Read each item carefully. Fill in the circle next to the best answer.

14. **Which of the following sentences has a possessive noun in it?** (14)

   (A) We are studying America's mountain ranges.
   (B) Mountain ranges are barriers to travel.
   (C) Daniel Boone led settlers across the Appalachian Mountains.
   (D) Lewis and Clark had difficulty crossing the Rockies.

15. **Read this sentence.**

   No driver of a stagecoach could handle a team of horses as skillfully as Charlie Parkhurst.

   Which of these nouns is a collective noun? (15)

   (A) driver
   (B) stagecoach
   (C) team
   (D) horses

16. **Read this sentence.**

   Charlie Parkhurst was the only female driver of stagecoaches at a time when women were excluded from that profession because of discrimination.

   Which of these nouns is a concrete noun? (15)

   (A) driver
   (B) time
   (C) profession
   (D) discrimination

17. **Read this sentence.**

   I need to borrow this atlas to use its relief maps.

   Which word in the sentence is a possessive pronoun? (16)

   (A) this
   (B) use
   (C) its
   (D) relief

18. **Which of the following sentences has an action verb in boldfaced type?** (17)

   (A) Mount Vernon **was** the home of America's first president, George Washington.
   (B) The main house **is** 2½ stories high.
   (C) Washington and his wife Martha **lived** in this mansion prior to the Revolutionary War.
   (D) Mount Vernon **became** home for the Washingtons again after George's second term as president.

19. **Read this sentence.**

   Before this week I had never seen a bison.

   What is the helping verb in this sentence? (18)

   (A) before
   (B) had
   (C) never
   (D) seen

Read each item carefully. Fill in the circle next to the best answer.

20. Read this sentence.

> We **might** have time for a visit to the Lincoln Memorial.

What is the special function of the modal auxiliary in boldfaced type? **(19)**

(A) to indicate ability
(B) to communicate an obligation
(C) to indicate possibility
(D) to give permission

21. Read this sentence.

> Thanks to its fine harbor, Charleston, South Carolina, is an important city.

Which of these words is an adjective in the sentence? **(20)**

(A) thanks
(B) fine
(C) South Carolina
(D) city

22. Read this sentence.

> Ships could dock safely and be protected from stormy seas.

Which of these words is an adverb in the sentence? **(21)**

(A) could
(B) dock
(C) safely
(D) stormy

23. Read this sentence.

> The American first flag had thirteen white stars on a field of blue.

How should this sentence be rewritten? **(22)**

(A) Change *American first* to *first American*.
(B) Change *thirteen white* to *white thirteen*.
(C) Change *American first* to *first American* and *thirteen white* to *white thirteen*.
(D) Make no change. The sentence is correct as written.

24. Which of the following sentences has a subordinating conjunction in it? **(23)**

(A) Ships carried rice from Charleston to distant ports.
(B) Rice planters in the Charleston area became prosperous.
(C) Field workers suffered, though; the work was hard and unhealthy.
(D) Because these workers were enslaved people, they could not leave their jobs.

25. Which sentence has a pair of correlative conjunctions? **(24)**

(A) My grandfather and grandmother came to the United States sixty years ago.
(B) Although they could barely speak English, they opened a small shop.
(C) Not only did they learn English, they also became fluent in Spanish.
(D) They learned Spanish because many of their customers were Spanish speakers.

TEST TIP: Eliminate answer choices that you know are incorrect.

(Numbers in parentheses identify related lessons.)

Read each item carefully. Fill in the circle next to the best answer.

1. Read this sentence.

   > Those athletes want to avoid injury, so ___ warming up carefully.

   Which word would complete the sentence correctly? **(25)**

   Ⓐ their   Ⓒ they're
   Ⓑ there   Ⓓ theyre

2. Which of the following sentences has *its* or *it's* used *incorrectly*? **(26)**

   Ⓐ It's important to stretch your muscles before competing.
   Ⓑ I am going to the gym to use it's exercise machines.
   Ⓒ The gym has its schedule posted on the door.
   Ⓓ I think it's fun to try new machines.

3. Which of the following sentences has *your* or *you're* used *incorrectly*? **(27)**

   Ⓐ Do you like you're gymnastics coach?
   Ⓑ I am amazed at your improvement!
   Ⓒ You're the best of anyone on the balance beam.
   Ⓓ Perhaps you have improved because you're a hard worker.

4. Read this sentence.

   > These drills will help me become a ___ soccer player.

   Which choice would complete the sentence correctly? **(28)**

   Ⓐ more good   Ⓒ more better
   Ⓑ gooder   Ⓓ better

5. Read this sentence.

   > The fishing rod ___ I use is old but effective.

   Which word would complete the sentence correctly? **(29)**

   Ⓐ that   Ⓒ who
   Ⓑ which   Ⓓ None of the above

6. Read each sentence. Look at the underlined word in it. Which sentence is written *incorrectly*? **(30)**

   Ⓐ We cannot play with a <u>real</u> baseball here.
   Ⓑ We would be <u>very</u> likely to break a window.
   Ⓒ This hollow plastic ball is <u>very</u> safe.
   Ⓓ It's <u>real</u> good for backyard ball games.

7. Read each sentence. Look at the underlined word in it. Which sentence is written *incorrectly*? **(31)**

   Ⓐ Please <u>set</u> your bag on the floor.
   Ⓑ <u>Sit</u> on the bench while I explain the rules.
   Ⓒ My sister has <u>sat</u> the paddles on the table.
   Ⓓ We have <u>sat</u> long enough; let's play!

Read each item carefully. Fill in the circle next to the best answer.

8. **Read this sentence.**

Saleem has ___ a lot about sports from his older brother.

   Which word would complete the sentence correctly? (32)

   - (A) learn
   - (B) teach
   - (C) learned
   - (D) taught

9. **Which of these sentences has *two, to,* or *too* used *incorrectly*? (33)**

   - (A) This canoe is made for two people.
   - (B) If one person paddles too hard, the canoe will not travel in a straight line.
   - (C) My sister and I paddled our canoe from the dock to the opposite shore of the lake.
   - (D) I love canoeing, and she does, to.

10. **Read each sentence. Look at the underlined word in it. Which sentence is written *incorrectly*? (34)**

   - (A) My aunt is <u>known</u> throughout the world as a champion.
   - (B) Her fame <u>grown</u> when she won a race last year.
   - (C) Few people <u>knew</u> how hard she had trained.
   - (D) She has <u>grown</u> stronger through exercise.

11. **Read each sentence. Look at the underlined word. Which sentence is written *incorrectly*? (35)**

   - (A) My uncle bought <u>hisself</u> a fishing boat.
   - (B) <u>Everyone</u> in our family likes to fish.
   - (C) There is <u>nothing</u> more relaxing than fishing for striped bass.
   - (D) I bought <u>myself</u> a fishing rod last month.

12. **Read these sentences.**

My uncle invited my sister and me on a fishing trip. He put ____ boat on a trailer and towed it to Pyramid Lake.

   Which pronoun should be used in the second sentence to refer to the boldfaced phrase? (36)

   - (A) him
   - (B) his
   - (C) our
   - (D) their

13. **Read this sentence.**

Many pitchers do exercises to strengthen ___ legs.

   Which word would complete the sentence correctly? (25)

   - (A) their
   - (B) there
   - (C) they're
   - (D) theyre

Read each item carefully. Fill in the circle next to the best answer.

14. **Which of the following sentences has *its* or *it's* used *incorrectly*? (26)**

    (A) This city is proud of its athletic fields.

    (B) It's important for students to get exercise.

    (C) Our school opens it's fields to the public.

    (D) They are filled with people, except when it's raining.

15. **Which of the following sentences has *your* or *you're* used *incorrectly*? (27)**

    (A) What is your favorite sport?

    (B) You're lucky to live near a soccer field.

    (C) How often do you play there with your friends?

    (D) Call me the next time your going to play there.

16. **Read this sentence.**

    > Our team has played hard, but we have the ___ record of all.

    Which choice would complete the sentence correctly? (28)

    (A) worse

    (B) baddest

    (C) most bad

    (D) worst

17. **Read this sentence.**

    > Myra is the batter ___ hit the home run.

    Which word would complete the sentence correctly? (29)

    (A) that

    (B) which

    (C) who

    (D) None of the above

18. **Read each sentence. Look at the underlined word in it. Which sentence is written *incorrectly*? (30)**

    (A) Is this a <u>real</u> golf club?

    (B) It isn't <u>very</u> heavy, and it's quite short.

    (C) It's for a young golfer; kids need <u>real</u> equipment to develop skills.

    (D) I will pay <u>real</u> careful attention to the instructor.

19. **Read each sentence. Look at the underlined word in it. Which sentence is written *incorrectly*? (31)**

    (A) I <u>sat</u> near mid-court at the basketball game.

    (B) I carelessly <u>sat</u> my sunglasses on the bench.

    (C) When Cici <u>sat</u> next to me, she broke them.

    (D) I should have <u>set</u> those glasses on my locker shelf.

Read each item carefully. Fill in the circle next to the best answer.

20. Read this sentence.

> Yesterday the coach ___ me how to run hurdles.

Which word would complete the sentence correctly? **(32)**

- (A) learn
- (B) teach
- (C) learned
- (D) taught

21. Which of these sentences has *two*, *to*, or *too* used *incorrectly*? **(33)**

- (A) I leaped too soon and hit the first hurdle.
- (B) I returned to the starting line and tried again.
- (C) I leaped over the first to hurdles.
- (D) I thought I would clear the third one, too, but I knocked it over.

22. Which of these sentences has *two*, *to*, or *too* used *incorrectly*? **(33)**

- (A) Each athlete may enter two events.
- (B) I will enter the high hurdles and compete in the long jump, too.
- (C) In a few minutes I will go too the starting line.
- (D) A blue ribbon will be given to the winner of each event.

23. Read each sentence. Look at the underlined word in it. Which sentence is written *incorrectly*? **(34)**

- (A) The home crowd <u>growed</u> quiet.
- (B) They <u>knew</u> that the next free throw could decide the game.
- (C) The star player swished the shot, and the home team's lead <u>grew</u>.
- (D) The fans all said they had <u>known</u> she'd make that free throw.

24. Read each sentence. Look at the underlined word or words. Which sentence is written *incorrectly*? **(35)**

- (A) Lakshmi wrote <u>herself</u> a note.
- (B) She did not want <u>anything</u> to go wrong.
- (C) With her mom's help, she had packed <u>every thing</u> needed for the hike.
- (D) She wanted to be sure her guests would enjoy <u>themselves</u>.

25. Read these sentences.

> Lakshmi took out **the trail map**. She unfolded ___ and studied the trail she had chosen for the day's hike.

Which pronoun should be used in the second sentence to refer to the boldfaced phrase? **(36)**

- (A) them
- (B) her
- (C) its
- (D) it

TEST TIP: Be sure to fill in the whole circle on the answer sheet.

(Numbers in parentheses identify related lessons.)

Read each item carefully. Fill in the circle next to the best answer.

1. **Read this sentence.**

   > When my dad saw me in the stands, he waved.

   Which word in the sentence is an object pronoun? (37)

   Ⓐ my
   Ⓑ dad
   Ⓒ me
   Ⓓ he

2. **Read each sentence. Look at the underlined word. Which sentence is written *incorrectly*? (38)**

   Ⓐ My dad takes my sister and <u>I</u> to the racetrack.
   Ⓑ <u>He</u> and my uncle are part of a pit crew.
   Ⓒ My sister and <u>I</u> are learning about auto mechanics.
   Ⓓ You may see <u>her</u> or mc in a pit crew someday.

3. **Read each sentence. Look at the underlined verb. Which sentence is *not* correct? (39)**

   Ⓐ Drivers on a track always <u>have</u> smooth pavement ahead.
   Ⓑ An off-road race for trucks <u>test</u> the drivers' reflexes.
   Ⓒ Only durable vehicles <u>enter</u> this type of race.
   Ⓓ A long race on dirt roads <u>punishes</u> vehicles and drivers.

4. **Read each sentence. Look at the underlined verb. Which sentence is *not* correct? (40)**

   Ⓐ That screeching noise <u>is</u> a warning.
   Ⓑ Your car's brake pads <u>are</u> ready for replacement.
   Ⓒ The mechanics in this shop <u>are</u> skillful.
   Ⓓ Repairs on an auto <u>is</u> never cheap.

5. **Read this sentence.**

   > My mom ___ our old car last Saturday.

   Which verb would complete the sentence correctly? (41)

   Ⓐ sells   Ⓒ sold
   Ⓑ will sell   Ⓓ has sold

6. **Read this sentence.**

   > By this coming Friday Monica ___ her new midget racer.

   Which verb would complete the sentence correctly? (42)

   Ⓐ was piloting   Ⓒ are piloting
   Ⓑ is piloting   Ⓓ will be piloting

7. **Read this sentence.**

   > So far she _____ only go-karts.

   Which verb would complete the sentence correctly? (43)

   Ⓐ had driven   Ⓒ have driven
   Ⓑ has driven   Ⓓ will have driven

Read each item carefully. Fill in the circle next to the best answer.

8. Read this sentence.

> By next Tuesday evening the trucking company ___ her midget racer.

Which verb would complete the sentence correctly? (44)

(A) had delivered
(B) has delivered
(C) have delivered
(D) will have delivered

9. Read this sentence.

> Today's resourceful teenagers find several ways to earn money, and they have saved most of the money they earn.

How should this sentence be changed to make it correct? (45)

(A) The verb *find* should be changed to *will find*.
(B) The verb *have saved* should be changed to *save*.
(C) The verb *have saved* should be changed to *saved*.
(D) No change should be made. The sentence is correct as written.

10. **Read each sentence. Which sentence has too many negatives? (46)**

(A) There isn't no room for any more decals on that car!
(B) I don't think it's possible to count all the decals.
(C) No one knows what that decal stands for.
(D) I would never drive a car covered with ads!

11. Read this sentence.

> My model racecar is ___ than my cousin's new model racecar.

Which choice would complete the sentence correctly? (47)

(A) beautifuler
(B) more beautiful
(C) beautifulest
(D) most beautiful

12. Read this sentence.

> This car uses fuel the ___ of any car I've tested.

Which choice would complete the sentence correctly? (48)

(A) more efficient
(B) more efficiently
(C) most efficient
(D) most efficiently

13. Read this sentence.

> My brother and I bring our car magazines with us on vacation.

Which word in the sentence is an object pronoun? (37)

(A) I
(B) our
(C) magazines
(D) us

Read each item carefully. Fill in the circle next to the best answer.

14. Read each sentence. Look at the underlined word. Which sentence is written *incorrectly*? (38)

(A) Tara and I went to a drag race with her parents.
(B) The noise didn't bother Tara or I.
(C) Tara shared her snack with her parents and me.
(D) She and her parents knew which cars would be the fastest.

15. Read each sentence. Look at the underlined verb. Which sentence is *not* correct? (39)

(A) Drivers in this class learn racing techniques.
(B) The instructor demonstrates the correct position for hands on the steering wheel.
(C) The eyes of a racecar driver looks ahead, to the sides, and in the mirrors.
(D) Any race with other cars requires concentration on the part of the driver.

16. Read each sentence. Look at the underlined verb. Which sentence is *not* correct? (40)

(A) A slick tire is unsafe in wet weather.
(B) An inspection of your tires are a good idea.
(C) Two tires on my car were bald.
(D) Fortunately, a tire sale was in progress.

17. Read this sentence.

In the future, Brian ___ better care of his car.

Which verb would complete the sentence correctly? (41)

(A) will take
(B) takes
(C) took
(D) has taken

18. Read this sentence.

Right now sunlight ___ on the track, but soon dark clouds will darken the sky.

Which verb would complete the sentence correctly? (41)

(A) shines
(B) shine
(C) shone
(D) will shine

19. Read this sentence.

Grandpa ___ a tire when we arrived.

Which verb would complete the sentence correctly? (42)

(A) is changing
(B) are changing
(C) was changing
(D) will be changing

Read each item carefully. Fill in the circle next to the best answer.

20. Read this sentence.

> Aunt Jill _____ an electric car because she wants to reduce her carbon footprint.

Which verb would complete the sentence correctly? **(43)**

(A) had bought
(B) has bought
(C) have bought
(D) will have bought

21. Read this sentence.

> Before yesterday I never _____ in an electric car.

Which verb would complete the sentence correctly? **(44)**

(A) had ridden
(B) has ridden
(C) have ridden
(D) will have ridden

22. Read this sentence.

> Jill read an article about carbon dioxide in the atmosphere, and she decides to buy a zero-emission vehicle.

How should this sentence be changed to make it correct? **(45)**

(A) The verb *read* should be changed to *reads*.
(B) The verb *decides* should be changed to *decide*.
(C) The verb *decides* should be changed to *decided*.
(D) No change should be made. The sentence is correct as written.

23. Read each sentence. Which sentence has too many negatives? **(46)**

(A) I haven't never ridden in such a big car!
(B) I don't think it will fit in our garage.
(C) It isn't easy to drive a big car on a narrow road.
(D) Nobody in our neighborhood owns a car this size.

24. Read this sentence.

> Enrique's soap box racer has the ___ time of all, but he is still proud of it.

Which choice would complete the sentence correctly? **(47)**

(A) slower
(B) more slow
(C) slowest
(D) most slow

25. Read this sentence.

> Clete drives _____ now than he did last year.

Which choice would complete the sentence correctly? **(48)**

(A) more careful
(B) more carefully
(C) most careful
(D) most carefully

TEST TIP: Mark your answers neatly. If you erase, erase completely and clearly without smudging.

(Numbers in parentheses identify related lessons.)

Read each item carefully. Fill in the circle next to the best answer.

1. Read this sentence.

   > What is the largest amphibian alive today!

   How should the sentence be changed to make it correct? (49)

   Ⓐ Change the exclamation point to a period.
   Ⓑ Change the exclamation point to a question mark.
   Ⓒ Make the first letter in amphibian an uppercase letter.
   Ⓓ Make no change. It is correct as written.

2. Read this sentence.

   > The japanese salamander is the largest amphibian on our planet.

   Which underlined word should be capitalized? (50)

   Ⓐ japanese
   Ⓑ salamander
   Ⓒ amphibian
   Ⓓ planet

3. Read this sentence.

   > Mister Niles Eugene Klein teaches us biology.

   How should the underlined name be written with abbreviations? (51)

   Ⓐ Mr N E Klein
   Ⓑ Mstr. n. e. Klein
   Ⓒ Mr. N.E. Klein
   Ⓓ Mstr. N.E. Klein

4. Read this sentence.

   > Soraya borrowed a pair of tough toads, a brand of rain boots, on labor day.

   How should the sentence be changed to make it correct? (52)

   Ⓐ Make the first letters in *rain, boots, labor,* and *day* uppercase letters.
   Ⓑ Make the first letters in *pair, tough, toads, rain,* and *boots* uppercase letters.
   Ⓒ Make the first letters in *tough, toads, labor,* and *day* uppercase letters.
   Ⓓ Make no change. The sentence is correct as written.

5. Read each sentence. Which sentence has the title in it written correctly? (53)

   Ⓐ The book "Prehistoric Amphibians and Their Ancestors" is amazing.
   Ⓑ Have you read the short story called *Don't Pet That Frog*?
   Ⓒ I just saw the movie "Revenge of the Reptiles."
   Ⓓ I am looking for the article titled "Stay Safe Around Snakes."

6. Read each sentence. Look at the underlined word. Which sentence is written *incorrectly*? (54)

   Ⓐ One local park's ponds are filled with frogs.
   Ⓑ Those frog's croaks are loud and deep.
   Ⓒ Frogs are many birds' favorite food.
   Ⓓ Some snakes feed on that park's frogs.

Read each item carefully. Fill in the circle next to the best answer.

7. **Read each sentence. Look at the commas. Which sentence is written correctly? (55)**

   (A) Snakes live on the ground, in trees, and in caves.

   (B) Whiptales, racers, and whipsnakes, are fast-moving reptiles.

   (C) Alligators crocodiles, and caimans are large, dangerous reptiles.

   (D) Snakes have distinctive eyes, tongues, and, tails.

8. **Read this sentence.**

   "Would you like to be a reptile watcher Sandra?" asked Mr. Tran.

   Where should a comma be placed in this sentence? (56)

   (A) after *you*   (C) after *reptile*
   (B) after *be*   (D) after *watcher*

9. **Read this sentence.**

   He told her to bring a notebook and a pencil he warned her to keep a safe distance from any snake she observed.

   Where should a semicolon be placed in this sentence? (57)

   (A) after *notebook*   (C) after *distance*
   (B) after *pencil*   (D) after *snake*

10. **Read each sentence. Which sentence needs to have quotation marks added to it? (58)**

    (A) Ariel said that she saw an Eastern hognose snake yesterday.

    (B) Rich asked her what the snake did when it noticed her.

    (C) It hissed and puffed itself up, Ariel replied.

    (D) She said that the snake then flipped on its back and stuck out its tongue.

11. **Read this sentence.**

    The great explorer and conservationist John Muir wrote "When one tugs at a single thing in nature, he finds it attached to the rest of the world."

    What should be done to make this sentence correct? (59)

    (A) Place a comma between *explorer* and *and*.

    (B) Place a comma between *Muir* and *wrote*.

    (C) Place a comma between *wrote* and the first quotation mark.

    (D) Nothing should be done. The sentence is correct as written.

12. **Read this friendly letter.**

    Dear Amy

    Did you borrow my reptile book? If so, please return it. I need it for the nature hike next weekend.

    Your friend,

    Louis

    Where should a comma be placed to make this letter correct? (60)

    (A) after *Amy* in the greeting
    (B) after *borrow* in the body
    (C) after *your* in the closing
    (D) All of the above

Read each item carefully. Fill in the circle next to the best answer.

13. **Read this sentence.**

> do most amphibians live in moist habitats?

How should the sentence be changed to make it correct? (49)

(A) Change the question mark to an exclamation point.

(B) Change the question mark to a period.

(C) Make the first letter into an uppercase letter.

(D) Make no change. It is correct as written.

14. **Read this sentence.**

> Central <u>america</u>, a warm, humid <u>area</u>, is home to many <u>species</u> of <u>salamanders</u>.

Which underlined word should be capitalized? (50)

(A) america

(B) area

(C) species

(D) salamanders

15. **Read this sentence.**

> I asked <u>Professor Jamal Lester Darby</u> about caecilians.

How should the underlined name be written with abbreviations? (51)

(A) Pro. J L Darby

(B) Prof. JL. Darby

(C) Pro JL Darby

(D) Prof. J.L. Darby

16. **Read this sentence.**

> The cool puddle company of portland, maine, produces rubber sandals called frog clogs.

How should the sentence be changed to make it correct? (52)

(A) Make the first letters in *cool, puddle,* and *company* uppercase letters.

(B) Make the first letters in *cool, puddle, company, portland,* and *maine* uppercase letters.

(C) Make the first letters in *cool, puddle, company, portland, maine, frog,* and *clogs* uppercase letters.

(D) Make no change. The sentence is correct as written.

17. **Read each sentence. Which sentence has the title in it written correctly? (53)**

(A) Larkin taught us the song <u>The Toad on the Road</u>.

(B) The movie titled <u>Jungle Squeeze</u> is about boa constrictors.

(C) "How to Raise Frogs" is a book I will not read.

(D) My poem <u>Turtle Journey</u> is the best one I've written.

18. **Read each sentence. Look at the underlined word. Which sentence is written *incorrectly*? (54)**

(A) An <u>amphibian's</u> skin has no scales.

(B) This <u>newt's</u> skin is smooth.

(C) Those <u>amphibians'</u> glands produce mucus, which covers the skin.

(D) That <u>toads'</u> skin feels like leather.

Read each item carefully. Fill in the circle next to the best answer.

19. Read each sentence. Look at the commas. Which sentence is written correctly? **(55)**

   Ⓐ Snakes, lizards, and iguanas, are reptiles.
   Ⓑ Eastern fence lizards can be seen on rocks, fences, and, trees.
   Ⓒ Many lizards eat tadpoles frogs and small fish.
   Ⓓ Female iguanas have brown, white, and black markings.

20. Read this sentence.

   "Oh every lizard has legs," said Stephanie.

   Where should a comma be placed in this sentence? **(56)**

   Ⓐ after *Oh*   Ⓒ after *lizard*
   Ⓑ after *every*   Ⓓ after *said*

21. Read this sentence.

   "Although it looks like a snake the glass lizard is a lizard that does not have legs," the ranger said to us.

   Where should a comma be placed in this sentence? **(56)**

   Ⓐ after *Although*
   Ⓑ between *lizard* and *is*
   Ⓒ after *snake*
   Ⓓ after *said*

22. Read this sentence.

   Spectacled caimans now live in southern Florida scientists believe they were brought from South America and released.

   Where should a semicolon be placed in this sentence? **(57)**

   Ⓐ after *caimans*   Ⓒ after *brought*
   Ⓑ after *Florida*   Ⓓ after *America*

23. Read each sentence. Which sentence needs to have quotation marks added to it? **(58)**

   Ⓐ Ron asked Kesh to tell him which reptile has the longest tail.
   Ⓑ Kesh said that the saltwater crocodile is the reptile with the longest tail.
   Ⓒ He explained that a large saltwater crocodile's tail can be 13 feet long.
   Ⓓ Ron said, I wonder how big its jaws are.

24. Read this quotation from a text:

   Lorraine Anderson expressed her appreciation of nature by writing, Nature has been, for me, for as long as I remember, a source of solace, inspiration, adventure, and delight; a home, a teacher, a companion.

   Where should quotation marks be placed to make this correct? **(59)**

   Ⓐ before *Lorraine* and after *companion*
   Ⓑ before *expressed* and after *companion*
   Ⓒ before *Nature* and after *companion*
   Ⓓ No quotation marks are needed. The quotation is correct as written.

25. Read this friendly letter.

   Dear Mrs. Elliot,

      I understand that you have a pet iguana. Would it be possible for me to come over and observe it? I am doing a report on that reptile for school.

   Sincerely

   David Jefferson

   In which part of the letter is a comma missing? **(60)**

   Ⓐ the greeting   Ⓒ the closing
   Ⓑ the body   Ⓓ It is correct as written.

Lesson 1 Underline the complete subject in each sentence once. Underline the complete predicate twice.

1. Hot sand covered Zoe's feet.

2. She rested beside a pile of driftwood.

3. This hidden beach was her favorite place.

4. Zoe fell asleep.

5. A noisy sea gull landed at her feet.

6. Someone's radio blasted loud music.

7. Some teenagers set up a volleyball net.

8. A crowd gathered.

9. Everyone cheered the players.

10. A quiet place is hard to find.

Lesson 2 In each sentence, draw one line under the simple subject and two lines under the simple predicate.

1. My alarm rang at 6:30 this morning.

2. I looked out the window.

3. Heavy black clouds threatened rain.

4. I dressed in warm clothes.

5. My father prepared a hot breakfast for everyone.

6. My mother packed an umbrella in my backpack.

7. A crowd waited impatiently for the bus.

8. The first raindrops were huge.

9. My umbrella snapped in the wind.

10. Randy shared his umbrella with me.

Extra Practice

Lesson 3 Each sentence below has either a compound subject or a compound predicate. Write *S* next to each sentence with a compound subject. Circle the two subjects. Write *P* next to each sentence with a compound predicate. Underline the two verbs.

1. The travelers <u>stopped</u> at the edge of the plateau and <u>looked</u> across the desert plain. __P__

2. (Grasses) and (shrubs) grew in clumps. __S__

3. The travelers <u>saw</u> a small oasis and <u>headed</u> in that direction. __P__

4. A (salamander) and a (lizard) slithered across their path. __S__

5. The lizard <u>crawled</u> onto a rock and <u>sat</u> warming itself in the sun. __P__

6. The (boy) and his (father) smiled at each other. __S__

7. The boy <u>grabbed</u> at the lizard and <u>missed</u>. __P__

8. (Trees) and green (grasses) grow in an oasis. __S__

9. The travelers <u>stopped</u> at the oasis and <u>rested</u> for a while. __P__

10. The fresh (water) and cool (shade) attract many travelers. __S__

Lesson 4 Circle the direct object in each sentence below.

1. The diver stretched her (muscles).

2. The announcer called her (name).

3. Her parents watched their (daughter) anxiously.

4. She quickly climbed the (ladder).

5. She focused her (concentration).

6. She executed the (dive) perfectly.

7. She entered the (water) smoothly.

8. The announcer called out a perfect (score).

9. The diver's fans clapped their (hands).

10. The girl hugged her (parents).

Lesson 5 The direct object in each sentence is printed in bold type. Circle the indirect object in each sentence.

1. Bif sent his (cousin) a **bag** of marbles.

2. His cousin sent (Bif) a thank you **note**.

3. She also sent (Bif) an **invitation** to her birthday party.

4. Bif's father gave (him) **permission** to drive to the party.

5. He mailed his (cousin) a **postcard** saying he could come.

6. Bif's mother handed (him) the **keys** to the car.

7. He gave his (family) one last **wave** and headed for Spokane.

8. He handed the (toll taker) a five dollar **bill** and waited for change.

9. When Bif arrived, his cousin gave (him) a big **hug**.

10. At the party Bif sang his (cousin) a special birthday **song** he wrote for her.

Lesson 6 Draw a box around the linking verb in each sentence. Then circle each boldfaced word that is a predicate noun. Underline each boldfaced word that is a predicate adjective.

1. Martin Luther King Jr. [was] an important (leader) of the civil rights movement in the United States.

2. He [was] a Baptist (minister).

3. He [was] the (leader) of a bus boycott in Montgomery, Alabama, in 1955–1956.

4. Dr. King's demonstrations [were] **nonviolent**.

5. Some Montgomery residents [were] **angry** about segregation.

6. The boycott [was] **successful** in ending segregated seating on public buses.

7. Dr. King [was] an eloquent (speaker).

8. His "I Have a Dream" speech [is] still an (inspiration).

9. Dr. King's assassination in 1968 [was] **tragic**.

10. People across the United States [were] **upset** by his death.

Lesson 7 Underline the prepositional phrase in each sentence. Circle the preposition that begins the prepositional phrase.

1. It had rained (for) 11 days.

2. Water gushed (into) creeks and streams.

3. We went (to) the river's edge.

4. The river carried huge logs (in) its current.

5. Many river residents spent the night (in) hotels.

6. We listened (to) the radio report.

7. The flood waters crested (at) midnight.

8. The next day, many people returned (to) their homes.

9. Our house had thick mud (on) the floor.

10. Perhaps we should move (to) higher ground.

Lesson 8 Write *S* next to each simple sentence and *C* next to each compound sentence. Then circle each conjunction or semicolon in each compound sentence.

1. Danny and Alicia went rafting on the Colorado River. __S__

2. The first day the water was calm, (and) Danny and Alicia enjoyed the scenery. __C__

3. At night they camped along the river bank, (and) the guides made a delicious dinner. __C__

4. The next morning the weather had turned cloudy. __S__

5. The river still looked calm, (but) the guides warned of dangerous rapids ahead. __C__

6. The rafters entered a very difficult part of the river. __S__

7. The raft shot past huge boulders and down small waterfalls(;) Danny and Alicia held on tightly. __C__

8. The wild roller-coaster ride lasted only 30 seconds, (but) it was long enough for them. __C__

9. Finally the raft reached calmer waters(;) everyone breathed a sigh of relief. __C__

10. Danny and Alicia loved the experience. __S__

Lesson 9 Each sentence below has one independent clause and one dependent clause. Draw one line under each independent clause and two lines under each dependent clause. Then circle the subordinating conjunction that begins each dependent clause.

1. Many people don't visit the desert (because) they are worried about its intense heat.

2. (If) you take proper precautions, you can enjoy a desert vacation.

3. (Because) summer heat is quite intense, you should plan your trip for the spring or fall.

4. (Because) it is hottest at noon, you should begin your desert exploration in the morning.

5. (After) the sun has set, the desert air grows cooler.

6. (As) the temperature drops, nocturnal animals come out in search of food.

7. (Although) most desert creatures are harmless, you must be cautious in open terrain.

8. Startled rattlesnakes sometimes attack, (though) they generally avoid people.

9. (When) you hike in the desert, you should always carry a snake-bite kit.

10. A desert vacation can be fun and safe (when) you put safety first.

Lesson 10 Write *CX* next to each complex sentence. Underline the dependent clause.

1. Although we've been to the park many times, we never get tired of it. ___**CX**___

2. My favorite ride is the roller coaster, but I also enjoy the Ferris wheel. _____

3. Liz does not like these rides because she is afraid of heights. ___**CX**___

4. While I fly high in the sky, she takes a spin on the merry-go-round. ___**CX**___

5. This ride is a hundred years old, and its horses are beautifully carved. _____

6. It is the most popular attraction in the park. _____

7. After we have lunch at the hotdog stand, we usually get ice cream. ___**CX**___

8. Then we ride the bumper cars, or we play some games. _____

9. I am especially good at the ring toss and at throwing darts. _____

10. When the sun begins to set, we head home tired but happy. ___**CX**___

Lesson 11 Circle the first word in each boldfaced dependent clause. Write *RP* if it is a relative pronoun. Write *RA* if it is a relative adverb.

1. The annual hiking trip is an event (that) our class looks forward to. ___RP___

2. We travel by bus to a park (where) there are several different habitats. ___RA___

3. We come across forests, prairies, and wetlands (when) we hike. ___RA___

4. Mrs. Jensen, (who) is a wildlife expert, points out many animals. ___RP___

5. She knows all the places (where) birds, deer, and snakes like to hide. ___RA___

6. She can also identify tracks, (which) is a good way to find animals. ___RP___

7. One counselor, Mr. Bates, is a botanist (who) knows all about plants. ___RP___

8. He takes us to a meadow (where) there are several kinds of wildflowers. ___RA___

9. He reminds us not to pick the flowers (when) we are in a state park. ___RA___

10. It is important not to disturb plants (that) grow naturally in a habitat. ___RP___

Lesson 12 Write *F* next to each fragment, *RO* next to each run-on sentence, and *CS* next to each comma splice.

1. While driving across Montana one dry summer. ___F___

2. We saw a herd of buffalo, we were amazed. ___CS___

3. In 1889 only 551 buffalo remained in the United States most had been killed by hunters. ___RO___

4. Extinction of the entire species. ___F___

5. Today more than fifteen thousand buffalo. ___F___

6. Most live on game preserves some run wild in national parks. ___RO___

7. The buffalo we saw in Montana lived on a private ranch, they are raised for meat. ___CS___

8. I have never eaten buffalo stew I'd like to try it. ___RO___

9. The animals we saw are called American bison, most people call them buffalo. ___CS___

10. These powerful, majestic animals. ___F___

Lesson 13 Circle the common nouns. Underline the proper nouns.

1. Langley Park is always crowded on (holidays).

2. The (fireworks) attract (people) on the Fourth of July.

3. The Smiths arrive early at the (park).

4. Janis and Nestor play (baseball).

5. Savannah practices (karate).

6. The outdoor (pool) opens in May.

7. My (brother) won the Best Swimmer Award.

8. His (strength) has helped make him the best (swimmer) in Nashville.

9. Labor Day signals that (summer) is over.

10. In September, we go back to (school).

Lesson 14 First put a box around each noun that is both plural and possessive. For the remaining nouns, underline each plural noun and circle each possessive noun.

1. The dancers practiced for the Lunar New Year for many months.

2. Volunteers sewed the ornate red costumes.

3. The (group's) leader gave the signal to drum loudly.

4. The firecrackers' smoke filled the air.

5. The women's movements were graceful.

6. Boys and girls crowded closer to see the dancing lions.

7. One father tried to hush his (baby's) cries.

8. The lions' heads seemed to roar.

9. Several photographers ran out in front of the crowd.

10. Then the acrobats' performance began.

Lesson 15 Read each sentence. Circle the boldfaced word that is the type of noun listed in parentheses.

1. "I can't think of a **topic** for my personal (**essay**)," complained Iris. (concrete noun)

2. "Have some (**patience**). It will come to you," her **father** replied. (abstract noun)

3. "My mind is blank. I have no (**ideas**)!" Iris said with a **frown**. (abstract noun)

4. "You could write about being in the school (**choir**)," her **father** said. (collective noun)

5. "Describe the (**joy**) you feel when you sing that **song**," he suggested. (abstract noun)

6. Iris considered the **idea**, but then she shook her (**head**). (concrete noun)

7. "I'd rather write a **paper** about joining the basketball (**team**)," she said. (collective noun)

8. "I have good (**memories**) of winning the championship **trophy**," she added. (abstract noun)

9. "Yes, remember the (**crowd**) that came to cheer you on?" her **father** asked. (collective noun)

10. "I think I have an **idea**!" Iris said as she picked up her (**pencil**). (concrete noun)

Lesson 16 Write a pronoun from the word bank that could take the place of the underlined word or phrase in each sentence. Remember to capitalize a word that begins a sentence.

her	him	he	she	they	them	we

1. <u>Kate</u> always sings off key. ____**She**____

2. Kate's brothers and sisters complain about <u>Kate's</u> singing. ____**her**____

3. <u>Nora, Emily, Carl, and Matt</u> asked for ear plugs. ____**They**____

4. "<u>Your father and I</u> enjoy her singing," their mother replied. ____**We**____

5. "Then you share a room with her!" <u>Nora and Emily</u> said. ____**they**____

6. Kate's music teacher encouraged her to practice with <u>Luisa and Dawn</u>. ____**them**____

7. On the day of the spring concert <u>Kate's</u> family sat in the front row. ____**her**____

8. <u>Mr. Higashi</u> gave a welcoming speech to the students and guests. ____**He**____

9. A baby girl screamed happily at <u>Mr. Higashi</u>. ____**him**____

10. "<u>That baby</u> will be a member of our chorus someday!" said Mr. Higashi with a smile. ____**She**____

Lesson 17 The verb in each sentence is underlined. Circle each action verb. Draw a box around each linking verb.

1. The Baltimore and Ohio [is] one of the oldest railroads in the United States.

2. In the 1820s, cities (needed) ways to transport goods around the country.

3. Some (constructed) waterways for shipping called canals.

4. Baltimore (started) a rail line to the Ohio River in 1828.

5. Until 1830, most trains [were] horse-drawn vehicles.

6. Then a new steam-powered train [became] a common sight on the tracks.

7. In August 1830, this steam locomotive (carried) passengers to Ellicott's Mills.

8. The passengers [were] speechless when they sped along at 15 miles per hour.

9. According to legend, a horse-drawn car (raced) the train back to Baltimore.

10. Because of a broken part on the locomotive, the horse [was] the winner.

Lesson 18 Circle the main verb in each sentence. Underline the helping verb.

1. Many creative pieces <u>were</u> (displayed) at the student art show.

2. Anna's oil paintings <u>were</u> (framed) for the event.

3. Other landscapes <u>were</u> (hung) on the wall next to them.

4. Visitors <u>could</u> (see) Gus and Maria's clay vases.

5. They <u>were</u> (dried) in the big kiln in the art room.

6. Colin <u>has</u> (carved) little birds and mice out of wood for years.

7. His animals <u>were</u> (arranged) on a table near the front.

8. Lance's picture of his sister <u>was</u> (drawn) with charcoal.

9. It <u>has</u> (received) a special prize for the best piece at the show.

10. All the talented student artists <u>should</u> (take) a bow!

Lesson 19 Underline the modal auxiliary in parentheses that best completes each sentence.

1. Now that the rink is open for the winter, we (can/must) finally skate!

2. If you cannot find your ice skates, you (can/may) borrow my sister's.

3. I (must/can) ask for her permission first, of course.

4. We (could/must) go skating on Friday after school or on Saturday morning.

5. My mom (may/can) drive you if you do not have a ride.

6. Mom says you (could/should) tell your parents where you are going to be.

7. Do you think the skating rink (might/must) be really crowded?

8. I know it will be cold, so I (can/will) wear a hat and gloves.

9. I (may/must) even wear my new wool sweater with the snowflakes on it.

10. You (should/could) make sure to dress warmly as well.

Lesson 20 Underline each adjective (including *a, an,* and *the*) in the sentences below.

1. Sam has a small, shady garden.

2. Three golden carp swim in a pond.

3. The cat stares at them with sharp eyes.

4. Many flowers bloom in pots.

5. Some flowers are white and blue; others are yellow and red.

6. Butterflies land on the tall grass.

7. Sam digs in the dark, moist earth.

8. Slimy earthworms curl into tiny balls.

9. Hungry robins dive at the slithery worms.

10. Sam enjoys this tiny garden.

Lesson 21 Circle the adverb that describes each underlined word.

1. The alarm clock <u>rang</u> (noisily) in my ear.

2. I (quickly) <u>rose</u> and dressed myself.

3. I (carefully) <u>checked</u> the departure time on my airline ticket.

4. Planes (rarely) <u>wait</u> for tardy passengers.

5. My cat <u>watched</u> (sadly) as I ate breakfast.

6. The taxi driver <u>honked</u> the horn (impatiently).

7. He <u>drove</u> (fast), and I held my breath and closed my eyes.

8. When the driver stopped the taxi, I (cautiously) <u>opened</u> my eyes.

9. I paid him and <u>tipped</u> him (generously).

10. I <u>walked</u> (directly) to the ticket counter and checked my baggage.

Lesson 22 Write the adjectives in parentheses in the correct order in each sentence.

1. Wyatt saw _____**seventy antique**_____ cars at the car show. (antique, seventy)

2. The _____**five boxy black**_____ cars were from the 1920s. (black, five, boxy)

3. The _____**large curvy**_____ cars were made in the 1940s. (large, curvy)

4. A 1950s station wagon had _____**smooth wooden**_____ panels. (wooden, smooth)

5. He really liked the _____**sporty red**_____ cars from the 1960s. (sporty, red)

6. Some were convertibles with _____**dark canvas**_____ tops. (canvas, dark)

7. They also had _____**shiny silver**_____ wheels. (silver, shiny)

8. The _____**giant rectangular**_____ cars from the 1970s were like boats. (rectangular, giant)

9. Many were painted a _____**dull green**_____ color. (dull, green)

10. _____**Three small colorful**_____ cars had been used for racing. (small, colorful, three)

Lesson 23 Underline each coordinating conjunction. Circle each subordinating conjunction.

1. Tyler <u>and</u> Zoe decided to make homemade pizza.

2. They usually buy it at Giorgio's <u>or</u> the Hopkins Cafe.

3. They thought it would be easy to make, <u>but</u> they weren't sure how to make the crust.

4. (Although) Tyler is an experienced cook, he wanted to follow a recipe.

5. (If) the pizza turned out badly, they would be very disappointed.

6. One cookbook had recipes for pineapple pizza <u>and</u> pesto pizza.

7. (Because) Zoe loves pineapple, it was an easy choice.

8. They put the pizza in the oven <u>and</u> turned on their favorite TV show.

9. (While) they watched TV, the pizza baked.

10. (Before) they tasted the pizza, they let it cool.

Lesson 24 Underline the pair of correlative conjunctions in each sentence.

1. <u>Neither</u> Ryan <u>nor</u> Gina made it to school today.

2. They <u>not only</u> are suffering from coughs <u>but also</u> have fevers.

3. Tonight's play must go on, <u>whether</u> they recover <u>or</u> cannot perform.

4. Ross is <u>both</u> ready <u>and</u> willing to stand in for Ryan.

5. He <u>not only</u> knows Ryan's part <u>but also</u> has rehearsed it a few times.

6. Replacing Ryan at the last minute is <u>both</u> scary <u>and</u> exciting.

7. Mr. Suarez thinks <u>either</u> Jill <u>or</u> Becca could stand in for Gina.

8. Gina's role is <u>neither</u> large <u>nor</u> difficult to learn.

9. Tonight's performance will <u>either</u> go smoothly <u>or</u> have some flaws.

10. Whatever happens, Mr. Suarez will be <u>both</u> proud <u>and</u> nervous.

Extra Practice

Lesson 25 Underline the word in parentheses that will correctly complete each sentence.

1. "Emi and her brother are going to Colorado for (<u>their</u>/there/they're) vacation," Kris said.

2. "I've never been (their/<u>there</u>/they're)," she added enviously.

3. "How are they getting (their/<u>there</u>/they're)?" asked Luis.

4. "(Their/There/<u>They're</u>) flying and then renting a car at the Denver airport," Kris replied.

5. "Do they need someone to water (<u>their</u>/there/they're) plants?" Luis asked.

6. "I live near (<u>their</u>/there/they're) house, so I could do it," he went on.

7. "I hope (their/there/<u>they're</u>) planning to take a lot of pictures," said Kris.

8. "Have you seen the pictures from (<u>their</u>/there/they're) trip to Georgia?" asked Luis.

9. "(Their/There/<u>They're</u>) lucky to be able to travel so much," sighed Kris.

10. "I don't envy (<u>their</u>/there/they're) travels. I like it here at home," said Luis.

Lesson 26 Write *its* or *it's* on the line to complete each sentence correctly. Remember to capitalize a word that begins a sentence.

1. "_____**It's**_____ called a tarantula," said Mr. Muñoz, holding up the large, hairy spider for the class to see.

2. "It makes _____**its**_____ home in warm areas around the world," he continued.

3. "_____**It's**_____ as big as my fist!" exclaimed Carlos.

4. "If you think this species is big, you should see the bird spider, which can spread _____**its**_____ legs about seven inches," said the teacher.

5. "_____**It's**_____ scary looking!" said Darrell.

6. "_____**It's**_____ really very friendly," said Mr. Muñoz, letting the spider walk up his arm.

7. "_____**Its**_____ bite can kill you!" shouted Alicia.

8. "_____**Its**_____ bite was once believed to cause a disease called *tarantism*," Mr. Muñoz explained.

9. "In reality, _____**it's**_____ no more dangerous than a bee," he continued.

10. "There's an Australian tarantula that's much more dangerous than this one," he added. _____**It's**_____ one of a group of tarantulas called *funnel-webs*."

Lesson 27 Write *your* or *you're* to complete each sentence correctly. Remember to capitalize a word that begins a sentence.

1. "Evie, may I borrow _____**your**_____ bike today?" asked Jason.

2. "Sure," said Evie, "but if _____**you're**_____ going to the park, be sure to lock it up."

3. "_____**You're**_____ late," Juan called when Jason arrived.

4. "Do you want me to play on _____**your**_____ team or on Dean's team?" Jason asked.

5. "_____**You're**_____ going to play on my team," answered Juan.

6. "_____**You're**_____ playing well today," Juan said when Jason caught his second fly ball.

7. "_____**Your**_____ advice about staying on my toes has really helped," Jason responded.

8. After reviewing the lineup, Juan told Jason, "_____**You're**_____ up third, so get ready."

9. "_____**You're**_____ up at bat next," Juan said.

10. "Keep _____**your**_____ eye on the ball!" he yelled.

Lesson 28 Underline the word in parentheses that correctly completes each sentence.

1. My sister thinks that birds make the (best/goodest) pets.

2. I like dogs much (better/gooder) than birds.

3. Dogs are (better/gooder) at playing games than birds.

4. My dog Lucy used to be the (worsest/worst) behaved dog in the world.

5. I took her to obedience school, and her behavior became (gooder/better).

6. Now Lucy is the (best/goodest) student in the class!

7. She's getting (better/gooder) at following my commands.

8. My sister used to complain that Lucy's fur made her allergies (worse/worser).

9. Spring is the (worsest/worst) time of year for allergies.

10. Having a dog in the house does make some people's allergies (worse/worser).

Extra Practice

Lesson 29 Write *who, which,* or *that* in the blank to complete each sentence correctly.

1. Halloween, __which__ takes place on October 31st, is my favorite holiday.

2. It's fun for children, __who__ get to dress up in costumes.

3. I like to wear costumes __that__ are wild and original.

4. My mother, __who__ is an artist, usually makes my costumes for me.

5. Last year I wore a dragon costume __that__ had a long tail and glittering scales.

6. My brother, __who__ is older than I, takes me trick-or-treating with him.

7. We only eat treats __that__ come wrapped in packages.

8. Last year my neighbor transformed her garage into a haunted house __that__ was very scary.

9. It had fake skeletons __that__ popped out from dark corners.

10. On Halloween night, my brother and I ate several pieces of candy, __which__ made me feel a little bit ill.

Lesson 30 Circle the word in parentheses that correctly completes each sentence.

1. My sister DeShawn is a (very/real) good horseback rider.

2. When my parents offered to pay for horseback riding lessons, she was (very/real) excited.

3. She showed (very/real) talent at the sport, even as a beginner.

4. She could ride horses that were usually (very/real) skittish with other riders.

5. She also practiced (very/real) hard.

6. DeShawn's riding instructor thought she could be a (very/real) champion someday, so she spent extra hours coaching her.

7. We were all (very/real) proud of DeShawn the day she won her first blue ribbon at a horse show.

8. Now she lives on a (very/real) horse farm and raises horses.

9. She is (very/real) lucky to be able to do something she loves.

10. I feel (very/real) happy whenever she asks me to visit.

Extra Practice

Extra Practice

Lesson 31 Write the correct form of *sit* or *set* in each blank.

1. When I got home from school, I ____set____ my backpack down on the kitchen table.

2. After getting myself a snack, I ____sat____ down at the table and pulled out my homework assignment.

3. "Jaime, can you please ____sit____ somewhere else?" Mom asked.

4. I took my belongings up to my room, ____set____ them on my desk, and tried to start my homework again.

5. A little while later, my mother called, "Jaime, please come help me ____set____ the table."

6. I carefully ____set____ eight dinner plates around the table.

7. Then I ____set____ the napkins, knives, forks, and spoons in their proper places.

8. Just then my father came home and ____set____ a bag of groceries on the counter.

9. Mom ____set____ the food on the table while Dad put the groceries away.

10. Finally, we all ____sat____ down and ate.

Lesson 32 Underline the word in parentheses that correctly completes each sentence.

1. Last summer my father took my sister to the pool to (learn/<u>teach</u>) her how to swim.

2. "First, I'm going to (learn/<u>teach</u>) you how to float on your back," he said to her.

3. My sister soon (<u>learned</u>/taught) that she could float without sinking.

4. After a few days he told her, "Now I'm going to (learn/<u>teach</u>) you some basic strokes."

5. First, he (learned/<u>taught</u>) her how to do the crawl.

6. "You need to (<u>learn</u>/teach) how to move your head correctly when you breathe," he said.

7. "When am I going to (<u>learn</u>/teach) how to dive?" my sister asked him.

8. "I'll (learn/<u>teach</u>) you to dive after you've learned how to swim well," he answered.

9. After that, my sister practiced hard and (<u>learned</u>/taught) her basic strokes very quickly.

10. By the end of the summer, my dad said she was ready to (<u>learn</u>/teach) how to do a swan dive.

Lesson 33 Circle the word in parentheses that best completes each sentence.

1. Kamika and I will get up early (**to**/two/too) make muffins for breakfast.

2. The recipe will yield over (to/**two**/too) dozen blueberry muffins.

3. We will need (to/**two**/too) cups of flour, milk, and eggs.

4. Is this bowl (to/two/**too**) small to mix all the ingredients?

5. Kamika will go out (**to**/two/too) the backyard and pick the blueberries.

6. She will wash them and fold them into the batter, (to/two/**too**).

7. The muffins will bake for at least thirty-(to/**two**/too) minutes.

8. We will be careful not to leave them in the oven (to/two/**too**) long.

9. They will still be warm when we bring them (**to**/two/too) the table.

10. I think I will eat at least (to/**two**/too) of these delicious treats.

Lesson 34 Underline the word in parentheses that correctly completes each sentence.

1. My aunt (<u>knew</u>/known) she wanted to be a policewoman when she was just a little girl.

2. "All my girlfriends wanted to be ballerinas or nurses when they (<u>grew</u>/grown) up," she said to me last week.

3. "I (<u>knew</u>/known) I did not want to dance or work in a hospital," she added.

4. She (<u>grew</u>/grown) up during a time when women didn't have as many job opportunities as they do today.

5. Many people she (<u>knew</u>/known) tried to discourage her from becoming a police officer.

6. "Luckily," she said, "I had (knew/<u>known</u>) several women who had interesting careers."

7. "I also (<u>grew</u>/grown) up in a family that encouraged me to follow my dreams," she added.

8. "I (<u>knew</u>/known) that being a girl wouldn't stop me from doing what I wanted to do," my aunt continued.

9. "You have (grew/<u>grown</u>) up in a time in which it's more acceptable for women to work in a variety of jobs," she told me.

10. I have (knew/<u>known</u>) many helpful people, but my aunt is the one who has encouraged me the most.

Lesson 35 Read the boldfaced pronoun in each sentence. Write *RF* if it is a reflexive pronoun. Write *IN* if it is an indefinite pronoun.

1. "I think we can teach **ourselves** how to surf," said Brad. ____RF____

2. "It looks so simple that **anyone** can do it," he exclaimed. ____IN____

3. "We should find **somebody** who can give us lessons," I warned. ____IN____

4. Keeping balanced on a surfboard is not easy for **everyone**. ____IN____

5. "You could hurt **yourself** if you don't know the right technique," I said. ____RF____

6. "I guess there might be **something** an expert can show us," Brad replied. ____IN____

7. "I would not want to make a fool of **myself** at the beach," he said with a laugh. ____RF____

8. "Yes, and **nothing** is more important than being safe," I said. ____IN____

9. I did not want Brad to get **himself** in trouble out in the water. ____RF____

10. "So, do you know **someone** who can teach us how to surf?" asked Brad. ____IN____

Lesson 36 Circle the antecedent or antecedents of each boldfaced pronoun.

1. The campers were ready for the annual canoe (race). Any minute now **it** would begin.

2. Five (canoes) were at the starting line. **They** surged forward at the sound of the whistle.

3. At first, (Lisa) and (Andre) were in the lead. One by one the other teams passed **them**.

4. The blue (canoe) did not stay long enough in the race. **It** tipped over, and its paddlers had to pull the canoe ashore.

5. The (lake) was calm and smooth. The only waves on **it** were created by the racers.

6. (Germaine) and (Jody) were in the red canoe. **They** had won last year, and many people thought they would win again.

7. (Lloyd) and (Veronica) were way ahead of the others. The crowd of campers cheered **them** on.

8. The finish (line) was still many yards away. Who would cross **it** first?

9. Suddenly, (Germaine) and (Jody) began catching up. **They** paddled hard until they had passed Lloyd and Veronica.

10. The red canoe crossed the finish line first. (Germaine) and (Jody) clapped and cheered as **they** floated toward the shore.

Lesson 37 Circle each boldfaced word that is a subject pronoun. Underline each boldfaced word that is an object pronoun.

1. Yesterday (I) helped my grandmother clean out her attic. (It) was full of interesting things.

2. My grandfather died a long time ago. (We) found an old photo of **him**.

3. (He) was wearing a naval uniform in the picture, and he looked handsome to **us**.

4. Grandmother gave the photo to **me**. (She) said she had another copy in her album.

5. (We) dragged a huge trunk out from behind some boxes. Inside **it** (we) found a pile of old-fashioned clothes.

6. (They) had plastic wrapped around **them**. (They) were perfectly preserved.

7. There was a kimono my grandfather had brought back with **him** from Japan. (He) visited Asia in the 1970s.

8. (I) unwrapped a beautiful blue evening gown that had been my grandmother's. I asked **her** if she would try it on.

9. (She) laughed and said that none of the dresses would fit **her** anymore.

10. We wrapped up the dresses and put **them** back in the trunk. Grandmother said that when (I) was big enough, they would belong to **me**.

Lesson 38 Circle the correct pronoun in each pair.

1. Laney and (me/(I)) made a treasure hunt for my little brother and sister.

2. We drew chalk maps on the sidewalk for him and (she/(her)) to follow.

3. My little sister is a good treasure hunter, so Laney and ((I)/me) had to make her clues hard.

4. My little brother is only four, so I helped (he/(him)) with the clues.

5. ((He)/Him) and I walked all over the yard, following clues.

6. My little sister and Laney worked as a team, competing against my brother and ((me)/I).

7. When my brother and sister got close to the treasure, Laney and (me/(I)) stopped helping.

8. They begged Laney and ((me)/I) to give away the last few clues, but we held firm.

9. Finally, she and (him/(he)) decided to help each other find the treasure.

10. They thanked Laney and ((me)/I) when they found out that the treasure was a big bag of popcorn.

Lesson 39 Underline the correct form of each verb in parentheses. Make sure the verb agrees with the subject.

1. In the south of France farmers (<u>grow</u>/grows) flowers for French perfume.

2. The Battle of the Flowers (take/<u>takes</u>) place there every February.

3. This twelve-day festival (include/<u>includes</u>) a parade through the city of Nice.

4. The people of Nice (<u>build</u>/builds) beautiful floats for the parade.

5. They (<u>use</u>/uses) flowers to decorate the floats.

6. Many Battles of the Flowers (<u>occur</u>/occurs) during the festival.

7. Each battle (last/<u>lasts</u>) all afternoon.

8. People (<u>bring</u>/brings) lots of flowers to the battle.

9. At the signal, everyone (throw/<u>throws</u>) flowers at one another.

10. Soon, colored petals (<u>cover</u>/covers) the ground.

Lesson 40 Underline the correct form of *be* in each sentence.

1. Traffic lights (is/<u>are</u>) an important safety device.

2. Before the invention of the traffic signal in the early 1920s, drivers (was/<u>were</u>) free to cross an intersection at any time. This caused accidents.

3. Garrett Morgan (<u>was</u>/were) an African American inventor.

4. His electric traffic signal system (<u>was</u>/were) the first of its kind.

5. One day Morgan saw a traffic accident in which several people (was/<u>were</u>) hurt.

6. Morgan (<u>was</u>/were) certain that he could improve traffic safety.

7. The modern traffic light system (<u>is</u>/are) only slightly different from Morgan's original system.

8. Today, this system (<u>is</u>/are) in operation all over the world.

9. Motorists everywhere (is/<u>are</u>) familiar with the traffic signal.

10. Driving (<u>is</u>/are) safer because of Morgan's invention.

Lesson 41 The verb in each sentence is boldfaced. Circle each present tense verb. Underline each past tense verb. Draw a box around each future tense verb.

1. Electric cars (use) energy stored in batteries instead of gasoline.

2. Many early cars <u>were</u> actually electric cars.

3. But gasoline-powered cars <u>became</u> popular in the early 1900s.

4. American companies <u>produced</u> them in large numbers.

5. They <u>remained</u> our car of choice for decades.

6. Critics (see) several problems with gasoline-powered cars, however.

7. Some day we [will run out] of the natural resources used to make gasoline.

8. And our cars' fumes (make) the air very dirty.

9. Electric cars (are) now ready to make a comeback.

10. They [will provide] a clean, reliable option for drivers for years to come.

Lesson 42 The verb in each sentence is boldfaced. Circle each present progressive verb. Underline each past progressive verb. Draw a box around each future progressive verb.

1. Aiden (is starting) a book club with a few of his friends.

2. They [will be meeting] every Saturday afternoon at three o'clock.

3. Aiden <u>was hoping</u> they could meet at the library, but it didn't work out.

4. Now he (is thinking) about inviting everyone to his house instead.

5. All the members [will be deciding] which books to read together.

6. Aiden (is trusting) that everyone will finish reading on time!

7. He <u>was expecting</u> that they'd begin with a novel, but they chose a play.

8. Although he prefers nonfiction, Aiden (is enjoying) the play.

9. He (is trying) his best to understand the characters and the theme.

10. He [will be leading] Saturday's discussion, so he must be prepared.

Lesson 43 Complete each sentence by writing the present perfect form of the verb (*has* or *have* plus the past participle) in parentheses. Watch for irregular verbs!

1. Jessie _____ **has flown** _____ model airplanes since she was eight. (fly)

2. Her dad _____ **has loved** _____ model airplanes since he was a little boy. (love)

3. Their neighbors _____ **have asked** _____ them how to fly model planes. (ask)

4. Jessie's mom _____ **has packed** _____ a picnic lunch for the flying lesson. (pack)

5. "I _____ **have heard** _____ that it may rain this morning," Jessie's mom warned. (hear)

6. "It _____ **has rained** _____ every Saturday!" Jessie complained. (rain)

7. "You _____ **have waited** _____ a long time to fly your plane," her father said. (wait)

8. "The neighbors _____ **have left** _____ for the park already," her mother said. (leave)

9. "Everyone _____ **has wanted** _____ to do this for a long time," Jessie pointed out. (want)

10. "I _____ **have reached** _____ my decision," Jessie's mother said. "Let's go!" (reach)

Lesson 44 Write the form of the verb that is described in parentheses to correctly complete each sentence.

1. Mai _____ **had finished** _____ her homework by four o'clock. (past perfect of *finish*)

2. She _____ **had walked** _____ our dog Fluffy as well. (past perfect of *walk*)

3. By dinnertime, she _____ **had cleaned** _____ her room. (past perfect of *clean*)

4. I _____ **had completed** _____ only my math worksheet. (past perfect of *complete*)

5. I _____ **had arrived** _____ home late from soccer practice. (past perfect of *arrive*)

6. By bedtime, Mai _____ **will have sent** _____ several e-mails. (future perfect of *send*)

7. She _____ **will have played** _____ her flute for an hour. (future perfect of *play*)

8. She _____ **will have watched** _____ a video on the computer. (future perfect of *watch*)

9. I _____ **will have failed** _____ to write my book report. (future perfect of *fail*)

10. Mai _____ **will have worked** _____ harder than I have again! (future perfect of *work*)

Lesson 45 Read each sentence. Are all the verb tenses correct, or is there an incorrect verb tense shift? Write *X* if the sentence contains an incorrect verb tense.

1. When Jeff's dog Cindy ran away, he loses all hope of finding her. __X__

2. Cindy had been missing for two days, and no one had seen her. _____

3. Jeff felt terrible because he is not watching her carefully at the park. __X__

4. He had looked away only a minute, but she still will disappear. __X__

5. His dad suggested that he put up flyers, but Jeff thought it was no use. _____

6. Just when Jeff believed the worst, he gets a call from a neighbor. __X__

7. The man had found Cindy while he is jogging near the park! __X__

8. Jeff was overjoyed, and he thanked the man over and over. _____

9. Now Jeff is not so hopeless when something bad happened. __X__

10. He believes that things will usually turn out fine in the end. _____

Lesson 46 Write *X* next to each sentence with two negative expressions. Then, on another sheet of paper, rewrite these sentences correctly. **Possible answers appear below. Accept all reasonable responses.**

1. "I haven't seen nothing that looks familiar for hours," David told Geena. __X__
    "I haven't seen anything that looks familiar for hours," David told Geena.

2. "I haven't never been so lost in my life," Geena agreed. __X__
    "I have never been so lost in my life," Geena agreed.

3. "This wouldn't have happened if we had paid more attention to the road signs," David said.

4. "There isn't no reason to panic," Geena told David. __X__
    "There isn't any reason to panic," Geena told David.

5. "I've never seen anyone look so confused," a police officer said to David.

6. "We didn't bring no map with us," David told the officer. __X__
    "We didn't bring a map with us," David told the officer.

7. The officer told them not to have no worries. __X__
    The officer told them not to have any worries.

8. "It won't take long to drive you back to your campsite," he said.

9. Police officers don't usually let no pedestrians ride in their police cars. __X__
    Police officers don't usually let pedestrians ride in their police cars.

10. Geena and David had never ridden in no real police car before, and they accepted the offer. __X__
    Geena and David had never ridden in a real police car before, and they accepted the offer.

Lesson 47 Underline the correct form of the adjective in parentheses.

1. Liza's dance troupe performed the (more creative/<u>most creative</u>) dance I have ever seen.

2. They combined ballet and gymnastics into a slow, balancing dance that was (most beautiful/<u>more beautiful</u>) than ballet alone.

3. Liza had designed the costumes, using the (lighter/<u>lightest</u>) fabric she could find.

4. The costumes flowed over the dancers' muscles, making them look (<u>more graceful</u>/gracefuler) than dancers in traditional leotards.

5. The music for their dance was (slowest/<u>slower</u>) than the music for the other dances.

6. Mia, the (<u>smallest</u>/smaller) girl in the whole company, amazed everyone.

7. She proved she was (strongest/<u>stronger</u>) than people thought by holding two dancers on her shoulders.

8. At the end of the piece, the applause was the (louder/<u>loudest</u>) I have ever heard.

9. Liza's dance troupe was definitely (<u>better</u>/best) than the other dance troupe.

10. They may be the (better/<u>best</u>) dance troupe in the city!

Lesson 48 Underline the correct form of the adverb.

1. Of all the swimmers at the starting line, Ellen waited the (<u>most nervously</u>/more nervously).

2. She had trained (hardest/<u>harder</u>) for this race than she had for any other race.

3. Ellen dove (<u>more swiftly</u>/most swiftly) than the swimmer next to her.

4. After falling behind in the first lap, Ellen came out of the turn (<u>more quickly</u>/most quickly) than any other swimmer in the race.

5. Her arms pulled her through the water, and soon she was swimming (<u>more smoothly</u>/most smoothly) than she had in the first lap.

6. Ellen's arms got tired (most easily/<u>more easily</u>) than her legs.

7. Still, she kept stroking (most persistently/<u>more persistently</u>) than she had in any other race.

8. Of all the people at the finish line, Ellen's dad cheered the (<u>loudest</u>/louder).

9. Ellen went home (most wearily/<u>more wearily</u>) than she ever had before.

10. Ellen ate the (<u>most hungrily</u>/more hungrily) at the dinner table that night.

Lesson 49 Correct each capitalization and punctuation error. Then label each sentence *declarative, interrogative, imperative,* or *exclamatory.*

1. please pass me the flour?._____ imperative _____
2. What are you making?_____ interrogative _____
3. I'm rolling out tortillas for dinner?._____ declarative _____
4. I love your homemade tortillas. _____ declarative _____
5. we are also having tamales for dinner and flan for dessert._____ declarative _____
6. is this a special occasion?_____ interrogative _____
7. Yes, uncle Leo got a new job today?._____ declarative _____
8. what great news that is!_____ exclamatory _____
9. don't tell anyone yet. _____ imperative _____
10. Is it a secret?_____ interrogative _____

Lesson 50 Draw three lines (≡) under each lowercase letter that should be capitalized. Draw a line through each uppercase letter that should not be capitalized.

1. The washington Monument was built in honor of george washington.
2. It stands between the united states Capitol building and the lincoln memorial.
3. The potomac river is Nearby.
4. Funds for the Washington Monument were raised by the Washington national monument society.
5. The Tower was designed by robert mills.
6. The Walls of the tower are covered in White marble from maryland.
7. Many of the stones for the Washington monument were Donated.
8. Pope pius IX sent a Stone from the Temple of concord in rome, italy.
9. This stone was stolen one night by members of a Group called the Know-Nothings.
10. Today the Washington Monument is a National memorial and is maintained by the National park Service.

Extra Practice

Lesson 51 Rewrite the items below on the lines. Use abbreviations where you can.

1. Doctor Alison Reid Calloway _____ Dr. A.R. Calloway _____

2. Tuesday, August 21 _____ Tues., Aug. 21 _____

3. Mister Mark Henry Novak _____ Mr. M.H. Novak _____

4. 333 Stone Avenue _____ 333 Stone Ave. _____

5. The Hungry Dog Company _____ The Hungry Dog Co. _____

6. Doctor Martin Luther King Junior _____ Dr. M.L. King Jr. _____

7. Peachtree Boulevard _____ Peachtree Blvd. _____

8. Piranhas Incorporated _____ Piranhas Inc. _____

9. Mister Joseph David Siegel _____ Mr. J.D. Siegel _____

10. Friday, February 8 _____ Fri., Feb. 8 _____

Lesson 52 Draw three lines (≡) under each letter in the sentence that should be capitalized.

1. "Class, what should we do to celebrate presidents' day this year?" asked ms. carle.

2. "I'm confused," said mindy. "Isn't the holiday called washington's birthday?"

3. "Yes, it was begun to mark george washington's actual birthday on february 22," Ms. Carle replied.

4. "But in 1968 it was moved to the third monday of the month by the united states congress," she explained.

5. Ms. carle continued, "People thought the day could also honor other presidents, such as abraham lincoln."

6. "His birthday is also in february, isn't it?" said quinn. "So what is the holiday's real name?"

7. "In many states, such as massachusetts and connecticut, the official name, washington's birthday, is used," Ms. Carle said.

8. "But here in tennessee we call it presidents' day. Each state decides which name to use," she concluded.

9. "Let's serve chelsea's cherry delites and cherries from mel's groceries," suggested Lee.

10. "george washington did chop down a cherry tree, right?" said jordan. Ms. Carle just smiled.

Lesson 53 Circle the letters that should be capitalized in each title. Underline or add quotation marks to each title.

1. Sarita wrote a summary of a story titled "legend of the okefenokee lizard."

2. Ami and Malvin went to the movie theater to see norton the alligator goes to france.

3. Jonas lent his book the poems of preston pig to his young cousin Emile.

4. Emile's favorite poem is called "mud is magnificent."

5. What is the best story in the book titled trailside adventures?

6. "Beware of the scorpion" is my favorite story.

7. Neuri watched the movie tornado avengers with Alvin and Rami.

8. They loved the movie's theme song, "the avengers are coming."

9. The librarian suggested Mari read the short story "a girl of the south" before traveling to Louisiana.

10. A magazine has decided to publish my poem "frog music."

Lesson 54 Underline the correct word in each pair. If the word is a possessive, write *possessive*. If the word is a contraction, write the two words it was made from.

1. (Let's/Lets') go to the dog show. _____ **Let us** _____

2. The (rottweiler's/rottweilers') bodies are massive. _____ **possessive** _____

3. That (pug's/pugs') face is cute. _____ **possessive** _____

4. All (pug's/pugs') noses are stubby. _____ **possessive** _____

5. That (chow's/chows') tongue is black! _____ **possessive** _____

6. Look, (he's/hes') wagging his tail. _____ **he is** _____

7. That is the biggest dog (Ive/I've) ever seen! _____ **I have** _____

8. (It's/Its') an Irish wolfhound. _____ **It is** _____

9. (Their/They're) the tallest of all breeds. _____ **They are** _____

10. I think that one is the four (judge's/judges') favorite. _____ **possessive** _____

Lesson 55 Add commas where they belong. Circle commas that don't belong.

1. This backpack has a, large inside pouch, a small outside pouch, and, a hidden pocket.

2. Its special lining can, keep food hot, warm, or cold.

3. I can use it for hiking, picnicking, or school.

4. When I bring it to school, I keep, my lunch in the small pouch, my books in the big pouch, and my keys, in the hidden pocket.

5. This backpack has belonged, to my uncle, my cousin, my brother, and me.

6. It has traveled to Africa, Asia, and Europe.

7. The places I've visited are, New Mexico, Canada, and Oregon.

8. Right now I have pajamas, a sleeping bag, and my toothbrush in the backpack.

9. I'm going on a sleepover with Evan, Michael, Lucas, and Josh.

10. We'll stay up late, eat pizza, and, tell scary stories.

Lesson 56 Add the missing comma to each sentence. Then decide why the comma is needed. Write *I* for introductory word or element, *C* for compound sentence, and *D* for direct address.

1. Dave, do you know what that bridge is called? __D__

2. No, I have no idea. __I__

3. I'll give you some hints, and you guess its name. __C__

4. Well, I'll try to guess. __I__

5. It was named after the channel it spans, and the channel was named during the California Gold Rush. __C__

6. Well, does that mean the word *gold* is in the title? __I__

7. Yes, you're getting warm. __I__

8. The second part of the name rhymes with *great*, but there's no *r* in the word. __C__

9. Mom, don't give such easy clues! __D__

10. Although you only gave me two clues, I already know that it's the Golden Gate Bridge. __I__

Lesson 57 Add a semicolon where it is needed in each sentence.

1. Soybeans come in many different colors; they can be red, green, yellow, or speckled.

2. Soybeans are easy to grow; they are a popular crop among farmers.

3. Soybean plants are good for the soil; they provide nitrogen, an important nutrient.

4. Many foods are made from soybeans; soy sauce, vegetable oil, soy flour, and tofu all have soy in them.

5. Soybeans can also be used for surprising things; some fire extinguishers contain foam made from soy.

6. Tofu is made by boiling, crushing, and pressing soybeans; this method was invented in China in 164 B.C.

7. The traditional Japanese diet includes tofu; Japan imports large amounts of soybeans.

8. In Japan tofu is served in beautiful ways; sometimes it is carved in the shape of leaves.

9. Tofu can be made to imitate many other foods; it can even be made to taste like ice cream.

10. Tofu is a healthy food; it provides more protein than lean beef.

Lesson 58 Write *I* after each indirect quotation and *D* after each direct quotation. Then add quotation marks and other punctuation to the direct quotations.

1. "I'd like to have a garden, but I live in the city," said Arno. __D__

2. Dinah said that plants will grow well in a sunny window. __I__

3. Arno opened the cupboard and asked, "Can I grow peas, beans, and peppers?" __D__

4. "You can grow all of those things in containers," Charlie said. __D__

5. "A bottle garden is another way to grow plants inside," said Martha. __D__

6. Martha explained that a bottle garden is called a *terrarium*. __I__

7. "First we need a big jar," said Charlie. __D__

8. Charlie said that Arno could put soil and plants in the jar. __I__

9. "What kind of small plants will you put in your terrarium?" asked Martha. __D__

10. "I think I'll put geraniums, moss, and ferns in it," said Arno. __D__

Extra Practice

Lesson 59 Add quotation marks and commas so that each direct quotation is written correctly.

1. "The new sculpture in front of Jefferson Public Library is the most creative art piece in the city," says critic Melinda Lu.

2. Ms. Lu also writes, "The modern style may not appeal to everyone, but it really is a beautiful work."

3. In an editorial for the Jefferson Post, however, artist Jesse King writes, "I hardly think that *beautiful* is the best word to describe this thing."

4. Librarian Todd Hunt agrees. "When I look out the window, all I see are ugly steel rods sticking up in the sky," he writes in his blog.

5. "Is it supposed to look like a bird, or maybe a giant butterfly?" adds a confused visitor to the library.

6. The library's official statement about the sculpture says, "We are fully behind the artist and are proud to display his work to the public."

Lesson 60 Rewrite this friendly letter correctly on the blanks below.

    Turkey Feather Ranch Peru, IN 46970 March 18, 20__ Dear Anya, My grandmother's ranch is so much fun! This morning, Grandma showed us where the baby turkeys grow. See you soon, Kristen

Turkey Feather Ranch _____

Peru, IN 46970 _____

March 18, 20__ _____

Dear Anya, _____

    My grandmother's ranch is so much fun! This morning, Grandma showed us where the baby turkeys grow. _____

_____

_____

See you soon, _____

Kristen _____

Read this text and answer the questions on the next page.

A Twister Is Formed

1   <u>An unusually hot and humid afternoon in mid-May.</u>

2   <u>The sun has been shining but now there are storm clouds in the</u>

3   <u>west.</u> Suddenly, your weather radio sounds a high-pitched alarm.

4   There is a tornado warning. <u>You know it is time to take cover, but</u>

5   <u>do you know what is happening in the atmosphere around you?</u>

6   <u>Most likely, a large thunderstorm is approaching, the air</u>

7   <u>is very unstable.</u> Warm air near the ground is rising and hitting

8   higher, cooler air. The water molecules in the warm air are in the

9   form of a gas. <u>When those molecules rise and cool off; they</u>

10   <u>change into a liquid and fall as rain.</u> Heat is also released when

11   the water molecules change. This causes updrafts, or strong

12   upward currents of air.

13   Something called wind shear is also present. <u>Wind shear</u>

14   <u>is created when winds at different heights blow in different</u>

15   <u>directions or at different speeds.</u> The varying wind speeds and

16   directions cause a tube of spinning air parallel to the ground.

17   <u>Conditions are now perfect. For the formation of a tornado.</u>

18   The updraft can pull on the spinning tube of air and make it

19   vertical. <u>The tube tightens and spins faster it turns into a twister</u>

20   <u>capable of damaging anything in its path.</u>

Read each item carefully. Fill in the circle next to the best answer.
(Numbers in parentheses identify related lessons.)

1. What change, if any, should be made to the underlined words in line 1? **(8, 12)**

   Ⓐ NO CHANGE
   Ⓑ Is an unusually
   Ⓒ Is an unusual
   Ⓓ It is an unusually

2. What change, if any, should be made to the underlined words in lines 2–3? **(8, 9)**

   Ⓐ NO CHANGE
   Ⓑ shining, but now
   Ⓒ shining, now
   Ⓓ shining but, now

3. What change, if any, should be made to the underlined words in lines 4–5? **(7)**

   Ⓐ NO CHANGE
   Ⓑ at the atmosphere
   Ⓒ from the atmosphere
   Ⓓ of the atmosphere

4. What change, if any, should be made to the underlined words in lines 6–7? **(8, 12)**

   Ⓐ NO CHANGE
   Ⓑ approaching the air
   Ⓒ approaching. The air
   Ⓓ approaching; The air

5. What change, if any, should be made to the underlined words in lines 9–10? **(8–10)**

   Ⓐ NO CHANGE
   Ⓑ cool off. They
   Ⓒ cool off? They
   Ⓓ cool off, they

6. What change, if any, should be made to the underlined words in lines 13–15? **(10, 11)**

   Ⓐ NO CHANGE
   Ⓑ is created. When winds
   Ⓒ is created which winds
   Ⓓ is created, when winds

7. What change, if any, should be made to the underlined words in line 17? **(12)**

   Ⓐ NO CHANGE
   Ⓑ perfect for the
   Ⓒ perfect; for the
   Ⓓ perfect, for the

8. What change, if any, should be made to the underlined words in lines 19–20? **(12)**

   Ⓐ NO CHANGE
   Ⓑ faster, it turns
   Ⓒ faster, but it turns
   Ⓓ faster. It turns

Read each item carefully. Fill in the circle next to the best answer.

9. Read the following sentences.

> The shark <u>swam gracefully around the tank</u>. Only the glass separated it from us.

What part of the sentence is underlined? **(1, 2)**

(A) complete subject
(B) complete predicate
(C) simple subject
(D) simple predicate

10. Read the following sentences.

> The full <u>moon</u> shone very brightly. It was more like day than night!

What part of the sentence is underlined? **(1, 2)**

(A) complete subject
(B) complete predicate
(C) simple subject
(D) simple predicate

11. Read the following sentences.

> I'm surprised Kyle did not win the writing contest. His story was <u>hilarious!</u>

What part of the sentence is underlined? **(4–6)**

(A) direct object
(B) indirect object
(C) predicate noun
(D) predicate adjective

12. Read the following sentences.

> Fossils are the remains of animals preserved in rock. They give <u>people</u> an idea of what ancient species looked like.

What part of the sentence is underlined? **(4–6)**

(A) direct object
(B) indirect object
(C) predicate noun
(D) predicate adjective

13. Read the following paragraph.

> [1] The skin is the body's largest organ. [2] It protects you. [3] It keeps you warm. [4] Your skin is important, so keep it healthy.

What is the best way to combine sentences 2 and 3? **(3)**

(A) It protects you, and keeps you warm.
(B) It protects you and keeps you warm.
(C) It protects you, it keeps you warm.
(D) It protects you but keeps you warm.

14. Read the following sentences.

> The ants crawled _____. There must have been hundreds of them!

Which is a prepositional phrase that completes the first sentence? **(7)**

(A) and gathered together
(B) across the floor
(C) when the light hit them
(D) frantically

Read each item carefully. Fill in the circle next to the best answer.

15. Read the following sentences.

> Is this the beach <u>where</u> you found that sand dollar? Let's dig around in the sand.

What kind of word is underlined? (11)

Ⓐ direct object
Ⓑ relative pronoun
Ⓒ predicate adjective
Ⓓ relative adverb

16. Read the following sentences.

> Lydia will keep studying <u>until she has learned all the words</u>. She wants to win the spelling bee.

What part of the sentence is underlined? (9)

Ⓐ dependent clause
Ⓑ independent clause
Ⓒ complete predicate
Ⓓ prepositional phrase

17. Read the following paragraph.

> [1] We can't wait to visit Grandma in Tucson. [2] It is still freezing here, but Arizona is warm and sunny. [3] We will see cacti and many desert animals. [4] Before we leave, Grandma will take us to the Arizona-Sonora Desert Museum.

Which sentence is a compound sentence? (8)

Ⓐ Sentence 1
Ⓑ Sentence 2
Ⓒ Sentence 3
Ⓓ Sentence 4

18. Read the following paragraph.

> [1] Although she loves dogs, Missy prefers cats. [2] The thing Missy likes most about felines is that they are proud and quiet. [3] They are also easy to care for.

Where is the best place to add the following sentence? (8–10)

> They do not run wildly and bark like dogs.

Ⓐ Before sentence 1
Ⓑ After sentence 1
Ⓒ After sentence 2
Ⓓ After sentence 3

19. Read the following sentence.

> Pedro sings in the local children's _____ once a week.

Which words and punctuation best complete the sentences? (12)

Ⓐ choir, they practice
Ⓑ choir. They practice.
Ⓒ choir. Practice
Ⓓ choir. They practice

20. Read the following sentences.

> The engine sputtered and died, the car wouldn't start again. Mom went inside to call the mechanic.

Why is the first sentence incorrect? (12)

Ⓐ It is a fragment.
Ⓑ It is a run-on sentence.
Ⓒ It should be a question.
Ⓓ It is a comma splice.

Read this text and answer the questions on the next page.

Daedalus and Icarus

1   Long ago, the cruel King Minos ruled the island of crete.

2   A ferocious monster called the Minotaur, who was half man and

3   half bull, terrorized its people. King Minos demanded that his

4   master craftsman, Daedalus, build a kind of maze called a labyrinth

5   to trap the Minotaur. The monster was lured to the maze and

6   trapped, but that was not enough for King Minos. He began to

7   throw his enemies in the labyrinth, where they would meet a

8   horribly end at the hands of the imprisoned monster.

9   King Minos did not want Daedalus to reveal the way out

10   of the maze. So he locked Daedalus and his son Icarus in a tower.

11   Father and son longed for escape. From their lofty window, he

12   looked with envy upon the birds flying free. Then one day Daedalus

13   had a brilliant idea. He and Icarus would fly from the tower just

14   like the birds. He will build them wings out of feathers and wax.

15   Daedalus soon completed the wings and gave Icarus his

16   pair with a warning. "Do not fly too close to the sun," he said.

17   Daedalus and Icarus jumped from the window, flapped

18   their white new delicate wings, and began to fly. Icarus ignored his

19   father's advice and boldly neared the sun. Daedalus watched in

20   horror as his sons wings melted and foolish Icarus fell into the sea.

Read each item carefully. Fill in the circle next to the best answer.
(Numbers in parentheses identify related lessons.)

1. What change, if any, should be made to the underlined words in line 1? **(13)**

   Ⓐ NO CHANGE
   Ⓑ Island of crete
   Ⓒ Island Of Crete
   Ⓓ island of Crete

5. What change, if any, should be made to the underlined words in lines 11–12? **(16)**

   Ⓐ NO CHANGE
   Ⓑ their looked with envy
   Ⓒ they looked with envy
   Ⓓ him looked with envy

2. What change, if any, should be made to the underlined words in lines 2–3? **(14)**

   Ⓐ NO CHANGE
   Ⓑ terrorized its person's.
   Ⓒ terrorized its people's.
   Ⓓ terrorized its person.

6. What change, if any, should be made to the underlined words in line 14? **(18, 19)**

   Ⓐ NO CHANGE
   Ⓑ He can build
   Ⓒ He may build
   Ⓓ He would build

3. What change, if any, should be made to the underlined words in lines 6–8? **(20, 21)**

   Ⓐ NO CHANGE
   Ⓑ meet a horrible end
   Ⓒ horrible meet an end
   Ⓓ meet an end horrible

7. What change, if any, should be made to the underlined words in lines 17–18? **(20, 22)**

   Ⓐ NO CHANGE
   Ⓑ delicate new white wings
   Ⓒ new delicate white wings
   Ⓓ white delicate new wings

4. What change, if any, should be made to the underlined words in line 10? **(16)**

   Ⓐ NO CHANGE
   Ⓑ its son Icarus
   Ⓒ him son Icarus
   Ⓓ their son Icarus

8. What change, if any, should be made to the underlined words in lines 19–20? **(14)**

   Ⓐ NO CHANGE
   Ⓑ his sons' wings
   Ⓒ his son's wings
   Ⓓ his sons's wings

Read each item carefully. Fill in the circle next to the best answer.

9. Read the following sentences.

> The sun was setting as we sped down the highway. We still had hope that we would get to <u>Denver</u> before dark.

What kind of noun is underlined? (13–15)

(A) proper (C) collective
(B) possessive (D) abstract

10. Read the following sentences.

> It was a hot day on the ranch. A <u>herd</u> of cattle gathered in a shady corner of the pasture.

What kind of noun is underlined? (13–15)

(A) proper (C) collective
(B) possessive (D) abstract

11. Read the following sentences.

> Through a process called molting, birds shed _____ feathers and grow new ones. This happens at least once a year.

Which pronoun best completes the first sentence? (16)

(A) them (C) her
(B) they (D) their

12. Read the following sentences.

> We <u>were</u> exhausted after our five-mile hike. We collapsed onto the soft grass and had a rest.

What kind of verb is underlined? (17–19)

(A) action (C) concrete
(B) linking (D) helping

13. Read the following paragraph.

> [1] We are having a used book sale on Saturday. [2] All money raised will be donated to the local food pantry. [3] We have organized many fundraisers for the food pantry through the years.

Where is the best place to add the following sentence? (17–19)

> Last year's car wash was a big hit.

(A) Before sentence 1
(B) After sentence 1
(C) After sentence 2
(D) After sentence 3

14. Read the following sentences.

> Taylor _____ try harder to get to practice on time. Doesn't he know the whole team is counting on him?

Which helping verb best completes the first sentence? (18, 19)

(A) might (C) should
(B) may (D) can

15. Read the following sentences.

> Sophia <u>often</u> takes this shortcut through the park. She can make it home in only five minutes.

What kind of word is underlined? (20, 21)

(A) noun (C) adjective
(B) verb (D) adverb

225

Read each item carefully. Fill in the circle next to the best answer.

16. Read the following sentences.

> I can't reach <u>those</u> storage boxes on the top shelf. Do you have a step ladder?

What kind of word is underlined? (20, 21)

Ⓐ noun   Ⓒ adjective
Ⓑ verb   Ⓓ adverb

17. Read the following sentences.

> We will need a _____ pan to bake the casserole. Let's find it before we begin to mix the ingredients.

Which series of adjectives completes the first sentence and is in the correct order? (22)

Ⓐ glass large rectangular
Ⓑ large rectangular glass
Ⓒ rectangular large glass
Ⓓ large glass rectangular

18. Read the following sentences.

> [1] Kurt might research electricity for his science project. [2] He might build a model of the solar system. [3] He is interested in both subjects.

What is the best way to combine sentences 1 and 2? (23)

Ⓐ Kurt might research electricity for his science project, or he might build a model of the solar system.
Ⓑ Kurt might research electricity for his science project, although he might build a model of the solar system.
Ⓒ Kurt might research electricity for his science project, he might build a model of the solar system.
Ⓓ Kurt might research electricity, or for his science project, he might build a model of the solar system.

19. Read the following paragraph.

> [1] The Pony Express began in 1861. [2] Its messengers rode on horseback to carry mail between Missouri and California. [3] Pony Express riders were known for their speed. [4] Though the service was reliable, the Pony Express lasted for only a year.

Which sentence contains a subordinating conjunction? (23)

Ⓐ Sentence 1
Ⓑ Sentence 2
Ⓒ Sentence 3
Ⓓ Sentence 4

20. Read the following sentences.

> Neither the drizzle _____ the chilly breeze kept people from attending the picnic. Everyone showed up with umbrellas and raincoats.

Which correlative conjunction best completes the first sentence? (24)

Ⓐ or
Ⓑ and
Ⓒ nor
Ⓓ but

Read this text and answer the questions on the next page.

To the Editor

1   There has been much debate lately concerning Westlake

2   Elementary's decision to require students to wear school uniforms.

3   <u>In particular, Mr. Cleary's fifth-grade class has been real angry</u>

4   <u>about the new rule.</u> They argue that forcing all students to dress

5   alike will rob them of the chance to be creative and unique. <u>This</u>

6   <u>is a good point, but I think there are some gooder reasons to</u>

7   <u>get behind school uniforms.</u>

8   <u>The fifth-graders should remember that we are attending</u>

9   <u>school to teach, not to walk in a fashion show.</u> Students should be

10   concentrating on math and science. <u>They should not be wondering</u>

11   <u>who has the latest name-brand jeans as they set at their desks.</u>

12   Likewise, time spent putting together the perfect outfit is wasted

13   time. <u>When everyone is dressed alike, there are no distractions.</u>

14   <u>Students are free to think only of they're studies.</u>

15   <u>The most good argument for school uniforms is that they</u>

16   <u>create equality in the classroom.</u> No students are more "in style"

17   or more privileged than others. No one will be teased about what

18   he or she is wearing. <u>If all students look the same, it will be easier</u>

19   <u>for them to respect and relate to each other.</u> Bullying will not be

20   such a worry. Doesn't that sound like a positive step for Westlake?

Read each item carefully. Fill in the circle next to the best answer.
(Number in parentheses identify related lessons.)

1. What change, if any, should be made to the underlined words in lines 3–4? **(30)**

   Ⓐ NO CHANGE
   Ⓑ has been well angry
   Ⓒ has been right angry
   Ⓓ has been very angry

5. What change, if any, should be made to the underlined words in line 13? **(35)**

   Ⓐ NO CHANGE
   Ⓑ When anyone is
   Ⓒ When themselves is
   Ⓓ When no one is

2. What change, if any, should be made to the underlined words in lines 5–7? **(28)**

   Ⓐ NO CHANGE
   Ⓑ some better reasons
   Ⓒ some best reasons
   Ⓓ some more good reasons

6. What change, if any, should be made to the underlined words in line 14? **(25)**

   Ⓐ NO CHANGE
   Ⓑ of there studies
   Ⓒ of these studies
   Ⓓ of their studies

3. What change, if any, should be made to the underlined words in lines 8–9? **(32)**

   Ⓐ NO CHANGE
   Ⓑ school to be learned
   Ⓒ school to learn
   Ⓓ school to be teached

7. What change, if any, should be made to the underlined words in lines 15–16? **(28)**

   Ⓐ NO CHANGE
   Ⓑ The most better argument
   Ⓒ The goodest argument
   Ⓓ The best argument

4. What change, if any, should be made to the underlined words in lines 10–11? **(31)**

   Ⓐ NO CHANGE
   Ⓑ sit at their desks
   Ⓒ sat at their desks
   Ⓓ setting at their desks

8. What change, if any, should be made to the underlined words in lines 18–19? **(36)**

   Ⓐ NO CHANGE
   Ⓑ easier for they
   Ⓒ easier for him
   Ⓓ easier for we

Read each item carefully. Fill in the circle next to the best answer.

9. Read the following sentences.

> I can't believe _____ going to miss the carnival. It will be so much fun!

Which word best completes the first sentence? (27)

(A) you   (C) you's
(B) your   (D) you're

10. Read the following sentences.

> The days were getting cooler and shorter. The trees were beginning to lose _____ leaves.

Which word best completes the second sentence? (25)

(A) there   (C) they're
(B) their   (D) its

11. Read the following sentences.

> The lion stalks _____ prey in the early morning hours. It hunts zebras, buffalo, and gazelles.

Which word best completes the first sentence? (26)

(A) it's   (C) their
(B) its   (D) they're

12. Read the following sentences.

> Jarrod is a boy _____ sits next to me in music class. He also lives in my neighborhood.

Which word best completes the first sentence? (29)

(A) that   (C) who
(B) which   (D) he

13. Read the following paragraph.

> [1] Jane thinks this is the best book the author has ever written. [2] She would argue that it is even better than his last novel. [3] Ivy does not agree at all. [4] In fact, she thinks it is the worse book she has ever read!

Which sentence contains an adjective that is incorrect? (28)

(A) Sentence 1   (C) Sentence 3
(B) Sentence 2   (D) Sentence 4

14. Read the following sentences.

> Elizabeth has _____ an inch since last year. She is the tallest girl in her class.

Which word best completes the first sentence? (34)

(A) grown   (C) grew
(B) growed   (D) grows

15. Read the following sentences.

> In the 1890s, millions of people came _____ America from Europe. Immigration was at an all-time high.

Which word best completes the first sentence? (33)

(A) to   (C) too
(B) threw   (D) two

Read each item carefully. Fill in the circle next to the best answer.

16. Read the following sentences.

> There were only ten seconds left in the game. The team _____ there was no hope for a victory.

Which word best completes the second sentence? **(34)**

(A) knows   (C) knowed
(B) known   (D) knew

17. Read the following sentences.

> Mr. Lorenzo _____ me how to throw a curveball. I'm ready to try out for the baseball team.

Which word best completes the first sentence? **(32)**

(A) teached   (C) learned
(B) taught   (D) learns

18. Read the following paragraph.

> [1] Anna studied her science notes for two hours. [2] John also studied for tomorrow's science test. [3] He completed a writing assignment as well.

Where is the best place to add the following sentence? **(36)**

> She is prepared for the test tomorrow.

(A) Before sentence 1
(B) After sentence 1
(C) After sentence 2
(D) After sentence 3

19. Read the following sentences.

> "We've locked ourselves out of the house," Dad said with a chuckle. "I'll call Uncle Rick and ask him to bring the spare key."

What kind of pronoun is underlined? **(35)**

(A) indefinite
(B) possessive
(C) reflexive
(D) relative

20. Read the following sentences.

> [1] It was too cold to play outside. [2] Darren spent the afternoon finishing his book report. [3] His mom was proud of him for making good use of his time.

What is the best way to combine sentences 1 and 2? **(23)**

(A) It was too cold to play outside, and Darren spent the afternoon finishing his book report.
(B) It was too cold to play outside when Darren spent the afternoon finishing his book report.
(C) It was too cold to play outside, but Darren spent the afternoon finishing his book report.
(D) Since it was too cold to play outside, Darren spent the afternoon finishing his book report.

Read this text and answer the questions on the next page.

Escaping the Dust

1   "Do we really have to leave, Papa?" I asked. The old car

2 was packed to the gills with all our belongings. My little sister Kay

3 sat quietly in the back seat beside a frying pan and a pile of sheets.

4 Her silence was strange. <u>She was only three, but she seems to</u>

5 <u>understand how sad and serious this day was for us.</u>

6   <u>It were the summer of 1935.</u> The drought had ruined yet

7 another year's crops. <u>We had see so many dust storms blow</u>

8 <u>through our tiny Oklahoma town that they were now a grim fact</u>

9 <u>of life instead of a rare event.</u> It's hard to explain just how terrible

10 a dust storm is. <u>A dark, sinister cloud—the darker cloud you've</u>

11 <u>ever seen—appears on the horizon.</u> Then you have only minutes

12 to take shelter and shut all the doors and windows as tightly as

13 possible. <u>Day turns into night as the dust blocks the sun.</u> Then

14 the dust works its way into every possible crack and crevice of

15 your house. It coats the floor, the furniture, and the dishes. It

16 covers your clothes and skin. You taste the grit in your mouth.

17   <u>"There's not nothing left for us here, Liza," Papa replied.</u>

18 <u>"The wheat is failing again.</u> The land has nothing left to give."

19 California sounded like a paradise where a farmer could

20 earn a good living. <u>We have no choice but to head west.</u>

Read each item carefully. Fill in the circle next to the best answer.
(Number in parentheses identify related lessons.)

1. What change, if any, should be made to the underlined words in lines 4–5? **(41, 45)**

   Ⓐ NO CHANGE
   Ⓑ but she seemed
   Ⓒ but she is seeming
   Ⓓ but she will seem

5. What change, if any, should be made to the underlined words in line 13? **(39, 41)**

   Ⓐ NO CHANGE
   Ⓑ Day turn into
   Ⓒ Day turned into
   Ⓓ Day have turned into

2. What change, if any, should be made to the underlined words in line 6? **(39, 40)**

   Ⓐ NO CHANGE
   Ⓑ It was the
   Ⓒ It be the
   Ⓓ It is the

6. What change, if any, should be made to the underlined words in line 17? **(46)**

   Ⓐ NO CHANGE
   Ⓑ There's anything left
   Ⓒ There's nothing not left
   Ⓓ There's nothing left

3. What change, if any, should be made to the underlined words in lines 7–9? **(43, 44)**

   Ⓐ NO CHANGE
   Ⓑ We will have seen
   Ⓒ We have seen
   Ⓓ We had seen

7. What change, if any, should be made to the underlined words in line 18? **(41, 42)**

   Ⓐ NO CHANGE
   Ⓑ wheat had been failing
   Ⓒ wheat was failing
   Ⓓ wheat is failed

4. What change, if any, should be made to the underlined words in lines 10–11? **(47, 48)**

   Ⓐ NO CHANGE
   Ⓑ the darkest cloud
   Ⓒ the more dark cloud
   Ⓓ the most darkly cloud

8. What change, if any, should be made to the underlined words in line 20? **(41, 45)**

   Ⓐ NO CHANGE
   Ⓑ We has no
   Ⓒ We had no
   Ⓓ We are having no

Read each item carefully. Fill in the circle next to the best answer.

9. Read the following sentences.

    > Today, Dad made lunch for _____.
    > We had turkey sandwiches and apple slices.

    Which words best complete the first sentence? (38)

    (A) Kevin and I
    (B) Kevin and me
    (C) me and Kevin
    (D) I and Kevin

10. Read the following sentences.

    > The librarian gave Jason a stern look.
    > She told <u>him</u> to keep his voice down.

    What kind of pronoun is underlined? (37)

    (A) subject
    (B) reflexive
    (C) indefinite
    (D) object

11. Read the following sentences.

    > Delaware is known as The First State.
    > It _____ the first state to approve the U.S. Constitution in 1787.

    Which form of the verb *be* best completes the second sentence? (39, 40)

    (A) is
    (B) are
    (C) was
    (D) were

12. Read the following paragraph.

    > [1] Last week, the class wrote poems about nature. [2] Li Min enjoyed the assignment because she loves poetry. [3] Li Min will not have as much fun writing nonfiction.

    Where is the best place to add the following sentence? (41)

    > Next week, the class will begin their research reports.

    (A) Before sentence 1
    (B) After sentence 1
    (C) After sentence 2
    (D) After sentence 3

13. Read the following sentences.

    > Katie has been given the lead in the school musical. She _____ a girl who is lost in a forest.

    Which word best completes the second sentence? (41, 42)

    (A) played
    (B) was playing
    (C) play
    (D) will be playing

14. Read the following sentences.

    > Martha's aunt <u>has worked</u> at the hospital for ten years. She runs medical tests in the lab.

    What verb form is underlined? (42–44)

    (A) past progressive
    (B) present progressive
    (C) past perfect
    (D) present perfect

233

Read each item carefully. Fill in the circle next to the best answer.

15. Read the following sentences.

> By the time this day is over, the troop _____ almost six miles. They will be ready for a rest.

Which verb best completes the first sentence? **(42–44)**

(A) had hiked
(B) will have hiked
(C) was hiking
(D) will be hiking

16. Read the following sentences.

> Kirsten _____ she knew in the crowd. She felt totally alone.

Which words best complete the first sentence? **(46)**

(A) didn't see no one
(B) didn't see anyone
(C) didn't not see anyone
(D) didn't see none

17. Read the following paragraph.

> [1] Abraham Lincoln was born in Kentucky in 1809. [2] Though he grew up on the frontier, he still found time to read. [3] He becomes a lawyer in 1836. [4] He was elected president of the United States in 1860.

Which sentence contains an incorrect verb tense? **(45)**

(A) Sentence 1
(B) Sentence 2
(C) Sentence 3
(D) Sentence 4

18. Read the following sentences.

> Jenny dove <u>deeper</u> into the lake than Harry did. She found a shiny pebble at the bottom.

What kind of word is underlined? **(47, 48)**

(A) comparative adjective
(B) superlative adjective
(C) comparative adverb
(D) superlative adverb

19. Read the following sentences.

> This is the _____ intersection in town. There have been two accidents here just this week.

Which word or words best complete the first sentence? **(47, 48)**

(A) dangerouser
(B) more dangerous
(C) most dangerous
(D) dangerest

20. Read the following sentences.

> [1] Today's soccer practice was long and hard. [2] Faye was never happier to see her own bed. [3] She dropped her backpack on the floor. [4] She leapt into her bed.

What is the best way to combine sentences 3 and 4? **(3)**

(A) She dropped her backpack on the floor after she leapt into her bed.
(B) She dropped her backpack on the floor and leapt into her bed.
(C) She dropped her backpack on the floor, and leapt into her bed.
(D) She dropped her backpack on the floor while leaping into her bed.

Read this text and answer the questions on the next page.

Local Shelter to Hold Fundraising and Adoption Event

1   <u>Volunteers from the Furry Friends Dog Shelter will be</u>

2   <u>washing cars for a cause this Saturday from noon to six in the</u>

3   <u>parking lot of Frank's gourmet foods. All proceeds from the</u>

4   <u>event will go toward food supplies, and upkeep of the shelter.</u>

5   Furry Friends will also bring along a few of their most adoptable

6   dogs and puppies for families considering a canine companion.

7   <u>The car wash is the third fundraiser Furry Friends has</u>

8   <u>organized this year, according to its director, Dr Marla A Simms.</u>

9   <u>The March bake sale and June's silent auction were successful,</u>

10   <u>but the shelter still urgently needs funds to keep operating.</u>

11   <u>"Last year we lost the support of two big donors, so</u>

12   <u>every penny counts Dr. Simms explained.</u> "Our cages are

13   almost always full, and it costs a lot to care for these animals."

14   And speaking of the animals, there will be some

15   wonderful dogs available for adoption this weekend. <u>"We ll be</u>

16   <u>bringing some cute puppies, but please consider giving a home</u>

17   <u>to an older dog," Dr. Simms added.</u> <u>"We have a sweet five-year-</u>

18   <u>old German shepherd that would be the perfect pet."</u>

19   <u>Furry Friends is requesting a ten-dollar donation for</u>

20   <u>each car washed!</u> Canine adoptions start at fifty dollars.

Read each item carefully. Fill in the circle next to the best answer.
(Number in parentheses identify related lessons.)

1. What change, if any, should be made to the underlined words in lines 1–3? **(50, 52)**

   Ⓐ NO CHANGE
   Ⓑ frank's gourmet foods
   Ⓒ Frank's Gourmet foods
   Ⓓ Frank's Gourmet Foods

2. What change, if any, should be made to the underlined words in lines 3–4? **(55)**

   Ⓐ NO CHANGE
   Ⓑ food, supplies, and upkeep
   Ⓒ food, supplies and, upkeep
   Ⓓ food supplies and upkeep

3. What change, if any, should be made to the underlined words in lines 7–8? **(50, 51)**

   Ⓐ NO CHANGE
   Ⓑ Dr. Marla A Simms
   Ⓒ Dr. Marla a. Simms
   Ⓓ Dr. Marla A. Simms

4. What change, if any, should be made to the underlined words in lines 9–10? **(56)**

   Ⓐ NO CHANGE
   Ⓑ were successful but
   Ⓒ were successful but,
   Ⓓ were, successful but

5. What change, if any, should be made to the underlined words in lines 11–12? **(58)**

   Ⓐ NO CHANGE
   Ⓑ counts, Dr. Simms explained. "
   Ⓒ counts." Dr. Simms explained.
   Ⓓ counts," Dr. Simms explained.

6. What change, if any, should be made to the underlined words in lines 15–17? **(54)**

   Ⓐ NO CHANGE
   Ⓑ We'll be bringing
   Ⓒ Well' be bringing
   Ⓓ W'ill be bringing

7. What change, if any, should be made to the underlined words in lines 17–18? **(50)**

   Ⓐ NO CHANGE
   Ⓑ Five-year-old German Shepherd
   Ⓒ Five-year-old german shepherd
   Ⓓ five-year-old german shepherd

8. What change, if any, should be made to the underlined words in lines 19–20? **(49)**

   Ⓐ NO CHANGE
   Ⓑ each car washed?
   Ⓒ each car washed.
   Ⓓ each car washed,

Read each item carefully. Fill in the circle next to the best answer.

9. Read the following sentences.

> <u>Where should we go on vacation this year?</u> I would rather hike in the mountains than sit on a beach.

What kind of sentence is underlined? (49)

(A) declarative
(B) interrogative
(C) imperative
(D) exclamatory

10. Read the following sentences.

> "I didn't know that <u>canadian</u> <u>money</u> was different from <u>ours</u>," said Tim. "We'll have to exchange our <u>dollars</u> in Toronto."

Which underlined word should be capitalized? (50)

(A) canadian
(B) money
(C) ours
(D) dollars

11. Read the following sentences.

> Have you heard Maya read _____? It is the first poem she ever wrote.

Which is the correct title that completes the first sentence? (53)

(A) "Ants on the March"
(B) Ants on the March
(C) "Ants On The March"
(D) Ants On The March

12. Read the following sentences.

> The <u>Sahara</u> <u>Desert</u> stretches across most of North <u>Africa</u>. It is almost the size of our entire <u>Country</u>.

Which underlined word should not be capitalized? (52)

(A) Sahara
(B) Desert
(C) Africa
(D) Country

13. Read the following sentences.

> The wind on the pier suddenly picked up. All the _____ hats blew off their heads.

Which word best completes the second sentence? (54)

(A) woman's
(B) womans'
(C) women's
(D) womens'

14. Read the following paragraph.

> [1] Wow, I can't wait to go to the water park tomorrow! [2] Brett are you excited, too? [3] I've already packed my swimsuit, towel, and sunscreen. [4] I've never been on the tallest waterslide, but I might try it this time!

Which sentence is missing a comma? (55, 56)

(A) Sentence 1
(B) Sentence 2
(C) Sentence 3
(D) Sentence 4

Read each item carefully. Fill in the circle next to the best answer.

15. Read the following sentences.

> "You forgot to feed the dog this morning didn't you?" said Mom with a frown. It was the second time I had forgotten that week.

Where should a comma be placed in the sentences? **(55, 56)**

(A) after *You*
(B) after *morning*
(C) after *said*
(D) after *forgotten*

16. Read the following friendly letter heading.

> 863 Green Tree Rd.
>
> _____
>
> August 6, 2014

Which address will correctly complete the heading? **(60)**

(A) Springfield IL 62704
(B) Springfield IL, 62704
(C) Springfield, IL 62704
(D) Springfield, IL, 62704

17. Read the following sentences.

> The rain was relentless it sounded like a million fists pounding on the roof. I knew I would get no sleep that night.

Where should a semicolon be placed in the sentences? **(57)**

(A) after *was*
(B) after *relentless*
(C) after *fists*
(D) after *get*

18. Read the following sentences.

> The rule book _____ who draws the highest number goes first." Because she drew an eight, Bridget will begin the game.

Which words and punctuation correctly complete the first sentence? **(59)**

(A) says, "The player
(B) says "The player
(C) says, the player
(D) says the player

19. Read the following paragraph.

> [1] The announcement was a welcome one. [2] The class breathed a collective sigh of relief. [3] No one was prepared for the spelling test that day.

Where is the best place to add the following sentence? **(58)**

> "I have decided to postpone the test," said Mr. Reed.

(A) Before sentence 1
(B) After sentence 1
(C) After sentence 2
(D) After sentence 3

20. Read the following sentences.

> [1] Karima put a lot of effort into her science project. [2] It took lots of planning. [3] It took several weekends to complete.

What is the best way to combine sentences 2 and 3? **(23)**

(A) It took lots of planning and several weekends to complete.
(B) It took lots of planning and it took several weekends to complete.
(C) It took lots of planning, and several weekends to complete.
(D) It took lots of planning, or it took several weekends to complete.

Grammar, Usage, and Mechanics Handbook
Table of Contents

Mechanics

- **Capitalize the first word in a sentence.**
  The kangaroo rat is an amazing animal.

- **Capitalize all *proper nouns,* including people's names and the names of particular places.**
  Gregory Gordon   Washington Monument

- **Capitalize titles of respect.**
  Mr. Alvarez   Dr. Chin   Ms. Murphy

- **Capitalize family titles used just before people's names and titles of respect that are part of names.**
  Uncle Frank   Aunt Mary   Governor Adamson

- **Capitalize initials of names.**
  Thomas Paul Gerard (T.P. Gerard)

- **Capitalize place names.**
  France   Utah   China   Baltimore

- **Capitalize *proper adjectives,* adjectives that are made from proper nouns.**
  Chinese   Icelandic   French   Latin American

- **Capitalize the months of the year and the days of the week.**
  February   April   Monday   Tuesday

- **Capitalize important words in the names of products and companies.**
  Blue Brook Cheese Spread   Heart of Gold Applesauce

  Little Hills Bakery   Anderson and Mumford, Inc.

- **Capitalize important words in the names of organizations.**
  American Lung Association   Veterans of Foreign Wars

- **Capitalize important words in the names of holidays.**
  Veterans Day   Fourth of July

- **Capitalize the first word in the greeting or closing of a letter.**
  Dear Edmundo,   Yours truly,

- **Capitalize the word *I.***
  Frances and I watched the movie together.

- **Capitalize the first, last, and most important words in a title. Be sure to capitalize all verbs including *is* and *was.***
  Island of the Blue Dolphins

  Away Is a Strange Place to Be

- **Capitalize the first word in a direct quotation.**
  Aunt Rose said, "Please pass the clam dip."

Section 2 | Abbreviations and Initials

Abbreviations are shortened forms of words. Many abbreviations begin with an uppercase letter and end with a period.

- **You can abbreviate titles of address and titles of respect when you write.**

  Mister (Mr. Brian Davis)   Mistress (Mrs. Maria Rosario)

  Doctor (Dr. Emily Chu)   Junior (Everett Castle, Jr.)

  Note: *Ms.* is a title of address used for women. It is not an abbreviation, but it requires a period (Ms. Anita Brown).

- **You can abbreviate words used in addresses when you write.**

  Street (St.)   Avenue (Ave.)   Route (Rte.)   Boulevard (Blvd.)   Road (Rd.)

- **You can abbreviate certain words in the names of businesses when you write.**

  Pet Helpers Incorporated (Pet Helpers Inc.)   Zykar Corporation (Zykar Corp.)

- **You can abbreviate days of the week when you take notes.**

  Sunday (Sun.)   Wednesday (Wed.)   Friday (Fri.)

  Monday (Mon.)   Thursday (Thurs.)   Saturday (Sat.)

  Tuesday (Tues.)

- **You can abbreviate months of the year when you take notes.**

  January (Jan.)   April (Apr.)   October (Oct.)

  February (Feb.)   August (Aug.)   November (Nov.)

  March (Mar.)   September (Sept.)   December (Dec.)

  (May, June, and July do not have abbreviated forms.)

- **You can abbreviate directions when you take notes.**

  North (N)   East (E)   South (S)   West (W)

An *initial* is the first letter of a name. An initial is written as an uppercase letter and a period. Sometimes initials are used for the names of countries or cities.

  Michael Paul Sanders (M.P. Sanders)   United States of America (U.S.A.)

  Washington, District of Columbia (Washington, D.C.)

Section 3 | Titles

- **Underline titles of books, newspapers, TV series, movies, and magazines.**

  <u>Island of the Blue Dolphins</u>   <u>Miami Herald</u>   <u>I Love Lucy</u>

  Note: These titles are put in italics when using a word processor.

- **Use quotation marks around articles in magazines, short stories, chapters in books, songs, and poems.**

  "This Land Is Your Land"   "The Gift"   "Eletelephony"

- **Capitalize the first, last, and most important words. Articles, prepositions, and conjunctions are usually not capitalized. Be sure to capitalize all verbs, including forms of the verb *be* (*am, is, are, was, were, been*).**

  A Knight in the Attic   *My Brother Sam Is Dead*

Section 4 Quotation Marks

- Put quotation marks (" ") around the titles of articles, magazines, short stories, book chapters, songs, and poems.
  My favorite short story is "Revenge of the Reptiles."

- Put quotation marks around a *direct quotation,* or a speaker's exact words.
  "Did you see that alligator?" Max asked.

- Do not put quotation marks around an *indirect quotation,* a person's words retold by another speaker. An indirect quotation is often signalled by *whether* or *that.*
  Max asked Rory whether he had seen an alligator. Rory said that he hadn't.

Writing a Conversation

- Put quotation marks around the speaker's words. Begin a direct quotation with an uppercase letter. Use a comma to separate the quotation from the speaker's name.
  Rory said, "There are no alligators in this area."

- When a direct quotation comes at the end of a sentence, put the end mark inside the last quotation mark.
  Max cried, "Look out!"

- When writing a conversation, begin a new paragraph with each change of speaker.
  Max panted, "I swear I saw a huge, scaly tail and a flat snout in the water!"

  "Relax," Rory said. "I told you there are no alligators around here."

- Put quotation marks around a quotation from a text.
  The great civil rights leader Martin Luther King said, "Injustice anywhere is a threat to justice everywhere."

Section 5 Spelling

Use these tips if you are not sure how to spell a word you want to write:
- Say the word aloud and break it into syllables. Try spelling each syllable. Put the syllables together to spell the whole word.
- Write the word. Make sure there is a vowel in every syllable. If the word looks wrong to you, try spelling it other ways.
- Think of a related word. Parts of related words are often spelled the same.
  Decide is related to *decision.*

When you use the word processing function of a computer to write something, you can use the spell-check feature. It will identify possible spelling errors in your writing. A spell checker will not catch errors with homophones, though. For example, if you type *break* instead of *brake,* the spell checker will not catch the mistake, because the word is spelled correctly.

Section 6 End Marks

Every sentence must end with a period, an exclamation point, or a question mark.

- Use a *period* at the end of a declarative sentence (statement) or an imperative sentence (command).

    Dad and I look alike. (*declarative*)   Step back very slowly. (*imperative*)

- Use an *exclamation point* at the end of an imperative sentence (a firm command) or at the end of an exclamatory sentence (a sentence that shows great feeling or excitement).

    Get away from the cliff! (*imperative*)   What an incredible sight! (*exclamatory*)

- Use a *question mark* at the end of an interrogative sentence (question).

    How many miles is it to Tucson? (*interrogative*)

Section 7 Apostrophes

An apostrophe (') is used to form the possessive of a noun or to join words in a contraction.

- **Possessives show ownership. To make a singular noun possessive, add** *'s*.

    The bike belongs to Carmen. It is Carmen's bike.

    The truck belongs to Mr. Ross. It is Mr. Ross's truck.

- **To form a possessive from a plural noun that ends in** *-s,* **add only an apostrophe.**

    Those books belong to my sisters. They are my sisters' books.

- **Some plural nouns do not end in** *-s.* **To form possessives with these nouns, add** *'s*.

    The children left their boots here. The children's boots are wet.

- **Use an apostrophe to replace the dropped letters in a contraction.**

    couldn't (could n<u>o</u>t)   it's (it <u>i</u>s)   hasn't (has n<u>o</u>t)

    didn't (did n<u>o</u>t)   I'm (I <u>a</u>m)   they'll (they <u>wi</u>ll)

Section 8 Commas and Semicolons

Commas in Sentences

- Use a comma after an introductory word or element in a sentence.

    Yes, I'd love to go to the movies.   Actually, we had a great time.

    Although it was raining, we still had fun at the zoo.

- Use a comma after a mild interjection at the beginning of a sentence. An *interjection* is a word that expresses emotion but is not part of an independent clause or a dependent clause in a sentence.

    Oh, it has started raining.   Hey, just grab an umbrella!

- Use a comma to separate items in a series. Put the last comma before *and* or *or.*

    The puppy whined, scratched at the door, and then barked loudly.

    Shall we eat cheese, bread, or fruit?

- Use a comma when speaking directly to a person.

    Akila, will you please stand up?   We would like you to sing, Akila.

- Use a comma to separate a direct quotation from the speaker's name.

    Harold asked, "How long do I have to sit here?"

"You must sit there until Anton returns," Vic said.

- Use a comma with the conjunctions *and, or,* and *but* when combining independent clauses in a compound sentence.
  Lisa liked the reptiles best, but Lyle preferred the amphibians.

Semicolons in Sentences

- You may use a semicolon in place of a comma and a conjunction when combining independent clauses.
  Lisa likes reptiles best; Lyle prefers amphibians.

Commas in Letters

- Use a comma after the greeting and closing of a friendly letter.
  Dear Reginald,   Your friend, Deke

Commas with Dates and Place Names

- Use a comma to separate the day from the date and the date from the year.
  We clinched the division championship on Saturday, September 19, 2015.

- Use a comma to separate the name of a city or town from the name of a state.
  I visited Memphis, Tennessee.

Sentence Structure and Parts of Speech

A *sentence* is a group of words that tells a complete thought. A sentence has two parts: a *subject* and a *predicate*.

- The subject tells *whom* or *what* the sentence is about.
  <u>The swimmers</u> race.

- The predicate tells what the subject *is* or *does*.
  The judges <u>watch carefully</u>.

There are four kinds of sentences: *declarative, interrogative, imperative,* and *exclamatory.*

- A sentence that tells something is a *declarative sentence.* It is also called a *statement.* A declarative sentence ends with a period.
  Jake swam faster than anyone.

- A sentence that asks something is an *interrogative sentence.* It is also called a *question.* An interrogative sentence ends with a question mark.
  Did Sammy qualify for the finals?

- A sentence that tells someone to do something is an *imperative sentence.* It is also called a *command.* An imperative sentence usually ends with a period, but a firm command can end with an exclamation point.
  Keep your eyes on the finish line.
  Watch out for that bee!

- A sentence that shows excitement or surprise is called an *exclamation* or *exclamatory sentence.* An exclamation ends with an exclamation point.
  Jake has won the race!

Section 10 Subjects

The *subject* of a sentence tells whom or what the sentence is about.

- A sentence can have one subject.
  <u>Mary</u> wrote a book.

- A sentence can have a *compound subject,* two or more subjects that share the same predicate.
  <u>Alex and Mark</u> have already read the book.

The *complete subject* includes all the words that name and tell about the subject.
  <u>Many different students</u> have borrowed the book.

The *simple subject* is the most important noun or pronoun in the complete subject.
  Many different <u>students</u> have borrowed the book.

  <u>They</u> discussed the book yesterday.

Note: Sometimes the simple subject and the complete subject are the same.

  <u>Ricardo</u> is writing a book about robots.

Section 11 Predicates

The *predicate* of a sentence tells what happened.

The *complete predicate* includes a verb and all the words that tell what happened.

- A complete predicate can tell what the subject of the sentence did. This kind of predicate includes an action verb.
  Mary <u>won an award</u>.

- A complete predicate can also tell more about the subject. This kind of predicate includes a linking verb.
  Mary <u>is a talented writer</u>.

- A *predicate noun* follows a linking verb and renames the subject.
  Our dog is a <u>retriever</u>.

- A *predicate adjective* follows a linking verb and describes the subject.
  Our dog is <u>friendly</u>.

The *simple predicate* is the verb that goes with the subject. It generally tells what the subject did, does, or will do.

Celia <u>won</u> an award for her performance.

She <u>will receive</u> a trophy next week.

A *compound predicate* is two or more predicates that share the same subject. Compound predicates are often joined by the conjunction *and* or *or*.

Ramon <u>sang</u> and <u>danced</u> in the play.

Mary <u>wrote</u> the play and <u>directed</u> it.

Section 12 Simple, Compound, and Complex Sentences

A sentence expresses one or more complete thoughts.

- A *simple sentence* tells one complete thought.
  Arthur has a rock collection.

- A *compound sentence* is made up of two simple sentences joined by a comma and a coordinating conjunction (*and, or, but*). Two simple sentences can be combined to form one compound sentence if the ideas in the simple sentences are related.
  Arthur has a rock collection<u>, and</u> Mary has a shell collection.
  Arthur collects rocks<u>, but</u> Mary collects shells.

- A *complex sentence* is made up of one *independent clause* (or simple sentence) and at least one dependent clause. A *dependent clause* is a group of words that has a subject and a predicate but cannot stand on its own.
  Dependent Clause: When Arthur visited southern Arizona

  Independent Clause: He learned a lot about desert plants and animals.

  Complex Sentence: When Arthur visited southern Arizona, he learned a lot about desert plants and animals.

Section 13 Fragments, Run-ons, and Comma Splices

A *fragment* is not a sentence, because it is missing a subject or a predicate. A fragment can also be called an incomplete sentence because it does not tell a complete thought.

Sumi and Ali. (*missing a predicate that tells what happened*)
Went hiking in the woods. (*missing a subject that tells who went hiking*)

A *run-on sentence* is two complete sentences that are run together.
Sumi went hiking Ali went swimming.

- To fix a run-on sentence, use a comma and a conjunction (*and, or, but*) to join the two sentences. (You may also join the sentences with a semicolon.)
Sumi went hiking, **but** Ali went swimming.

A *comma splice* is two complete sentences that have a comma between them but are missing a conjunction such as *and, or,* or *but.*
Sumi went hiking yesterday, Ali went swimming.

- To fix a comma splice, add *and, or,* or *but* after the comma.
Sumi went hiking yesterday, **and** Ali went swimming.

Try not to string too many short sentences together when you write. Instead, combine sentences and take out unnecessary information.

Incorrect: I stared at him and he stared at me and I told him to go away and he wouldn't so then I called my big sister.

Correct: We stared at each other. I told him to go away, but he wouldn't. Then I called my big sister.

Section 14 Nouns

A *common noun* names any person, place, thing, or idea.
Ira visited an auto **museum** with his **friends**. Ira has always had an **interest** in **cars**.

A *proper noun* names a certain person, place, thing, or idea. Proper nouns begin with an uppercase letter.
Ira wants to visit the **Sonoran Desert** in **Mexico**.

A *collective noun* names a group of people or things that act as one unit.
jury   family   committee   audience   crowd

- Most often, a collective noun is treated as a singular subject.
The track **team** is the strongest one we've had in years.

A *concrete noun* names something you can see, touch, hear, smell, or taste.
dog   meadow   pebble   stove

An *abstract noun* names an idea, a quality, or a characteristic.
freedom   bravery   freshness   excellence

Section 15 Adjectives

An *adjective* is a word that tells more about a noun.
- Some adjectives tell what kind.
Jim observed the **huge** elephant. The **enormous** beast towered above him.

- Some adjectives tell how many.
The elephant was **twelve** feet tall. It weighed **several** tons.

- Sometimes an adjective follows the noun it describes.
Jim was **careful** not to anger the elephant. He was **happy** when the trainer led it away.

- Two or more adjectives can be used to describe a noun. When you use two or more adjectives to describe a noun, put the adjectives in an order that sounds natural. This chart can help you.

how many	what quality	how big	how old	what shape	what color	what material	→ noun
three	*beautiful*	*small*	*new*	*round*	*pink*	*silken*	→ petals

- *A, an,* and *the* are special kinds of adjectives called *articles.* Use *a* and *an* to refer to any person, place, or thing. Use *the* to refer to a specific person, place, or thing. Use *a* before a singular noun that begins with a consonant sound. Use *an* before a singular noun that begins with a vowel sound.

  <u>An</u> elephant is heavier than <u>a</u> rhino. <u>The</u> elephant in this picture is six weeks old.

- *Demonstrative adjectives* tell which one. The words *this, that, these,* and *those* can be used as demonstrative adjectives. Use *this* and *these* to talk about things that are nearby. Use *that* and *those* to talk about things that are far away.

  <u>This</u> book is about rhinos.   <u>These</u> rhinos just came to the zoo.
  <u>That</u> rhino is enormous!   <u>Those</u> funny-looking creatures are wildebeests.

  Note: Never use *here* or *there* after the adjectives *this, that, these,* and *those.*

- A *proper adjective* is made from a proper noun. Capitalize proper adjectives.
  <u>Italian</u> cooking   <u>Democratic</u> convention   <u>Apache</u> legend

Section 16   Pronouns

A *pronoun* can replace a noun naming a person, place, thing, or idea. Personal pronouns include *I, me, you, we, us, he, she, him, her, it, they,* and *them.*

- A *subject pronoun* takes the place of the subject of a sentence. The subject pronouns are *I, you, he, she, it, we,* and *they.*
  Rita is an excellent soccer player. <u>She</u> is an excellent soccer player.

- Do not use both the pronoun and the noun it replaces together.
  Incorrect: <u>Rita she</u> made the team.
  Correct: <u>Rita</u> made the team. OR <u>She</u> made the team.

- An *object pronoun* replaces a noun that is the object of a verb or preposition. The object pronouns are *me, you, him, her, it, us,* and *them.*
  Rita's team played the Bobcats. Rita's team beat <u>them</u>.

- Use a subject pronoun as part of a compound subject. Use an object pronoun as part of a compound object. To test whether a pronoun is correct, say the sentence <u>without</u> the other part of a compound subject or object.
  Incorrect: Rita told Ellen and <u>I</u> it was a close game. (Rita told <u>I</u> it was a close game.)
  Correct: Rita told Ellen and <u>me</u> it was a close game. (Rita told <u>me</u> it was a close game.)

- An *antecedent* is the word or phrase a pronoun refers to. The antecedent always includes a noun.
  <u>The Bobcats</u> are excellent players. (They) won every game last season.

- A pronoun must match its antecedent. An antecedent and a pronoun agree when they have the same *number* (singular or plural) and *gender* (male or female).
  <u>Nick</u> won the game for our team. <u>He</u> kicked a goal at the last minute.
  <u>Nick's mother</u> cheered. <u>She</u> was very excited.
  <u>The Bobcats</u> were upset. <u>They</u> had not lost a game all season.

- *Indefinite pronouns* refer to persons or things that are not identified as individuals. These pronouns include *all, anybody, both, anything, few, most, no one,* and *somebody*.
  <u>Somebody</u> lost the key to the gym. We can't do <u>anything</u> unless we find it.

- *Reflexive pronouns* refer back to the subject of a sentence. A reflexive pronoun contains the word part *self* or *selves*.
  My brother bought <u>himself</u> a new puck. We cheered for <u>ourselves</u>.

- *This, that, these,* and *those* can be used as demonstrative pronouns. Use *this* and *these* to talk about one or more things that are nearby. Use *that* and *those* to talk about one or more things that are far away.
  <u>This</u> is a soft rug.
  <u>These</u> are sweeter than <u>those</u> over there.
  <u>That</u> is where I sat yesterday.
  <u>Those</u> are the new chairs I told you about.

- *Possessive pronouns* show ownership or connection. The words *my, your his, her, its, their,* and *our* are possessive pronouns.
  Those skates belong to <u>my</u> brother. Those are <u>his</u> kneepads, too.

- The interrogative pronouns *who, what,* and *which* are used to ask questions.
  <u>Who</u> has brought the volleyball?   <u>What</u> is a wicket used for?
  <u>Which</u> is the net for volleyball?

- When the pronouns *who, whom, whose, which,* and *that* are used to introduce a dependent clause, they are called *relative pronouns*. A relative pronoun always follows the noun it refers to.
  The player **who** <u>brought the volleyball</u> can serve first.
  I joined the team **that** <u>chose me</u>.
  This net, **which** <u>I found in my closet</u>, will be perfect for our volleyball game.

Note: For more information on using who, whom, which, and that, see Section 27, Problem Words.

Section 17 Verbs

An *action verb* shows action in a sentence.
  Scientists <u>study</u> the natural world.   They <u>learn</u> how the laws of nature work.

- Sometimes a *helping verb* is needed to help the main verb show action. A helping verb comes before a main verb.
  Scientists <u>are</u> studying glaciers.   The studies <u>will</u> help us learn about Earth's history.

- Verbs can tell about the present, the past, or the future.
  Few people <u>travel</u> in Antarctica. (*present tense*)
  Explorers first <u>traveled</u> to the South Pole over 100 years ago. (*past tense*)
  Other explorers <u>will travel</u> to the South Pole in the future. (*future tense*)
  Scientists <u>have studied</u> Antarctica for many years. (*present perfect tense*)

Certain helping verbs have special functions. The helping verbs *may* and *might* can be used to ask or give permission. The helping verbs *can* and *could* can be used to indicate ability. The helping verbs *should* and *must* can be used to communicate a duty or an obligation. The helping verbs *may, might, could, should,* and *will* can be used to indicate possibility—how likely something is to happen. Helping verbs that have these special functions are called *modal auxiliaries.*

- The *present tense* is used to show that something happens regularly or is true now.
  Squirrels <u>bury</u> nuts each fall.

  Add *-s* to most verbs to show present tense when the subject is *he, she, it,* or a singular noun. Add *-es* to verbs ending in *s, ch, sh,* or *x.* Do not add *-s* or *-es* if the subject is a plural noun or if the subject is *I, you, we,* or *they.*

add *-s*	add *-es*	change *y* to *i* and add *-es*
speak/speaks	reach/reaches	carry/carries
look/looks	mix/mixes	bury/buries

- The *past tense* shows past action. Add *-ed* to most verbs to form the past tense. Verbs that do not add *-ed* are called *irregular verbs.* Here are some common irregular verbs.

Present	Past	With *has, have,* or *had*
blow	blew	blown
bring	brought	brought
catch	caught	caught
come	came	come
find	found	found
give	gave	given
go	went	gone
grow	grew	grown
hide	hid	hidden
know	knew	known
leave	left	left
set	set	set
sing	sang	sung
sit	sat	sat
sleep	slept	slept
take	took	taken
teach	taught	taught
tell	told	told
throw	threw	thrown

- The future tense indicates future action. Use the helping verb *will* to form the future tense.
  Mom <u>will visit</u> Antarctica next year. She <u>will photograph</u> penguins.

- Perfect-tense verbs are used to indicate certain time relationships.

  The *present perfect tense* shows action that began in the past and may still be happening. To form the present perfect tense, add the helping verb *has* or *have* to the past participle of a verb.

  Mom <u>has studied</u> Antarctica for years. Her articles <u>have appeared</u> in science journals.

  The *past perfect tense* shows action that was completed by a certain time in the past. To form the past perfect tense, add the helping verb *had* to the past participle of a verb.

  Before she visited Antarctica, Mom <u>had imagined</u> it as a wasteland.

  The *future perfect tense* shows action that will be complete by a certain time in the future. To form the future perfect tense, add the helping verbs *will have* to the past participle form of a verb.

  By the end of the year, Mom <u>will have published</u> a book on Antarctic sea creatures.

- The subject and its verb must agree in number.

  An Antarctic explorer needs special equipment.

  (*singular subject:* **An Antarctic explorer**; *verb + -s or -es:* **needs**)

  Explorers carry climbing tools and survival gear.

  (*plural subject:* **Explorers**; *verb without -s or -es:* **carry**)

A *linking verb* does not show action. It connects the subject of a sentence to a word or words in the predicate that tell about the subject. Linking verbs include forms of the verb *be,* such as *am, is, are, was,* and *were. Seem* and *become* are linking verbs, too.

Explorers <u>are</u> brave.   That route <u>seems</u> very long and dangerous.

Note: *Feel, taste, smell, sound,* and *look* can be action or linking verbs.

- Choose verb tenses carefully so that the verb forms you use work together to indicate time accurately and consistently. When you describe events that happen in the same time frame, do not shift tenses. When you describe events that happen at different times, use verbs in different tenses to indicate the order in which the events happened.

  Malcolm wanted to stay dry on the hike, so he <u>packed</u> a poncho. (not <u>packs</u>)

  The doves begin their calls early in the morning, and they <u>continue</u> them past noon. (not <u>continued</u>)

Section 18 Adverbs

An *adverb* is usually used to describe a verb or an adjective. Most adverbs tell how, when, where, or how much.

- Many adverbs end in *-ly*.

  Andrew approached the snake cage <u>slowly</u>. He <u>cautiously</u> peered inside.

- Some adverbs do not end in *-ly*.

  Andrew knew that snakes can move <u>fast</u>.

- *Very* is an adverb. It means "extremely." Never use *real* in place of *very*.

  Incorrect   Correct

  The snake's fangs were <u>real</u> sharp.   The snake's fangs were <u>very</u> sharp.

- When the word *when, where,* or *why* begins a dependent clause that tells about a place, a time, or a reason, it can be called a *relative adverb*.

Tucker Avenue is a street **where** many accidents happen. (place)

Friday is the day **when** my report is due. (time)

This article gives five reasons **why** you should drink water instead of soda. (reason)

Note: A word that is a relative adverb can also be classified as a subordinating conjunction.

Section 19 Prepositions

A *preposition* shows a relationship between a word in a sentence and a noun or pronoun that follows the preposition. Prepositions help tell when, where, what kind, how, or how much.

- Prepositions include the words *in, at, under, over, on, through, to, across, around, beside, during, off,* and *before.*

  Jeff left the milk **on** the table. He knew it belonged **in** the refrigerator.

- A *prepositional phrase* is a group of words that begins with a preposition and ends with its object. The object of a preposition is a noun or a pronoun. A prepositional phrase can be at the beginning, middle, or end of a sentence.

  Jeff knew his mother would be home **in five minutes**.

  Within three minutes Jeff had put the milk away.

The *object of a preposition* is the noun or pronoun at the end of a prepositional phrase.

Milt gave a pen to his **sister**. (*Sister* is the object of the preposition *to*.)

Section 20 Direct Objects and Indirect Objects

A *direct object* is the word or words that receive the action of the verb. Direct objects follow action verbs. (A linking verb never has a direct object.) To find the direct object, say the verb followed by "Whom?" or "What?" A direct object is always a noun or pronoun.

Jacques painted a **picture.** (Painted whom or what? Picture. *Picture* is the direct object.)

A sentence with a direct object may also have an *indirect object*. An indirect object is a noun or pronoun and usually tells to whom something is given.

Jacques gave his **mom** the painting.

Section 21 Conjunctions

The words *and, or,* and *but* are *coordinating conjunctions*. They connect words or groups of words that have the same function.

- Coordinating conjunctions may be used to join words within a sentence.

  My favorite reptiles are snakes **and** lizards.   Najim doesn't like snakes **or** lizards.

- A comma and a coordinating conjunction can be used to join two or more simple sentences. (The conjunction *and* does not need a comma if both sentences are short.)

  I like snakes, **but** he says they're creepy.   We can get a snake, **or** we can get a lizard.

A *subordinating conjunction* shows how one clause (a group of words with a subject and predicate) relates to another clause. Many dependent clauses begin with a subordinating conjunction. Subordinating conjunctions include *although, because, if,* and *before.*

Before his mom left, Bo cleaned his room. **Because** he had a favor to ask, he vacuumed, too.

Correlative conjunctions always appear in pairs. They connect words or groups of words and provide more emphasis than coordinating conjunctions. Some correlative conjunctions are *both…and, either…or, neither…nor, not only…but (also),* and *whether…or.*

You can **either** wash the car **or** mow the lawn.
Emma is using **both** the broom **and** the vacuum cleaner.

Usage

Section 22   Negatives

A *negative word* says "no" or "not."

- Often negatives are in the form of contractions.
  Do **not** enter that room.   **Don't** even go near the door.

- In most sentences it is not correct to use two negatives.

Incorrect	Correct
We **can't** see **nothing**.	We **can't** see anything.
We **haven't** got **no** solution.	We **haven't** got a solution.

- Do not use the word *ain't*.

Section 23   Comparisons

- The *comparative form* of an adjective or adverb compares two people, places, or things. The comparative form is often followed by "than." To compare two people, places, or things, add *-er* to short adjectives and adverbs.
  An elephant is **tall**. A giraffe is **taller** than an elephant. (*Giraffe* is compared with *elephant*.)

  A lion runs **fast**. A cheetah runs **faster** than any other land animal. (*Cheetah* is compared with *any other land animal*.)

- The *superlative form* of an adjective or adverb compares three or more people, places, or things. The article "the" usually comes before the superlative form. To compare three or more items, add *-est* to short adjectives and adverbs.
  The giraffe is the **tallest** land animal.

  The cheetah runs the **fastest** of any animal now alive.

- When comparing two or more things using the ending *-er* or *-est,* never use the word *more.*

Incorrect	Correct
She is **more faster** than he is.	She is **faster** than he is.

- The word *more* is used with longer adjectives to compare two persons, places, or things. Use the word *most* to compare three or more persons, places, or things.
  Mario is **excited** about the field trip.

  Duane is **more excited** than Mario.

  Kiki is the **most excited** student of all.

- Sometimes the words *good* and *bad* are used to compare. These words change forms in comparisons.

Mario is a **good** athlete.	The basketball court is in **bad** shape.
Kiki is a **better** athlete.	The tennis court is in **worse** shape than the basketball court.
Bill is the **best** athlete of all.	The ice rink is in the **worst** shape of all.

Note: Use *better* or *worse* to compare two things. Use *best* or *worst* to compare three or more things.

Section 24 Contractions

When two or more words are combined to form one word, one or more letters are dropped and replaced by an apostrophe. These words are called *contractions*.

- In the contraction below, an apostrophe takes the place of the letters *wi*.
  he will = he'll

- Here are some other common contractions.

cannot/can't	have not/haven't	she would/she'd
could not/couldn't	I will/I'll	they have/they've
does not/doesn't	it is/it's	we are/we're

Section 25 Plural Nouns

- A *singular noun* names one person, place, thing, or idea.

girl	pond	arrow	freedom

- A *plural noun* names more than one person, place, or thing. To make most singular nouns plural, add *-s*.

girl<u>s</u>	pond<u>s</u>	arrow<u>s</u>	freedom<u>s</u>

- For nouns ending in *sh, ch, x,* or *z,* add *-es* to make the word plural.
  bush/bush<u>es</u>   box/box<u>es</u>
  lunch/lunch<u>es</u>   buzz/buzz<u>es</u>

- For nouns ending in a consonant and *y*, change the *y* to *i* and add *-es*.
  penny/penn<u>ies</u>   army/arm<u>ies</u>

- For nouns that end in *f* or *fe*, replace *f* or *fe* with *ves* to make the noun plural.
  shelf/shel<u>ves</u>   wife/wi<u>ves</u>

- Some words change spelling when the plural is formed.

man/men	woman/women	mouse/mice	goose/geese

- Some words have the same singular and plural form.
  deer   sheep

Section 26 Possessive Nouns

A *possessive noun* shows ownership.

- To make a singular noun possessive, add an apostrophe and *-s*.
  John<u>'s</u> bat   the girl<u>'s</u> bike

- When a singular noun ends in *-s,* add an apostrophe and *-s*.
  Ross<u>'s</u> project   James<u>'s</u> glasses

- To make a plural noun that ends in *-s* possessive, add an apostrophe.
  the soldiers<u>'</u> songs   the girls<u>'</u> bikes

- When a plural noun does not end in *-s,* add an apostrophe and *s* to show possession.
  the men<u>'s</u> ideas   the children<u>'s</u> shoes

Section 27 Problem Words

These words are often misused in writing.

sit	*Sit* means "rest or stay in one place." Sit down and relax for a while.
sat	*Sat* is the past tense of *sit.* I sat in that chair yesterday.
set	*Set* is a verb meaning "put." Set the chair here.

may	*May* is used to ask permission or to express a possibility. May I have another hot dog? I may borrow that book someday.
can	*Can* shows that someone is able to do something. I can easily eat three hot dogs.

learn	*Learn* means "to get knowledge." Who will help you learn Spanish?
teach	*Teach* means "to give knowledge." Never use *learn* in place of *teach.* **Incorrect:** My sister will learn me to speak Spanish. **Correct:** My sister will teach me to speak Spanish.

is	Use *is* to tell about one person, place, or thing. Alabama is warm during the summer.
are	Use *are* to tell about more than one person, place, or thing. Also use *are* with the word *you.* Seattle and San Francisco are cool during the summer. You are welcome to visit me anytime.

doesn't	The contraction *doesn't* is used with the singular pronouns *he, she,* and *it.* He doesn't like sauerkraut. It doesn't agree with him.
don't	The contraction *don't* is used with the plural pronouns *we* and *they.* *Don't* is also used with *I* and *you.* They don't like swiss cheese. I don't care for it, either.

I	Use the pronoun *I* as the subject of a sentence. When using *I* or *me* with another noun or pronoun, always name yourself last. I am going to basketball camp. Renée and I will ride together.
me	Use the pronoun *me* after action verbs. Renée will call me this evening. Also use *me* after a preposition, such as *to, at,* and *with.* Pass the ball to me. Come to the game with Renée and me.

good **well**	*Good* is an adjective. *Well* is an adverb. These words are often used incorrectly. **Incorrect:** Renée plays good. **Correct:** Renée is a good basketball player. She plays well.

like	*Like* means "similar to" or "have a fondness for." Do not use *like* in places where it does not belong. **Incorrect:** I enjoy, like, all kinds of water sports. **Correct:** I like swimming and water polo.
you know	Only use the phrase *you know* when it helps a sentence make sense. Try not to use it in places where it does not belong. **Incorrect:** We can, you know, go canoeing. **Correct:** Did you know that my family has a canoe?
let	*Let* is a verb that means "allow." Please let me go to the mall with you.
leave	*Leave* is a verb that means "go away from" or "let stay." We will leave at noon. Leave your sweater here.
was	*Was* is a past tense form of *be*. Use *was* to tell about one person or thing. Hana was sad yesterday.
were	*Were* is also a past tense form of *be*. Use *were* to tell about more than one person or thing. Also use the word *were* with *you*. Hana and her friend were both unhappy. Were you home yesterday?
has	Use *has* to tell about one person or thing. Rory has a stamp collection.
have	Use *have* to tell about more than one. Also use *have* with the pronoun *I*. David and Lin have a rock collection. I have a bottle cap collection.
who	Use *who* to refer to people. The man who picked me up is my father.
which	Use *which* to refer to things. His rear tire, which was flat, had to be repaired.
that	*That* can refer to people or things. Use *that* instead of *which* to begin a clause that is necessary to the meaning of the sentence. The picture that Stephon drew won first prize.
very	*Very* is an adverb. It means "extremely." I was very tired after the hike.
real	*Real* is an adjective. It means "actual" or "true to life." Never use *real* in place of *very*. **Incorrect:** The hike was real long. **Correct:** I used a real compass to find my way.

Section 28 Homophones

Homophones sound alike but have different spellings and meanings.

are	*Are* is a form of the verb *be*.	We are best friends.
our	*Our* is a possessive pronoun.	Our favorite color is green.
hour	An *hour* is sixty minutes.	Meet me in an hour.

its	*Its* is a possessive pronoun.	The horse shook its shaggy head.
it's	*It's* is a contraction of the words *it is*.	It's a beautiful day for a ride.

there	*There* is an adverb that usually means "in that place." It can also be used in the expressions "there is" and "there are."	
	Please put the books there.	There are three books on the table.
	There is a library nearby.	
their	*Their* is a possessive pronoun. It shows something belongs to more than one person or thing.	
	Their tickets are in my pocket.	
they're	*They're* is a contraction made from the words *they are*.	
	They're waiting for me inside.	

two	*Two* is a number.	Apples and pears are two fruits I like.
to	*To* means "toward."	I brought the pot to the stove.
too	*Too* means "also."	I'd like some lunch, too.
	Too can mean "more than enough."	That's too much pepper!

your	*Your* is a possessive pronoun.	
	Where are your socks?	
you're	*You're* is a contraction made from the words *you are*.	
	You're coming with us, aren't you?	

whose	*Whose* is a possessive pronoun.	
	Whose raincoat is this?	
who's	*Who's* is a contraction made from the words *who* and *is* or *who* and *has*.	
	Who's at the front door?	Who's taken my book?

ate	*Ate* is a form of the verb *eat*.	We ate lunch together.
eight	*Eight* is a number word.	She had eight marbles.

principal	A *principal* is a person with authority.
	The principal made the rule.
principle	A *principle* is a general rule or code of behavior.
	He lived with a strong principle of honesty.

waist	The *waist* is the middle part of the body.
	She wore a belt around her waist.
waste	To *waste* something is to use it in a careless way.
	She would never waste something she could recycle.

aloud	*Aloud* means "out loud" or "able to be heard."
	He read the poem aloud.
allowed	*Allowed* is a form of the verb *allow*.
	We were not allowed to swim after dark.

Letters and E-mails

A *friendly letter* is an informal letter written to a friend or family member.
In a friendly letter, you might send a message,
invite someone to a party, or thank someone for a gift.
A friendly letter has five parts.

- The *heading* gives your address and the date.

- The *greeting* includes the name of the person you are writing to.

- The *body* of the letter gives your message.

- The *closing* is a friendly or polite way to say good-bye.

- The *signature* is your name.

> 35 Rand Street
> Chicago, IL 60606
> July 15, 20__
>
> Dear Kim,
>
> Hi from the big city. I'm spending the summer learning to skateboard. My brother Raj is teaching me. He's a pro.
>
> I have one skateboard and hope to buy another one soon. If I can do that, we can practice together when you come to visit.
>
> Your friend,
> *Art*

A *business letter* is a formal letter.
You would write a business letter to a company, an employer, a newspaper, or any person you do not know well. A business letter looks a lot like a friendly letter, but it also includes the name and address of the business you are writing to, substitutes a colon for a comma after the greeting, omits paragraph indentations, and aligns all of the letter parts along the left-hand margin.

> 35 Rand Street
> Chicago, IL 60606
> July 15, 20__
>
> Swenson Skateboard Company
> 10026 Portage Road
> Lansing, MI 48091
>
> Dear Sir or Madam:
>
> Please send me your latest skateboard catalog. I am particularly interested in your newest models, the K-7 series.
>
> Thank you.
>
> Sincerely yours,
> *Arthur Quinn*
> Arthur Quinn

The envelope below shows how to address a letter.
A friendly letter and a business letter are addressed the same way.

> ARTHUR QUINN
> 35 RAND ST
> CHICAGO IL 60606
>
>   KIM LEE
>   1555 MONTAGUE BLVD
>   MEMPHIS TN 38106

259

Section 30　E-mails

An *e-mail* is a note sent from one person to another person, a group, or a company via a computer network. Many people use e-mail to stay in touch with friends and family. An e-mail should contain four parts.

- An e-mail contains a *greeting*, a *body*, a *closing*, and your *name*.
- An e-mail *header* contains your e-mail address, the e-mail address of the person you are writing to, the date, and a subject line.

| Send | Save as a Draft | Cancel |

From:	arthur_quinn@communicago.net
To:	info@swenskate.com
Date:	July 15, 20__
Subject:	Skateboard catalog

Attach Files

Dear Sir or Madam:

Please send me your latest skateboard catalog. I am particularly interested in your newest models, the K-7 series.

My address is 35 Rand Street, Chicago, IL 60606. Thank you.

Sincerely,
Arthur Quinn

Research

Section 31 Library Research

You can find information for a report or a project in a library.

- Many libraries have an information desk. The person at the desk can help you look for information.
- Libraries have many reference books, including dictionaries, thesauruses, and encyclopedias. You can use these to find information about words, and basic information about topics.
- Libraries have nonfiction books about all kinds of subjects. You can find books on a particular subject by entering that subject into a computer connected to the library's database. This database lists all the publications in the library. The computer will usually list several books on the subject you entered. Each listing will have a code that tells where in the library that book can be found.

Section 32 Internet Research

You can use online dictionaries, thesauruses, and encyclopedias to find basic information about words and topics. You can also find information for a report or a project by using an Internet *search engine*.

- Think of **key words** that tell what you are looking for. For example, if you need information on animals that live in the rain forest, you might use the key words **rain forest animals**. Type these words into the search engine's text box.
- The search engine will provide you with links to **websites**. You can click on a link to visit a website.
- When you get to the website, you need to judge whether it will be a good source of information.
  — Notice the last three letters of the website's Internet address. Sites with a **.gov** and **.edu** are usually more reliable than sites with **.com**.
  — Think about who has written the information. Is the writer an expert on the topic? Is the writer giving facts, or just expressing opinions?
  — Check to see if the information is up-to-date. The site should tell you when it was last updated.

Internet Safety

Be sure to follow safety rules whenever you use the Internet. These rules will help you keep personal information private.

- When you log on to a school computer, you may type your own name as a username. However, when you go on the Internet, you use a screen name. That should never be your real name or nickname. You will also use a password, a secret word or symbol that identifies who you are. Keep your password safe. Do not share it with anyone. Never use your address, birthday, phone number, or pet's name as a password. Those are too easy for someone else to figure out.

- Have you ever received e-mail with an attachment? Usually you must click the attachment to load it into your computer. Never download attachments from strangers. These may harm your computer.

Guidelines for Listening and Speaking

Section 33 **Listening**

These steps will help you be a good listener:

- **Listen carefully** when others are speaking.
- **Keep in mind your reason for listening.** Are you listening to learn about a topic? To be entertained? To get directions? Decide what you should get out of the listening experience.
- **Look directly at the speaker.** Doing this will help you concentrate on what he or she has to say.
- **Do not interrupt** the speaker or talk to others while the speaker is talking.
- **Ask questions** when the speaker is finished talking if there is anything you did not understand.

Section 34 **Speaking**

Being a good speaker takes practice. These guidelines can help you become an effective speaker:

Giving Oral Reports

- **Be prepared.** Know exactly what it is that you are going to talk about and how long you will speak. Have your notes in front of you.
- **Speak slowly** and **clearly.** Speak **loudly** enough so everyone can hear you.
- **Look** at your audience.

Taking Part in Discussions

- **Listen** to what others have to say.
- **Disagree politely.** Let others in the group know you respect their point of view.
- **Try not to interrupt others.** Everyone should have a chance to speak.

Language Index
Conventions of Standard English